THE BUSINESS OF PLEASURE
A HISTORY OF PAID SEX IN THE HEART OF EUROPE

THE BUSINESS OF PLEASURE

A HISTORY OF PAID SEX IN THE HEART OF EUROPE

Edited by
Elwin Hofman,
Magaly Rodríguez García,
and Pieter Vanhees

Leuven University Press

Authorised translation of the Dutch edition published in 2022 by Uitgeverij Prometheus, Amsterdam.
Original title: Seks voor geld. Een geschiedenis van prostitutie in België
© 2022 Dutch edition by Elwin Hofman, Magaly Rodríguez García, and Pieter Vanhees
© 2024 English edition by Leuven University Press / Universitaire Pers Leuven / Presses Universitaires de Louvain. Minderbroedersstraat 4, B-3000 Leuven (Belgium)

ISBN 978 94 6270 410 7
eISBN 978 94 6166 557 7 (ePUB)
https://doi.org/10.11116/9789461665577
D/2024/1869/39
NUR: 695
Typesetting: Crius Group
Cover design: Daniel Benneworth-Gray
Cover image: André Favory, Le Cristal Palace à Anvers, 1922

CONTENTS

Ostend

BRUGES

East Flanders

Scheldt

GHENT

Yser

West Flanders

Aalst

CITY OF

Lys

Scheldt

*1

Kortrijk

BCR

Tournai

Walloo

Hainaut

La Louviè

MONS

Charler

◆ Capital

■ Provincial capitals

● Other major cities

☐ Province boundaries

------ Main rivers

- - - Language border
      *1 Dutch (north) - French (south)
      *2 French (west) - German (east)

BCR: Brussels-Capital Region

0   25   50 km

Cartography: Felix Vanderleenen, KU Leuven

RP *Antwerp*

len

LS

LEUVEN

sh Brabant

WAVRE
it

NAMUR

ambre

Limburg

HASSELT

*1

LIÈGE

Meuse

Namur

Dinant

*1

*1

*2

Verviers

Liège

*2

Luxembourg

ARLON

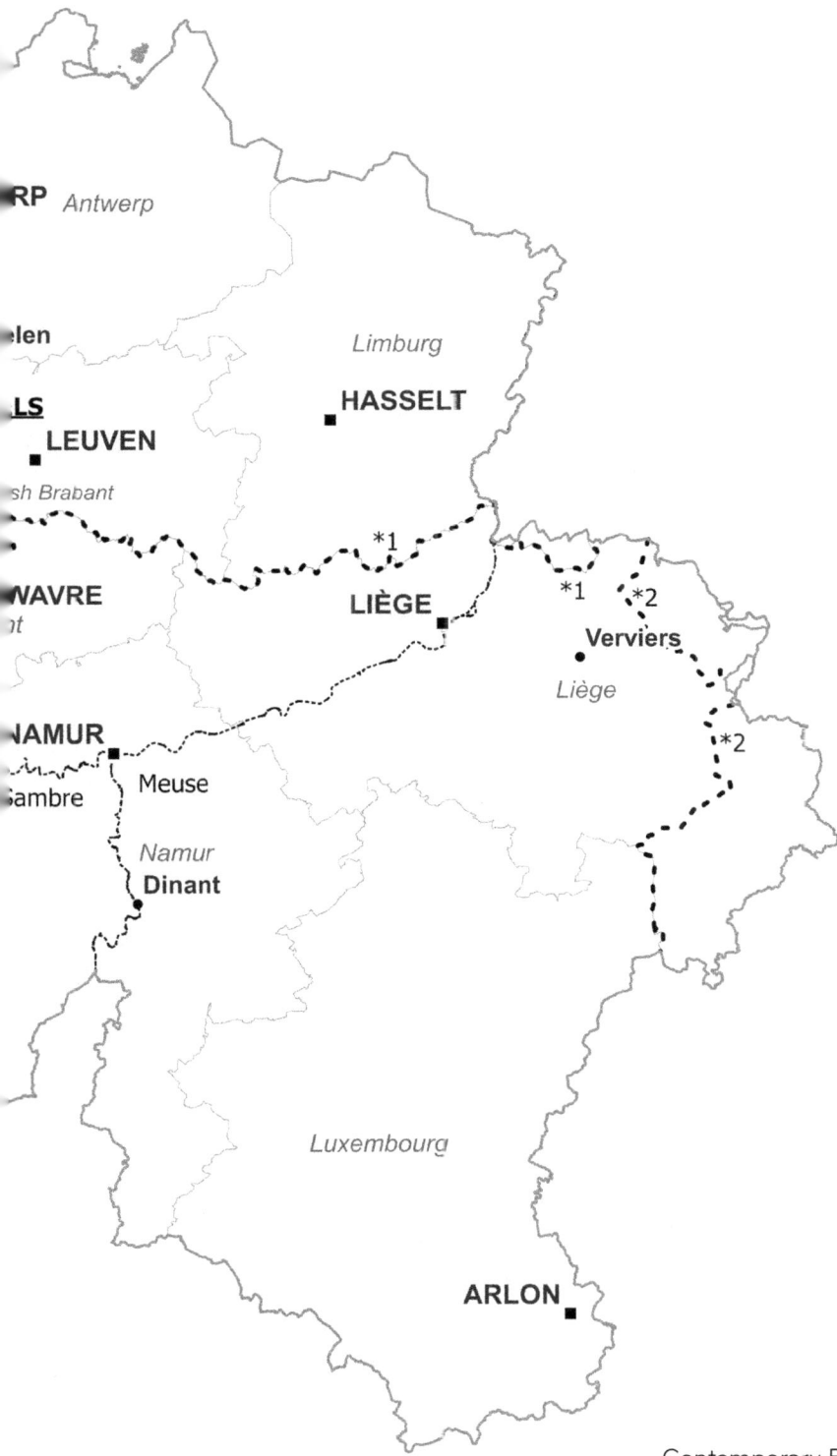

Contemporary Belgium.

INTRODUCTION: ANNE-MARIE'S TRIBULATIONS

Elwin Hofman, Magaly Rodríguez García, and Pieter Vanhees

During her father's absence in 1888, eighteen-year-old Anne-Marie pulled the door of her childhood home shut. There were troubles in the family: life was not easy in a poor household of twelve siblings, most of them younger than her. She found a room with her older sister in the Antwerp port district, near what is now the Red Star Line Museum. It was anything but a respectable home. According to the neighbours, only 'wantons' lived there. Anne-Marie made her living selling sex. She walked the streets and picked up customers in the many bars of the port district. This brought her to the attention of the vice police. An officer who had spotted her promptly registered her as a 'loose woman' and issued her a 'prostitution booklet', a kind of passport allowing her to sell sex, on the condition that she report for weekly medical examinations. Through this regulatory system, the government hoped to prevent the spread of venereal disease.

Anne-Marie found the weekly examinations painful and humiliating. She tried to avoid them. After only a few months, however, fate struck: not only was she pregnant with a stranger's child, but she had also contracted syphilis. As soon as the examining doctor diagnosed the infection, he had her forcibly admitted to Saint Elizabeth's Hospital. The humiliations, illness, and pregnancy had devastated her. Having reconciled with her parents, her father petitioned the mayor to take her off the list of prostitutes. While he could not watch over her because was a sailor and often absent, Anne-Marie would help her mother with her work as a laundress.

The police, however, after assessing the request, argued that Anne-Marie's infection was evidence of 'immoral behaviour' and refused to remove her from the register. Thus, after being discharged from the hospital, Anne-Marie returned to her parents' home. She also stayed regularly with her sister and continued to sell sex until her advanced pregnancy made this impossible. In early 1889, she gave birth to a boy, Charles-Louis, who died a few months later. It must have been a terrible blow.

Soon after her baby's death, Anne-Marie began a relationship with a deserting soldier. As the deserter wanted to avoid the police, the couple moved to London in June 1889. We don't know exactly what happened there, but they returned to Antwerp in October. Anne-Marie, with her boyfriend's approval, continued to sell sex, according to a vice squad report. She did help her mother with the laundry, but in the eyes of the police, this was just a front. Anne-Marie carried laundry to and from the ships docking in Antwerp, which gave her the opportunity to get to know the sailors, whom she then received in her room.

Anne-Marie and her father kept on trying to have her removed from the prostitution list so that she would no longer have to undergo the notorious medical examinations. But the harder they tried, the closer the vice police kept watch over her. One police officer even followed her for several days, enabling him to give detailed accounts of her streetwalking. At times she seemed inactive, but then an officer would again see her engaging in sexual activity with sailors. Witnesses described her as a 'total street whore'. A colleague, too, said that Anne-Marie was 'as much a whore as we are, because she never works yet has her pockets full of money'.

Anne-Marie's life at the end of the nineteenth century raises many questions. Why did she sell sex? Was she forced to do it, or was it her free choice, or was it more complicated? Did prostitution really pay that well? Why did the police and municipal administration go to such lengths to keep her under surveillance? We cannot answer all these questions. But as the previous account shows, historical sources do provide valuable details about Anne-Marie and countless other actors in the sex industry. Archival evidence allows us to better understand the lives of people who became involved in the 'business of pleasure'. Their backgrounds and survival strategies often resemble those of contemporary sex workers, though time and space always influenced how people sold intimacy.

Indeed, calling prostitution 'the world's oldest profession', is inaccurate because it suggests that little has changed, almost as if commercial sex has no history. Nothing could be further from the truth. How women and men exchanged sex for money or goods was linked to urbanisation, nation building, and the professionalisation of police forces; to developments in the labour market and in transport; to notions about disease, sexuality, and love; and to migration flows and new technologies. The history of prostitution thus runs parallel to major historical changes, yet often remains in the shadows.

Elwin Hofman, Magaly Rodríguez García, and Pieter Vanhees

This book recounts the history of sex work in what is now Belgium, from the late Middle Ages to the present. Located at the heart of Europe, Belgium's history reveals much about attitudes to commercial sex in neighbouring regions. Booming cities like Antwerp, Bruges, and Brussels have attracted foreigners – sex workers and clients alike – since the Middle Ages, while policymakers and journalists have often reacted to developments abroad. We are therefore telling both a Belgian and a European story – a story of politics, tolerance, and repression – but above all a lived history of women and men who saw commercial sex as a way of escaping the tedium of conventional work. It is a story of policing and creative ways of avoiding surveillance, of ambitions and false promises, of 'easy money' and disappointments. In this book, we consider the social profiles, motivations, and working conditions of people in prostitution, as well as society's response to this alternative way of life. We look at the material culture and evolution of brothels, street, window and private prostitution, and at the changing ideas and practices of sex.

The sex industry has always been – and still is – characterised by an enormous diversity, even in a relatively small place like present-day Belgium. There was no such thing as 'the' sex worker, and prostitution policies were anything but clearcut. Local authorities largely decided for themselves how to deal with commercial sex. Women like Anne-Marie had to take this into account, but their behaviour also influenced local policies. This book focuses on these diverse practices and personalities, revealing the interaction between sex workers, clients, pimps, brothel owners, neighbours, police officers, and policymakers. We bring the history of sex work in Belgium out of the shadows where it has long lingered. We are not motivated by voyeurism, but by a desire to come to a better understanding of the difficult situations and choices people faced in the past and still face today.

Prostitution Unravelled

Commercial sex came to the attention of historians in the 1970s, mainly under the influence of feminist historians. The timing was not accidental, but coincided with the birth of the sex worker movement. Prostitution then became what US historian Timothy Gilfoyle called a 'metaphor of modernity'. The history of the sex industry offers a window into broader political, socio-economic, and cultural changes. In other words, the history of people in the margins provides a new perspective on classic historical themes.

Initially, historians focused mainly on policy and the thorny debates on the best way to deal with prostitution. Regulationists (who advocate the regulation of the trade by local authorities), abolitionists (who oppose regulation), and prohibitionists (who want to ban commercial sex altogether) fought one another since the nineteenth century. Despite their vocal disagreements, they all shared the belief that commercial sex was inherently problematic. Both those in favour and against regulation associated prostitution with venereal diseases, violence, exploitation, alcohol, and drugs.

The various positions on prostitution often masked a hidden agenda. Sellers of sex had a symbolic political value, as they endangered the patriarchal order. Improving the fate of sex workers was rarely a concern of policymakers. Historians have, therefore, especially during the last two decades, paid more attention to the underlying intentions of actors who called for the regulation or oppression of prostitution. Christine Machiels, for instance, has studied feminist discussions and concrete initiatives to abolish the system of prostitution in Belgium, France, and Switzerland from 1860 to 1960. She describes how feminist municipal councillors tried to weigh in on the political agenda during the interwar period. Their actions led to an abolitionist experiment in 1920s Brussels and to the actual abolition of the regulation system in Belgium in 1948.

Despite the persistent view of prostitution as a problem, historians have shifted their focus from policy and media debates to the opportunities the sex trade offered and the difficulties it posed to people engaged in it. Following the lead of activists, they understood commercial sex as an economic activity and integrated the phrase 'sex work' in their analyses. Beginning in the late 1980s, social historians have studied how the sector operated; who was involved in it; where transactions took place; how sex workers, pimps, and clients interacted; and how much was paid and earned. The works of Judith Walkowitz on late Victorian London, Luise White on colonial Nairobi, or Sophie De Schaepdrijver on nineteenth-century Brussels revealed the economic workings and social implications of the sex industry in various places and periods.

By the turn of the century, media attention to globalisation and international crime led to neo-abolitionist efforts to combat prostitution. As the sale of sex was perceived as synonymous to human trafficking, historians saw parallels with the outcry over 'white slavery' at the end of the nineteenth century. The story of English underage girls found in Belgian brothels and of the sensationalist British and Belgian reporting resonated with the mediatisation of human trafficking in Belgium and elsewhere in the 1990s. Historians and other social scientists then concluded that neither secularisation nor sexual emancipation had dissipated the fear that commercial sex provoked among elites and the public at large.

All these studies reveal the diversity of historical research on sex work. However, much uncharted territory remains, and a long-term perspective is lacking.

Elwin Hofman, Magaly Rodríguez García, and Pieter Vanhees

Karin Borghouts, *Abandoned brothel*, Antwerp, 2001.

Moreover, the voices of the main actors of the sex industry are frequently absent in the available literature. This is no coincidence, for brothel owners, pimps, and sex workers have often tried to stay in the shadows. We know Anne-Marie and many other women and men active in the sector because their attempts to escape surveillance failed, so that their stories ended up in the archives of local authorities, medical, and social institutions.

Much of our knowledge about the history of paid sex – including in this book – is based on sources from the domain of law and order. Over the centuries, authorities in their various guises have tried to 'manage' sex work. Policies oscillated between various degrees of tolerance and repression, and between strict systems of control and the ad hoc imposition of fines and penalties. Such policies produced a wealth of historical sources, of which many have been lost, but others preserved for posterity. Police reports, lists of fines and taxes, prostitution registers, accountancy books, court records, and medical files provide us with fascinating details about the sex trade, the people involved, and the policing thereof.

Depending on the historical period, artists, doctors, scientists, jurists, preachers, and secular reformers also discussed prostitution. For some, the sex worker was a muse who stimulated artistic creativity, for many others a source of disease, immorality, and decay. These sources have in common with those produced by the authorities that the sex industry's main actors themselves rarely, if ever, wielded pen or brush: their voices can only be discerned between the lines. For more recent periods, however, a greater number of personal accounts exists, in the form of autobiographies and interviews by journalists or historians. Thus, insights gained from oral history appear later in this book. Moreover, the final chapter is exclusively devoted to the testimony of a former Belgian sex worker and activist, Sonia Verstappen.

Using such a diverse range of sources and reading them in an original way allows us to get as close as possible to the people we are interested in. We can analyse why they chose a different path in life, and the opportunities commercial sex provided them. Yet sometimes we can only speculate. Even though Belgian archives provide remarkable details about the sex trade, our historical knowledge remains quite asymmetrical. For instance, we know much less about male sellers of sex than about women involved in prostitution and, vice versa, we know much more about men in their roles of brothel owners, pimps, or clients, than about female customers. We also know little about the presumably countless persons for whom the sale of sex only had a temporary and limited impact on their lives. Still, the available sources do permit us to paint a richly detailed, and at the same time nuanced, picture of paid sex in the heart of Europe from the Middle Ages to the present.

What's in a Name?

The attentive reader has probably already noticed that we use several terms to describe our topic: the sex industry (or trade), commercial sex, paid sex, sex work, prostitution. This is not stylistic sloppiness. While many contemporary historians and social scientists avoid the term 'prostitution', we choose to use it alongside other terms. We are aware of the negative connotation attached to the word, suggesting that people who sold sex were somehow 'deviants'. Yet as historians we recognise the importance of a concept that, since the end of the eighteenth century, specifically referred to the exchange of sexual services for payment in cash or kind.

The word 'prostitution' derives from the Latin *prostituere*, *prostare*, or *prostibulum* and refers to the method of customer recruitment: sitting or standing in the front door of a brothel. But in the Greek and Roman world, as well as during the Middle Ages and the early modern period, other terms were used, such as *hetaira* (courtesan), *meretrix* (literally, 'she who earns'), and *amica* (female

Elwin Hofman, Magaly Rodríguez García, and Pieter Vanhees

friend), or 'whore' and 'lewd woman' in English, Middle Dutch, and many other languages. Such terms referred not only to women who sold sex, but to all women who engaged in atypical sexual relations. 'Whoring' is a word that often appears in medieval sources, and it is not always easy to distinguish between sex workers, adulteresses, and women who were sexually active before marriage. This changed in the eighteenth century, in Belgium and in many other European countries. Henceforth, authorities considered stricter surveillance necessary and began to stress the financial transaction. Notably, the authorities increasingly began to use the term 'prostitute' to refer specifically to women who sold sex. At the same time, authorities were not always sure about the monetary transaction, so any 'suspect woman' was at risk of ending up in the prostitution registers.

Hence, historical terms like 'prostitution' and 'prostitute' are important because they reflect the stigma surrounding commercial sex and the persons engaged in it. Tolerance of paid sex varied, depending on time and place. Sometimes, purveyors of sex were considered part of the working population, but more often than not, they were depicted as 'public women', very different from 'respectable' ones. Furthermore, the sale of sex was almost invariably linked to women. Until quite recently, prostitution was considered a typically female activity, whereas men or trans women who exchanged sex for money or material goods were often associated with homosexuality.

In the late twentieth century, the terms 'sex work' and 'sex worker' gained importance, emerging in the context of the socio-political and cultural changes of the 1960s and 1970s. The growth of new social organisations and the rise of a human rights discourse contributed to the development of the international sex worker movement. At its cradle were the legalisation of prostitution in Senegal in 1969 and the creation of organisations such as the US-based COYOTE (Call Off Your Old Tired Ethics) in 1973 and Britain's PUSSI (Prostitutes United for Social and Sexual Independence) in 1975. That same year, a group of sex workers occupied the Church of Saint-Nizier in Lyon, to protest police violence and lack of government protection. They received much media attention and were also supported by locals, who provided them with food and clothing. Their activism received a further boost when American artist, filmmaker, and author Carol Leigh, also known as 'The Scarlot Harlot', protested against the one-sided depiction of commercial sex as sexual abuse by men. At a feminist conference in San Francisco in 1979, Leigh coined the terms 'sex work' and 'sex worker', which in her view emphasised the service provider rather than the client. Other feminist attendees were not amused: many of them followed an abolitionist logic and remained faithful to their notion of prostitution and pornography as blatant symbols of patriarchy. The clash heralded the beginning of what is sometimes called the 'sex wars'.

In Belgium, the sex worker movement got off to a slower start. As a result of the AIDS epidemic, the activism of the 1980s and 1990s revolved mainly around health and safety. Social workers started to focus on harm reduction and, for the first time, paid attention to male and trans sellers of sex. While activists like Sonia Verstappen joined hands with other Belgian and foreign sex workers who demanded respect and state protection, a real movement only appeared in the new millennium. UTSOPI, the Union des Travailleur.euse.s du Sex Organisé.e.s pour l'Indépendance ('Union of Organised Sex Workers for Independence'), was founded in Brussels in 2015 to defend the rights of all those who engaged in commercial sex, regardless of their gender identity. Just a few years after its foundation, UTSOPI, in coalition with social workers, public authorities, scholars, and other stakeholders, achieved a major success. In 2022, the Belgian government approved a law that decriminalised commercial sex and opened the door to the formal recognition of prostitution as independent or wage labour.

In this book, too, we understand prostitution as a form of work. That means we see it as an activity that requires effort and has an economic value. This broad definition of work allows us to place commercial sex within the framework of labour history, even when sex workers from the Middle Ages to today experienced their activity as unpleasant, degrading, oppressing, or even coercive. Forced labour, after all, is also labour. Of course, this does not mean that we condone forced prostitution. Nor does it mean that all people who sold or sell sex saw or see their occupation as work.

Both archival sources and oral testimonies show that many sellers of sex did not define their activities as work. Anne-Marie's colleagues, for example, pointed out that she 'never worked' but made a lot of money from prostitution. For them – and perhaps for Anne-Marie, too, prostitution was something else. Many sources, from Belgium and abroad, contain accounts of women who justified their involvement in commercial sex with the argument that they 'did not find work'. Many used terms such as 'easy money', which they contrasted with the negative perception of the traditional jobs available to them. For others, particularly in times of crisis, the sale of sex simply meant survival.

The development of the sex worker movement has not changed this. Today, many people active in prostitution do not define themselves as sex workers. Some refer literally to the phenomenon ('sex for money'); others distance themselves from the profession by stressing the activity ('I sell sex', 'I engage in prostitution'…). This is not unique to the world of prostitution. In various sectors, many do not consider their daily activities as work or as meaningful for their self-perception and self-esteem. But that does not deter social scientists from studying those human efforts as work, both in the present and in the past.

Elwin Hofman, Magaly Rodríguez García, and Pieter Vanhees

From the Middle Ages to Today

The story we tell in this book begins in the late Middle Ages, around 1200. Of course, women and men exchanged sexual services for money or goods before this time. We choose to start in the thirteenth century because it was around that time that the Low Countries took on a shape that is still recognisable today. Important medieval cities still exist today, and the territory that would later become Belgium developed into a densely populated area, a crossroads of trade and cultures. In the late Middle Ages, cities were the first to issue prostitution policies, ensuring a certain, though not absolute, continuity with regards to public attitudes towards commercial sex. Urbanisation led to an expanding administration and more complex governing bodies promulgating rules aimed at promoting economic activities and safeguarding public order. At the same time, the importation of paper from China allowed merchants and other private individuals to create their own records and keep track of their transactions. More and more was written down and preserved.

It is therefore from about 1200 that we encounter the primary sources mentioned above. Indeed, the thirteenth century saw the birth of the first legal texts on prostitution, written accounts of the punishment violators of these laws received, as well as detailed accounts of some brothel keepers. These sources demonstrate that early attempts at regulation existed outside France, which has often been considered the cradle of the modern system of prostitution control. The late Middle Ages ushered in an era of increased societal interest in commercial sex, viewed as a 'necessary evil' by some and as a 'business of pleasure' by many others.

From that point of departure, this book is structured more or less chronologically. Each chapter is written by an expert on the period in question, but always deals with similar themes. In the first chapter, we show how sex work was organised from the thirteenth to the sixteenth centuries. Prostitution occupied an ambiguous place in late medieval society. While the Low Countries were known for their rich commercial sex culture and brothels were often tolerated, there was also a strong stigma on 'whoredom'. Paid sex was sinful, according to Christian doctrines, but also necessary to protect decent women. The policy of tolerance in most cities in the region that corresponds to what is now Belgium allowed so-called bathhouses to flourish.

From the end of the fifteenth century – and especially in the sixteenth century – the policy of tolerance came under pressure. With the rise of Protestantism and its Catholic reaction, Church authorities began to reject commercial sex more explicitly. As the Northern Netherlands (roughly today's Netherlands) split off from the Southern Netherlands (roughly today's Belgium) at the end of the sixteenth century, more and more cities tried to restrict prostitution or even ban it altogether. In the seventeenth and eighteenth centuries, they sometimes decreed harsh punishments for brothel owners, pimps, and sex workers. In practice, however, even in the early modern era, the authorities left most sex workers alone if they maintained a modicum of discretion. The second chapter in this book explores how the main actors of the sex industry navigated that climate.

From the sixteenth century, another difficulty confronted the sector: venereal disease. The rise of syphilis increasingly worried sex workers, clients, and authorities alike. This was one of the reasons why, at the end of the eighteenth century, attempts were made to move away from unsuccessful repressive measures and to develop a more sophisticated regulation system. As roving armies carried syphilis all over Europe, authorities desperately sought to protect their soldiers through registration lists and compulsory medical checks for sex workers. Napoleon became a champion of regulation, and many others followed his example. Around 1800, many Belgian cities drafted their own prostitution regulations, which remained in place after the official creation of Belgium in 1830. Indeed, the young nation early on earned international notoriety for its 'hyperregulation', affecting Anne-Marie and many others. The third chapter focuses on the regulation system and media scandals at the end of the nineteenth century, as well as the impact of the First World War on the policing, selling, and buying of sex.

The Belle Époque – late 1800s and early 1900s – was also the heyday of European imperialism. Belgian territory expanded to include a colony in Central Africa, seventy-seven times the size of the motherland. The Congo became the private property of Belgian King Leopold II in 1885 and then, from 1908 until 1960, stood under the rule of the Belgian state. In the fourth chapter, we highlight how the colonisers made new prostitution practices possible in Central Africa, a fact so far little studied by historians. Sex work by white women was prevented quite successfully by the authorities in the Congo. To their frustration, Black women developed practices of their own, which the colonisers eventually preferred to regulate rather than curb. At the same time, Belgian authorities classified all sorts of intimate relationships foreign to them as 'prostitution'.

Meanwhile, as we show in the fifth chapter, much was changing at home. After the First World War, American institutions such as The Rockefeller Foundation, and international organisations like the League of Nations, were fervently involved in the fight against global crime and the hedonism of the Roaring Twenties. Belgium's prostitution policy was a thorn in the eye of abolitionist activists who saw a direct link between the system of regulation and traf-

Elwin Hofman, Magaly Rodríguez García, and Pieter Vanhees

ficking. As prostitution control took an even harsher form during the German occupation of the 1940s, abolitionists convinced Belgian and French authorities to abandon the system. Nonetheless, the abolition of state regulation after the Second World War did not lead to many changes on the ground. In fact, the popularisation of new technologies, such as the telephone, fluorescent lights, and the automobile, meant that new forms of organisation became possible in sex work, too.

For historians, the recent past is always the most difficult to grasp. In the last chapters, we examine two complementary aspects of sex work since the 1970s. In chapter six, we provide an overview of changing policies and practices in commercial sex. At the end of the twentieth century, new opportunities and challenges emerged as Belgian society became increasingly globalised. Multi-national companies and European institutions settled in Brussels; migrants from Central and Eastern Europe arrived in Belgium after the fall of the Berlin Wall; and so did refugees from former Yugoslavia, Afghanistan, Rwanda, and other parts of the world. Cheaper transport and the Internet also facilitated the arrival of sellers of sex and intermediaries of prostitution who saw in Belgium the perfect location to pursue their interests. Belgian authorities, residents, and business owners in red-light districts and local sex workers responded in different ways to this new reality.

In chapter seven we present Sonia Verstappen's testimony. Her personal account of the circumstances that led to her engagement in commercial sex from the 1970s to the early 2000s provides a unique inside look at the recent history of prostitution. Her views on the arrival of large numbers of migrants from all parts of the world, the struggles with authorities wishing to relegate commercial sex to cities' outskirts, and the difficulties in developing new sex work policies that would protect all sex workers tell us much about the challenges of the twenty-first century. Verstappen's testimony is hence not only about prostitution, but also about alternative forms of intimacy, workers' organisation, and labour in general.

Much has changed over the past eight hundred years in how sex work was organised, policed, and experienced in the area that is Belgium today. But there is also continuity. Commercial sex has always been the subject of debate. What was the 'business of pleasure' for some was often viewed as a problem, which in Belgium was mainly a concern of local authorities. Yet, time and again, women and men found their way to prostitution, for longer or shorter periods, by choice or under duress. Time and again, they had to look for ways to escape the tight grip of authorities, neighbours, pimps, or brothel owners. They did so in very diverse ways. This book is an ode to that diversity.

1. GUILTY PLEASURE (1200–1550)

Jelle Haemers

Yde Veermans and her partner Willem Neeten were in trouble. They ran The Rose in Leuven, a well-known brothel that bore the name of the medieval symbol par excellence of lovemaking. In 1460, Yde and Willem handed over a sum of money to the town's hangman in exchange for the hacked-off hand of an executed criminal. They had hung a bag containing the skinned bones in a kettle used to heat bathing water. According to their lurid superstition, guests who washed themselves with this water would be inclined to quickly revisit their establishment. However, Yde and Willem were caught by the sheriff of Leuven, the representative of the Duke of Brabant. The couple was arrested, not only for stealing body parts from a hanged man, but also because this unsanitary practice had endangered the health of their customers. The Rose was closed and confiscated by the sheriff.

At first sight, this colourful incident seems to confirm several clichés about medieval sex work. The couple engaged in magical and criminal practices, conforming to the image of prostitution as a marginal trade and those involved in it as 'marginal people' or even 'witches'. However, historians have now demonstrated that commercial sex was not a peripheral phenomenon, but omnipresent in medieval cities. We now know that medieval sex workers were integrated into the society around them to a surprising degree. From this perspective, Yde and Willem look like independent operators of a family business embedded in the city's social fabric, providing a service indispensable for its proper functioning.

Yde and Willem collided with the authorities, but this was not because of the brothel's primary activities. Densely populated towns maintained strict measures to prevent epidemics and watched over the hygiene of their inhabitants, as Yde and Willem experienced first-hand. Moreover, can we accuse the couple of marginal practices if we bear in mind that they had only adopted a widespread custom? After all, the Church itself tried to attract believers in a similar way: with bones and other relics on display, it hoped to attract a large influx to pilgrimage sites. However, letting people bathe in water in which bones had steeped was clearly unacceptable, as was using a deceased person's hand for profane purposes. Contrary to the stereotypes, medieval people trying to avoid the outbreak of disease did not tolerate unsanitary practices. It was this concern that led to the imprisonment of Yde and Willem.

Sex work was considered sinful and dishonourable in the Low Countries, as elsewhere in medieval Europe, but it was not a crime. The relatively high tolerance of commercial sex created opportunities for brothel owners to attain wealth and status, though they did not escape government control, as the case of Yde and Willem reveals. Wealthy women, such as female brothel keepers, enjoyed relative freedom in the Low Countries. In towns, single women were able to work relatively freely. Daughters had the same inheritance rights as sons, and many female citizens invested in trade, just as they freely expressed their opinions in the streets. A brothel keeper like Yde often clashed with the authorities, but she clearly belonged to the wealthier citizens of the town. Though some citizens may have considered these women morally inferior, we will see that their material culture bears witness to their economic power and social status. Much like today, an ambiguous attitude thus characterised the medieval treatment of prostitution.

Women and Sex

Medieval elites often looked down on sex workers, using what was seen as their God-given body for the sale of 'unnatural' sex that was not aimed at procreation. This disdain is apparent in the designations given to female sex workers in Middle Dutch: *vrouwen van lichte* or *oneerlijk leven* ('women of light or dishonest life'), *deerne van oneerlijk leven, meyssen van zonden* ('sinful women'), *gemeen wijf* or *wereltwijf* ('common woman' or 'worldly woman'). Middle French echoed this contempt, but also reveals desire: from *femme folle* ('foolish woman'), over *femme de deshoneste* or *mauvaise vie* ('dishonourable lady'), to *fille de joye* or *fille de l'amoureuse vie* ('girl of pleasure' or 'loving girl'). Sometimes an insult was used, such as 'whore' (*hoer, baisselette* or *putain*), or a more curious name, like 'priest's women' (*papenwiven, mesquines de prêtres*). Women who sold sex were told to *folier leur corps* – abuse their God-given body. Tellingly, such words were not used by the sex workers themselves when they took up the pen in lease contracts and the like. They called themselves *vrouw, wijf,* or *femme*, the neutral words used to describe a woman in Dutch and French.

There is no general name for male sex workers, as they barely appear in the sources. There were (rare) tales of adulterous women, knocking on the doors of handsome lovers. In *Van den cnape van Dordrecht*, a tale told in fourteenth-century Brussels, a male sex worker calls himself a 'lad' who 'fucked wives for money'. In a French-language version, he describes himself as a *foteor* or *fouteres as loier*, freely translated: 'a fucker for hire'. Men like him possibly offered their services clandestinely, as little is known about their lifestyles.

The same applies to homosexual intercourse. Since intolerance towards 'buggery' (*buggerye*) was high, men and women who had intercourse with someone of their own sex were disapprovingly labelled 'sodomites'. It is possible that some of the men who were sentenced to severe punishments had worked for money, but evidence is lacking. In 1391, for example, at a major trial in Mechelen, Jan Stoelkin, along with seventeen other men, was sentenced to death for having committed 'buggery'. The verdict was silent on whether any payment had been involved. The judges wanted to make an example of someone who had clearly challenged the prevailing sexual norms, but they were also lenient, acquitting Stoelkin's partners. As long as people did not overtly have sexual relations with others of their sex, the Middle Ages were sometimes more lenient than is often imagined. Nevertheless, tolerance for female prostitution was much greater.

Ambivalence towards prostitution had its origins in medieval thinking about sex. Some religious thinkers were not averse to pre-marital relations or prostitution. Leading religious thinkers like Augustine and Thomas Aquinas argued that the presence of 'sinful women' in society could prevent greater evils. At the same time, there were rabid opponents within the Church. The sacred status of marriage and celibacy for clerics were non-negotiable. Husbands and celibates were thus expected to avoid 'lewd' places. Yet this did not prevent many clerics from seeking out brothels, and vice versa: street prostitution often flourished in the vicinity of monasteries. Yde and Willem's brothel, for instance, was located close to the cloister of the Augustinians, who, in terms of sexuality, may have put their master's advice into practice.

Taboos around sex within marriage were rare, except perhaps for an aversion to anal sex. According to a common Church-inspired view, unlike today, sex was not an act of two people. Rather, it was something men did to women via penetration. The man was the active partner, the woman submitted. In didactic stories, mostly written by clerics, the man had to lie on top of the woman to promote procreation. However, this did not prevent the circulation, among the population, of numerous poems and songs that glorified both male and female pleasure in bed and parodied the traditional positions. One poem about female sex from one of the oldest collections of poetry in Dutch (1528) was quite lyrical, for instance: 'My red lips, blushing cheeks, stiff breasts and soft body'. A lusty and wild woman sings about the joys of lovemaking in marriage. Sex is wild, unbound by Church doctrine.

Numerous extant booklets include recipes for increasing lust in men and women, sections on the use of contraceptives, and, in disguised form, instructions for inducing abortion. The book *Der vrouwen heimelijcheit* (1405) – about the 'hidden thing' of women, namely their genitals – is full of semi-gynaecological information, including technical information about coitus. In this book, sex is a cheerful means of keeping the body healthy and women pleased. Although sex work also appears in such texts, the attitude is again ambiguous: on the one hand, it is surrounded with a hint of shame; on the other, women appear in them as creative initiators. As they dance, they perform curious stances: with their legs in the air, like a rider on horseback, or turned around with the buttocks up. Medieval literature, at least the texts circulating among the common people, is thus full of sexual pleasure. But what was it like in practice?

Stews, Sex Work, and Pimps

Let's take a closer look at the place where women like Yde worked, the medieval brothel or 'stew'. In the southern Low Countries, as in England and France, stews were the most common type of brothel. In Southern, Central, and Eastern Europe, the sex industry was mainly organised in public brothels: the *prostibulum publicum*, like the Frauenhaus in the German Empire, founded by urban or regional authorities, and leased out to wealthy people. The house on the Berlich in Cologne, the so-called Casteletto in Dubrovnik, and the Château Vert in Toulouse, to name but a few well-known examples, were leased by the city to private operators, who in turn employed the women. Private brothels, most of which were illegal, were also active in some of these towns. In the Low Countries, however, private individuals could operate brothels legally, and public brothels were very rare.

These bathhouses and brothels were both known by the name *stove* in Dutch or *étuve* in French. This was because of their distinctive feature: the 'stove' that heated the building and distributed warm air through a system of pipes. The best English translation for *stove* is 'stew', a word that appears in Middle English in the middle of the fourteenth century to describe a hot room and by extension a place where people took hot baths. Stews existed all over Europe, but in the Low Countries they had grown into huge establishments where one could not only bathe, but also eat, drink, dance, and find other pleasures. Some of these stews were run as brothels, as in London, where bathhouses were so notorious that by the middle of the fourteenth century a whole neighbourhood came to be called 'Les Stuwes'. Etymologically, 'stew' comes from *estuve* or even from the Dutch *stove* – the latter term also being used in Middle English to refer to a heated room or building. This may be because migrants from the Netherlands and Northern France brought the invention with them. Sellers of sex from Flanders, Artois, Brabant, and Liège were active in many European cities, and brothels in Southwark were also packed with Flemish women. A fourteenth-century chronicle, for instance, describes how the London rebels in 1381 attacked a 'stew house', used by Flemish women, near London Bridge. To emphasise their origin, the chronicler referred to these sex workers by the Dutch term for women (*vrouwen*): the *frows* of Flanders.

It has rightly been suggested that sex workers might have highlighted their 'exotic' origins to be more attractive to their clients. But while it is quite possible that women claiming to be from the other side of the channel were in fact not from there, many women from Flanders and Brabant did engage in prostitution in England, including running brothels in the harbour towns of England, France, and Italy. For instance, 'whores' from Flanders, Brabant, and Liège were very popular in fifteenth-century Florence, where pimps from Brabant had even founded a kind of association that organised social activities. These migrants did not introduce brothels to these places but, given the preference for the exotic in the sex trade, it is quite possible that English or Italian brothel keepers were inspired by the stew culture of the Low Countries.

The cities of the Low Countries, and Bruges in particular, were certainly renowned throughout Europe for their bathing culture, and many merchants, noblemen, and soldiers described visiting a stew. For instance, when the Spanish nobleman Pero Tafur visited Bruges in 1438, he was struck by the fact that 'they take the bathing of men and women together to be as honest as we do churchgoing'. The Low Countries were a crossroads for traders, and from a commercial point of view, brothels offered male travellers attractive facilities. Students, merchants, mariners, and the like were given what could be called 'home comforts' in the stew. These services included hospitality and meals as well as 'paid love'.

The name 'stew', however, did not automatically mean that a bathhouse was also a brothel. Sometimes it was only clear for visitors 'in the know' that sexual services were available in a particular establishment, rather like massage parlours or saunas today. That is why lease contracts of stews usually refer to 'honourable stews' or explicitly state that women there did not offer sex. For example, in 1476 the priest Jan Ballinc from Leuven and his sister let a bathhouse in the Steenstraat to Jacob van der Moeyen and his wife. The lease contract explicitly states that the tenants of the stew should not let any 'dishonourable company' enter the establishment.

Authorities in the Low Countries only acted as watchdogs and, as stated above, usually did not manage stews themselves. An exception was a public brothel in Liège, the Matrognard, owned and farmed out by the prince bishop. It had a monopoly on prostitution within the city walls, but the punishments of private brothel keepers show that the rule was not respected. The city government in Breda in 1496 also opened a bathhouse, having financed its construction, but that may have been part of a general reconstruction programme after a large fire burned down a section of the town. Elsewhere, stews were part of the private market. In some towns, such as Bruges, stew keepers were theoretically prohibited from employing sex workers, but the fine they paid for this 'crime' was in practice a lucrative tax for the town. The tax records list thirty-four such stews over a period of 150 years. Since they paid this tax, we can be certain they were brothels.

Few cities had similar fiscal legislation, but almost everywhere regulations were in place regarding stews. Some stews were open to men only, some only to women, and others accepted a mixed clientele. For example, an ordinance of 1415 from Aalst permitted mixed stews on Saturdays only, while women were welcome on Mondays, men the next day, and so on. A provision from 1398 stipulated that the stews of Mons should display a placard depicting a man or woman to indicate who was welcome on that day. Of the forty well-known Ghent stews, sixteen operated as women's stews, and thirteen as men's; the others were probably mixed. It is unclear in which of these houses women offered sexual services. For instance, a 1471 ordinance from Mechelen states that mixed bathhouses would henceforth not be permitted. Married women could accompany their husbands to men's stews, but couples were no longer welcome in the women's stews. Female servants were allowed in both types of establishments, but this could refer to women filling the baths with hot water. Presumably sex workers were mainly active in men's or mixed stews. Men were not allowed in the women's stews, but in men's stews 'dishonourable' women did their work.

If sex work and keeping a brothel were mostly tolerated, the law had little mercy for pimps (*putiers* in Middle Dutch, or *hurier* in French). A pimp was someone who 'kept women for his own profit', as Antwerp law stated. The appropriate punishment for them was banishment. The houses of whoever hid pimps had to be demolished to show that they no longer belonged to the community. The oldest criminal law of Oudenaarde (1328) even stipulated that an ear of the condemned should be pierced with a glowing iron if they did not leave town. The regional authorities also regularly intervened. In August 1459, for example, the Burgundian duke Philip the Good, who then ruled most of the

Jelle Haemers

Low Countries, issued an ordinance stipulating that 'whoever lives off dishonourable women' had to leave the country for ten years.

Yde Veermans from Leuven had fallen victim to this law, too, because she paid a fine to the sheriff that year for the 'profit' she had taken from the women working in her brothel. Presumably the sheriff had found the kettle with the bones when he investigated her brothel to find out whether she had complied with the Ducal ordinance. In this case, she bought off her punishment, demonstrating that authorities did not punish too severely if the offender promised henceforth to abide by the law. But that did not prevent pimps from being regularly targeted. In 1428, for example, the Maastricht city council stipulated that a search would be conducted twice a year in each parish for residents who engaged in 'pimphood'. In Maastricht, as elsewhere, authorities regularly punished men as well as women for this crime, which shows that the practice was difficult to eradicate. 'Trafficking in women' on a massive scale was rare in the Middle Ages, although abuse of trust was all too prevalent. In any case, a legal framework existed to counter such practices.

Places of Prostitution

The fine that Yde Veermans paid in 1459 was not her first confrontation with the local authorities. Six years earlier, Yde and Willem had already caused nuisance in Leuven when, according to the aldermen, they had attracted 'worthless and dishonourable women' to their street. However, when defending her case at the town hall, Yde argued that the nuisance was not as bad as the neighbours had claimed: she had only been acting 'courteously', or in a civilised manner by making rooms available to these girls in her own home. Her response reveals that some stews in the Low Countries did not have bathing facilities, though such houses seem to have been rare. That is also what Yde's next remark revealed. In response to the neighbours' complaints, she promised to expand her building into an actual stew, permitting the girls to offer their services on the premises. The aldermen accepted her defence and decided that Yde and her partner were no longer allowed to rent out rooms in their house to girls but would instead be permitted to 'keep a stew as others do in the town'. However, if the couple was caught committing any irregularities, the town council would intervene.

Yde and Willem's brothel was located in the northern port area of Leuven. As with most stews in the Netherlands, it was on a waterway, the river Dyle. Water and the infrastructure to heat it were essential in stews. A 1449 inventory of a Cambrai brothel contained items such as ashtrays and pokers, a large bathtub, six smaller tubs, barrels, numerous buckets of wood, leather, and iron, as well as fuel. For Ghent, the description of a visit in 1912 to the ruins of Castle Wandelaert, the largest women's stew in the city, testifies to the existence of ovens in the building. Climbing a stone staircase giving access to two floors, the visitor found that each floor had two large rooms. He also discovered a large round stone tub in an outhouse near the water, which he suspected was a reservoir filled with water from the Scheldt to supply the baths.

In 1528, a literary work printed by Jan van den Dale, called *De stove*, locates the story in a Brussels' men's bathhouse, which was, however, only separated from a women's bathhouse by a thin wall. As in a sauna today, it was probably a wooden partition, which, according to the account, allowed guests to eavesdrop on conversations in the adjoining room. While the wooden interiors no longer exist, archaeological remains of stews confirm that their architecture in the Low Countries followed a general pattern. Excavations in the Nederstove, a large stew in Aalst, for instance, uncovered two round stone ovens. Under a mud floor, excavators made a remarkable discovery: the skeleton of a baby less than six months old, buried in a cloth. We do not know the cause of death, but it may have been a newborn of one of the sex workers.

Like the brothels mentioned above, most of these establishments could be found in a particular part of town. Indeed, zoning commercial sex was common. The goal was to keep street prostitution out of some neighbourhoods, but also to control nuisance. In this way, men looking for commercial sex knew where to find the right women. In general, it is striking that the prostitution district was never located right in the city centre, but also not far outside town. Many cities consisted of an old core that usually dated back to a twelfth-century settlement, and was surrounded by a new, wider wall in the fourteenth century. The wealthiest citizens, who lived within the core, may have made use of the services of sellers of sex, but preferred to meet them in the suburbs. This is clearly the case in Leuven, for example, where the area outside of the twelfth-century ramparts – like the Halvestraat where Yde lived – were well-known streetwalking districts.

In Antwerp and Brussels, convents were popular meeting places. In Brussels, the streets around the Franciscan convent (today's Bourse or Brussels' Stock Exchange Building) were known hotspots for commercial sex. Sex workers were also active in the cemetery around Antwerp's Church of Our Lady, just as Maastricht's 'hot neighbourhood' was located at the church of the same name. In 1406, the city stipulated that sex workers had to move within a defined area in the square in front of the church, so that they would no longer occupy the entire street. In Mons, the (still existing) Rue des Fillettes was located near the

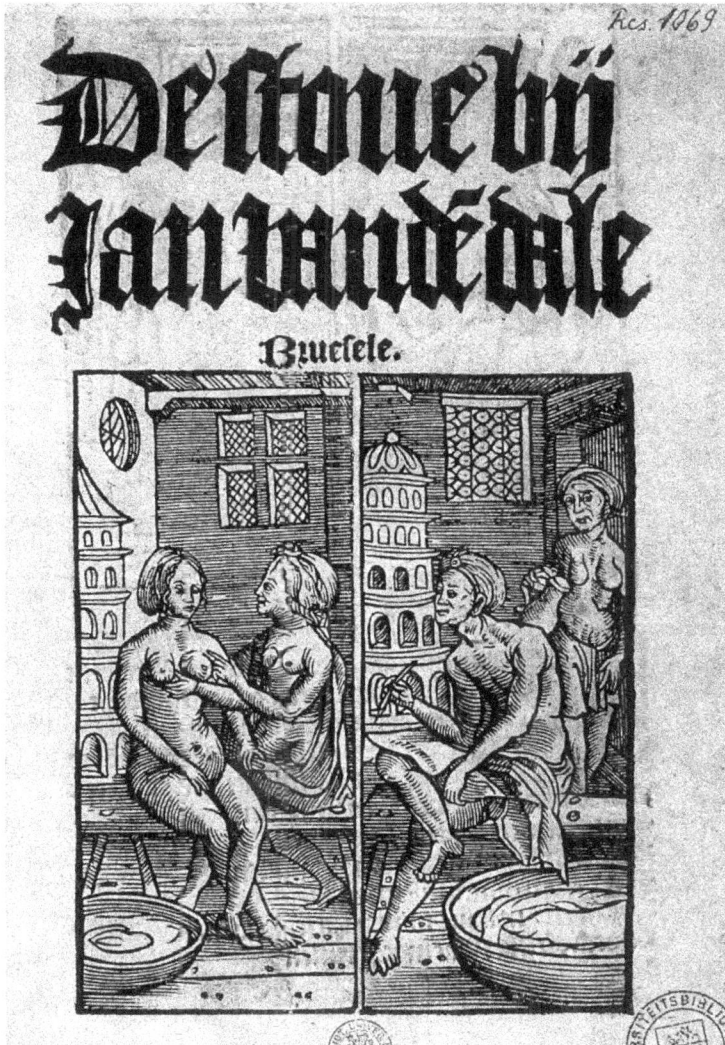

The cover page of the popular tale *De Stove*, printed by Jan van den Dale in 1528, shows the interior of a women's stew in Brussels, separated from a men's stew by a thin wall. A visitor in the latter carefully notes down a conversation of two women in the adjoining room, while a female servant is filling the bath (*Jan van den Dale. Gekende werken met inleiding, bronnenstudie, aanteekeningen en glossarium*, ed. Gilbert Degroote, De Nederlandsche boekhandel, 1944, p. 147).

Dominican monastery; in Mechelen, customers sought out their haunts in the area around St John's Church. In short, the presence of celibate men attracted sellers of sex.

At the end of the fifteenth century, in particular, the proximity of commercial sex to religious institutions posed a problem for municipal and convent administrations, as a growing moral revival drove a wedge between the religious world and sex workers. In 1471, for example, the Antwerp city government stipulated that no new brothels would be permitted in the streets where the annual procession passed. 'Sinful women' were not allowed to buy houses or yards there to carry out their activities, nor to hold meetings of 'men, women, and young girls'. But it was to no avail, because six years later, and again in 1516, the city had to renew the ordinance. Local authorities hoped to limit the nuisance of prostitution, especially during religious festivals.

Given the central location and sheer size of stews, their owners must have come from wealthy families. As in other regions, stew owners in the Low Countries boasted a high social status. Many wealthy families made a nice living by renting out bathhouses. Take the example of In den Wierinc, the largest brothel in Leuven, which lay in the city centre, directly opposite the ducal palace. The Beyaert family had been managing the property for a long time before the brothers Jan and Peter Beyaert in 1459 let it to a tailor, Jacob van Stertebeke, and his wife. Jan and Peter belonged to the economic elite of Leuven, lending money to many families and leaving a significant inheritance. We know that Yde Veermans also lent money to others and acted as a guarantor in lease contracts. Like other wealthy women in the Low Countries, Yde became involved in finances, capital markets, and the world of petty trade. From that perspective, Yde was just another businesswoman like many others in town, though her business was to entertain men with sex.

Into the Brothel

Stews like Yde's were famous for their sexual entertainment. This is evident in the poem 'Adieu Bruxelles' ('Goodbye Brussels') of the fourteenth-century French troubadour Eustache Deschamps. When back in Paris after a journey to Brussels he wrote down his memories of a visit to one of the town's brothels. He recounts how the visitor to the stews could have a pleasant bath, drink Rhine wine, sing and dance, and have fun with willing girls in beautiful rooms with soft beds. One verse praises the brothel's 'rabbits, plovers, capons, and pheasants', terms that almost certainly do not refer to the food Deschamps ate, but to the sweet company he found there.

Jelle Haemers

Medieval literature and iconography frequently associated animals, especially birds, and flowers with love, in either a spiritual or a sexual sense. In Cambrai, Douai, Arras, and Saint-Omer, citizens and travellers could visit brothels named after lilies, roses, and swans. Others had grandiose names, such as The Crown, The God of Love, The Sun, The Devil, The Angel, or The Paradise. The same was true of brothels in Dutch-speaking towns: The Peacock or The Falcon (Sluis), In the Rose (Leuven), In the Lamb and the Deer (Bruges). Just about every town had a brothel called The Parrot, the symbol par excellence of the game of love. Not only did this colourful bird refer to sexual entertainment, it was also the target in a popular shooting game, the parrot symbolising the 'male act'. Archers of the shooting guilds aimed at parrots made of wood or cardboard, fixed at the end of a long pole. Even French brothels had adopted the Dutch name. Such was the case in Douai, where the Etuve des Papegais was a well-known place of entertainment; while in Avignon one could visit a brothel with a room called Papegai. In the Low Countries too, whole brothels as well as separate rooms had symbolic names referring to sex. The room names of In den Wierinc in Leuven appealed to the imagination: the falcon, the peacock, the parrot, the lily room, or the rose hat. There was also a St George's chamber, perhaps an allusion to the 'juice' of St George, a popular euphemism in Dutch fiction for male seed. Such names and metaphors were meant to create the kind of elegant atmosphere that would please customers like the courtly poet Eustache Deschamps.

What did the interior of these rooms look like? Many lease contracts, both from bathhouses and brothels, mention beds among their furniture. In Leuven, the largest brothel had no less than forty-two beds. In other cities there was also significant sleeping space in stews. Casteel Wandelaert in Ghent contained thirty-seven beds, while smaller establishments, such as The New Stew and The Crown, had from ten to twenty beds. Brothels in other towns offered similar numbers. Among the movables in stews, contracts list linen, bedding, and many sleeping caps. The 1425 lease of The New Stew in Ghent, for instance, lists nineteen blankets and fourteen pillows. The presence of a furnace kettle in the Leuven stew Gulden Mouwe ('Golden Sleeve') reveals that cooking went on there, but aside from a few drinking pots, no cutlery is mentioned in the contract, presumably because the tenants brought their own. Another stew in Leuven has the only inventory containing kitchen supplies (a pantry, with all kinds of boxes and kettles), as well as a (portable?) latrine.

The stew's 'private' rooms were clearly not individual spaces, as they often contained several beds, which could accommodate a family, a small group, or a few couples. If a couple wished to be separate from others, in bed, screens or

The interior of a medieval stew, run as a brothel, in the Low Countries. The miniature was made in Bruges in the third quarter of the fifteenth century (Paris, Bibliothèque nationale de France, Ms. Réserve, n° 5196, 378r; from Valerius Maximus' *Dits et faits mémorables*, translated by Simon de Hesdin and Nicolas de Gonesse).

curtains (listed in several lease contracts) could render their intimate encounter invisible to others. The room contents described in the sources match the well-known iconography: couples dining together in a luxurious room full of baths and curtained beds. Fine furnishings were necessary in brothels if women were entertaining noblemen, who probably expected to be pleasured in a place that was not only comfortable, but also appropriate to their social status. It is also possible that men outside the town's upper social stratum were attracted by the luxury on

Jelle Haemers

offer, as it promised the joy of an unforgettable experience. The so-called Dukes' room in the Leuven stew In den Wierinc contained three beds, a sofa, and a comfortable armchair, while another room also boasted a sofa. Since the brothel was near the ducal palace, members of the duke's entourage might have booked it. Perhaps members of court behaved like dukes when visiting these rooms and sitting in their cosy armchairs? The information we have about the rooms' names and interiors suggests that they were designed to appeal, above all, to men.

At the same time, the material culture of brothels might also have reflected the identity and aspirations of the women working there. It is hard to find information about their living conditions, but some brothels had rooms with names referring to their occupants. There was not only a 'women's room' with six beds in In den Wierinc, but also separate rooms with women's names, such as Anne's room and Marioen's room, each containing three beds. While these were probably the names of women who worked there, the 'women's room' might have been a room for other members of the brothel's staff. The inventory of a Cambrai brothel also lists a 'girls' room'. The servants in most of these houses were female, as we know from stories and iconography. Some carried water and others served food, while sex workers and masseuses pleasured men. A Brussels ordinance of 1424 suggests that many of the servants were poor, for the town councillors forbade servants of the stews to beg on the streets or to ask for bread at the doors of citizens' homes. Perhaps some of the women working in stews, both as servants or as sex workers, accumulated so much debt that they were unable to free themselves from a life of semi-slavery. Information about how they were paid is sparse in the Low Countries, but research on Bruges seems to confirm that many sex workers were financially dependent on the brothel's tenant. As we have seen, legislation regularly forbade pimps from taking goods from sex workers, but the fact that such ordinances were regularly promulgated shows that women who worked in brothels often faced exploitation.

Still, not all sex workers lived a life of misery. Official government documents recording the sales of sex workers' personal belongings offer unique insight into their material goods. These public sales were organised to pay off the women's debts when they died unexpectedly. We can, for instance, investigate the wardrobe of Bette Caens from Sluis, who died in 1396, because the accounts detail the goods found at her home. She certainly numbered among the wealthier brothel owners; the sale of her belongings brought in 393 pounds. While the account describes Bette as a 'lady of women' (*dame de femmes*), meaning she offered facilities to sex workers in her house, her possessions suggest that she also offered commercial sex herself. In addition to silver dishes and precious chests, the clerk found in the wardrobe of her bedroom a green overdress, a grey hat with gilded silver buttons, and a red cloak lined with squirrel fur. Clothing reflected the woman's status, and such finery was an investment that could be readily transported. In addition, as an erotic outfit it would render the woman attractive to clients. Unsurprisingly, abbot Gilles Li Muisis of Tournai even insinuated that the new fashion of rows of buttons on the sleeves and cut-out cleavages from the 1340s had come into vogue because of sex workers.

Accounts recording the sale of the worldly goods of four 'common women' from Valenciennes add more detail to the belongings of those who worked in brothels. Alongside more common furniture, such as beds and cupboards, they also possessed luxury objects. A certain Marie, for instance, who worked as a masseuse in a stew, left chairs, an oil lamp, bed linen, candlesticks and a 'woman's suitcase' when she died in 1491. She also owned a comb, a shrine, and two posh dresses, one of which was lined with rabbit fur. Another sex worker, also named Marie, had a bed, linen, a mirror, a laundry basket, a grey dress, and an image of St John. Similar goods were found in the house of Micquelette, who also possessed an ointment box and much pottery. Women (including, perhaps, fellow sex workers) were among those who purchased her goods, along with craftsmen and sellers of second-hand goods.

Belotte de Sirau, another *fille de vie* of Valenciennes, died in a hospital in 1498. The profits from the sale of her movables (cupboards, shelves, cooking pots, a waffle iron, a black lady's mantle, a decorated belt, and so on) went to the owner of her apartment for unpaid rent, to the priest who performed the funeral mass, and to the undertaker who had ordered two porters to carry her body from the hospital to the cemetery and dig her grave. The sale brought in a total of 14 pounds, a decent sum situating Belotte squarely among the middling groups in town. For Belotte, and for Bette Caens from Sluis, a mass was organised, and alms distributed to the poor, as was usual when well-respected people died.

Sex Work and the Authorities

Several interesting sources are extant, providing insight into the life sex workers led inside and outside the brothel. Some resulted from the punishment of sex workers who violated urban regulation – as was the case with Yde Veermans from Leuven. Others are normative texts, or even inventories of the property of women who were active in the stews. In what follows, we briefly survey the information such documents provide, allowing us to reconstruct the lives of sex workers.

Several normative texts enlighten us on how sex workers were, or at least should be, dressed. In Mons, for example, 'common women' (sometimes mentioned with the addition 'who made money with their body') were required to wear a piece of yellow cloth, as distributed by the town receiver himself in 1480 to those who practised this 'joyful profession'. In Namur, a green band had to adorn the right sleeve of the dress of 'women with a dishonourable life', and they were forbidden to wear headgear. In Maastricht, too, the city council decided in 1389 that all women who let themselves 'be married for money' had to pin on a yellow cloth. That way, residents could immediately recognize who they were dealing with. This measure served to protect 'honourable women' from harassment by men looking for paid sex.

The policy also saved men from unpleasant surprises, as, for example, a priest from Tongerlo near Antwerp experienced in 1455. By his own account, he did not know he was dealing with a sex worker when he started talking to a woman at an Antwerp inn. She offered him a drink, which he willingly accepted. Moreover, according to the account of the Antwerp sheriff, the woman invited the clergyman to stay with her. The two went off together, but after a while the woman asked for money, which the priest would not give her. To settle the ensuing argument, the couple eventually ended up at the sheriff's office, who let them go after an amicable settlement. We do not know the exact circumstances of this incident, but it was precisely to avoid such cases that cities developed a clear 'recognition policy'. Still, the question remains to what extent sellers of sex complied with these regulations.

Documented punishments of sex workers found in government archives do reveal that some women caused trouble. These were often women who had gotten into fights or entered areas forbidden to them. Yet lumping these women together with criminals goes too far. The government mainly targeted repeat offenders and intervened when public order was threatened. This is also reflected in the severity of the punishments: the 'criminals' often got off with a fine or an obligatory pilgrimage. The latter, a typically medieval punishment, of course had a religious purpose but also a practical one: the source of the evil was sent out of town for a while. In Diest, for example, Noykene Basteels in 1490 was condemned to a double pilgrimage: having committed immoral acts at the beguinage and also wounded a man, she had to travel both to Ferrara and Rome. Indeed, sex workers could get into fights, as happened in Sluis (the outport of Bruges) in 1392. Maye Deminne had with her nails scratched open Line van der Londe's face, for having slept with her boyfriend. She was fined.

The authorities had no mercy for people who facilitated commercial sex with children. The following cases show that while judges did act against abuse, some practices were difficult to curb. In 1436, for instance, Marie Brachelette from Mons had offered some men sex with her daughter in exchange for money. A common punishment in Hainaut for such a crime was public humiliation. The executioner locked Marie up in a large basket, which he then immersed in a small lake or barrel of water. The intention was not to drown the woman, but to publicly shame her and scare off bystanders. Afterwards, the woman was banished. Avezoete, a woman who had first been expelled from Ypres in 1314, was again convicted five years later, this time for having allowed men to sleep with her daughter, and for receiving the money the daughter had 'won with her body', as the condemnation put it. In 1431, two people from Brussels faced severe punishment for the same reason. Miller Oste De Dekker and Katelijn Faes had led away a 'good man's child', that is, an underage girl from a good family, and had 'disgraced' her in Katelijn's house on the road to Leuven. This was obviously unacceptable: a heavy fine and a banishment were imposed on them. In 1483, the aldermen of Bruges convicted brothel keeper Cornelie van den Hecke for employing 'young virgins'. When a client raped a fifteen-year-old girl there, Cornelie had even snapped at the victim to stop shouting.

A further government initiative, albeit this time to curb sex work in the city, involved the establishment of so-called houses of 'converted women'. Such houses, into which sex workers could enter if they promised to put an end to their activities, existed all over Europe. Avignon alone numbered seven such houses when the pope had his residence there. To avoid nuisance on the streets and the possible suffering of those involved, Duchess Margaret of York, in cooperation with the Mons city council, in 1481 founded a home there for sex workers who would henceforth go through life as 'repentant women'. The founding act states that the duchess not only wanted to keep the *filles de l'amoureuse vie* away from her own palace, but also that she wanted to prevent the many quarrels and riots that took place among them. After the women had renounced their activities, they could move into the house, with a one-month probationary period. The maximum age was thirty, which suggests that the founders wished mainly to rescue young women from a difficult situation.

The 'repenties', as they were known throughout Europe, were not a religious order, because although the inhabitants were known as 'poor sisters of Magdalena' or, in Lille 'Madelonnettes' (after Mary Magdalene, the patron saint of sex workers), the women could leave the house and retire. Henceforth they were married to God, it was said, but they could also marry a 'real man' on condition that they left the community. Sometimes, however, women left the house to take up sex work again, as the story of Calotte Desfontaines shows. In 1489, she was banished for three years from the town of Lille because she had left the house and had sex with a married man.

The number of women in the houses of converted women could vary considerably. In the beginning, for example, twenty-four were allowed to stay in

Jelle Haemers

Lille, while in Prague the number could reach eighty. In the Low Countries, the houses of repentance did not survive the religious reforms of the seventeenth century: in 1613 the Tournai house closed its doors, and in 1650 that of Valenciennes followed. Although the Couvent de Repenties of Mons existed until the end of the eighteenth century, it had previously been transformed into an ordinary convent for women.

Whether the government actually established such houses out of charity, remains an open question. But it is notable that their establishment, as in the example of Mons, was the result of complaints about the (alleged) nuisance caused mainly by visiting customers. This seems to be the general trend: the government mainly took action after local residents complained about nuisance. In 1444, for example, the city council of Leuven decided, at the request of the inhabitants, that women who 'held public company' had to move to the place assigned them, near the city walls. Discontent grew especially in the Halvestraat, located on the eastern city wall near the Dyle. The city banned streetwalking as early as 1426, because the nuns of a nearby convent could no longer tolerate dealing with the 'dishonourable women'. A few decades later, it seems the nuisance in Leuven's Halvestraat had still not dissipated. Indeed, as we saw above, it was in that precise street that Yde Veermans had caused trouble.

Customers

What do we know about Yde's customers and the 'nuisance' they caused? Were they really attracted by her lurid practices? For information about the visitors to brothels, we can again draw upon legal texts. Antwerp legislation, for example, sentenced married people found in brothels to a fine. This applied both to adulterous husbands and to wives who offered their services. In Sint-Truiden, the punishment for nocturnal brothel visits consisted of one *real* (a local coin) for a town's inhabitant, a relatively small sum, and double for a stranger. In practice, therefore, the fine may here have amounted more to a kind of residence tax.

There were also other practical rules for clients. Paid sex could attract unruly people and lead to brawls. In Diest and Sint-Truiden, therefore, brothel-goers were forbidden to carry weapons; in Lille and Huy, men who went out on the streets after ten o'clock in the evening could be arrested in these neighbourhoods. The fact that in many other cities sex workers were forbidden to be active on the streets after curfew, on pain of a fine, suggests that visits had to take place mainly during the day.

Such measures were intended not only to limit street violence, but also to protect sellers of sex. Thus, in 1394, Jan de Zaghere ran up against a three pound fine in Nieuwpoort after Maykin Janssoons denounced him for having refused to pay for her services. In Brussels in 1480, Gillis van Ieghem went on a compulsory pilgrimage to Milan because he had beaten a certain Juliane on her bed in a stew. Admittedly, Juliane was also fined because she had grossly overcharged him. An Antwerp sex worker called Paxken, who was not only 'light of morals' but also 'light of senses', according to the sheriff's bookkeeping, was not so lucky. She died in 1459 after a run-in with a drunk man who had thrown a pot against her head. This and many other examples testify to the aggression to which sellers of sex were subjected.

A diverse array of extant sources, including verdicts of condemned citizens, travel journals, or tales sung by troubadours about the mischief-mongering of male cronies testify to the fact that soldiers, travellers, and even nobles spent the night in cabarets or other places of ill repute. Thus, in 1479 the city council of Tournai exiled two residents after they ran amok in one of the city's largest brothels, the Estuves du Molinel. Gillot de Hem and Jacqueot Navel had an altercation with some mercenaries from the army of the French king (Tournai belonged to France), whom they found in the bedrooms. When both men also pulled a knife on the city's procurator, who had come to put things in order, they were obliged, among others, to make a trip – appropriately – to the pilgrimage site of Saint Mary Magdalene in the Provence.

The sixteenth-century travel accounts of the Bohemian baron Leo of Rozmital, for one, attest to the fact that not only soldiers and lower-class people, but also traders and itinerant diplomats, enjoyed the services of sex workers. Arriving in Mechelen in 1466, he noted in his travel journal that he first discovered the Bruges baths. Much to his joy, as another visitor from the Holy Roman Empire, Yeronimus Münzer from Nuremberg, noted in his accounts in 1495, very willing women could be found in those baths. The Flemish women, attractively dressed, were very adept at lovemaking, Münzer mused. In his eyes, they were 'real daughters of Venus'.

Of course, locals themselves also visited stews, as brothel attendance was an integral part of day- and nightlife. The accounts of private individuals contain telling traces of brothel visits. The personal accounts of Wenceslas of Bohemia, Duke of Brabant, reveal that in the years 1363 and 1364, he visited Nicolas Pedelere's stew in Brussels a total of twenty-seven times, each time 'with knights and armed men from his retinue'. It is unclear, however, whether these were ordinary bathhouses or brothels. The fourteenth-century cash book of Simon de Rikelike, a wealthy farmer and widower from Sint-Pieters-op-den-Dijk, near Bruges, is more explicit. Personal expenses from May 1327, for instance, document that he often went to the 'bride', an expression denoting a visit to a concubine or sex worker, both in Bruges and in the surrounding countryside. On a Sunday, for example, Simon visited Hanne Motins' inn; on the following Tuesday he went back; on Thursday he visited the stew Ten Vachte; on another Tuesday Simon went to bathhouses in Bruges; and shortly afterwards again in a neighbouring village. So, during this merry month of May, Simon spent much time in commercial sex venues, which explains why he copied verses from the *Roman de la Rose* that sang of free love in his cashbook. Moreover, the expenses incurred provide an idea of the cost of a brothel visit: prices varied from one-third to two-thirds the daily wage of a skilled artisan. The visit, therefore, did not weigh heavily on Simon's budget and was affordable for artisans.

Quite a few sellers of sex tried to lure clients not only with a 'democratic' price, but also with an 'exotic' origin, a luxurious interior, or with magic. In 1434, for instance, Antwerp aldermen sent Jan Dackenans' wife on a pilgrim-age to Rome because she had used 'magic powder' and spices to attract men to women. In later periods, too, we find women using magical practices to lure customers. Thus, in 1544 the aldermen of Bruges punished a woman for bringing some bones of an executed person to their brothel, in a bid to attract more clients. Superstition is of all times, but apparently (black) magic figured in medieval folklore as a stimulant for brothel attendance.

And so, we are back to Yde from Leuven. How did her confrontation with the authorities end? As the earlier clash with the town council in 1453 demon-strated, Yde was not a woman to sit by idly. Indeed, after her subsequent impris-onment by the sheriff in 1460, she immediately demanded her release, hoping to revoke the confiscation of her property with a trial before the alderman's court. During the trial she argued that the mayor had no right to seize houses belonging to people from Leuven. She added that she was willing to accept con-demnation, provided it was done (in her own words) 'with justice'. Yde admitted that she had put the bones in a bathtub, but she hoped, as was her right, for an amicable settlement. Although the sheriff objected, the Leuven aldermen vindicated Yde: the town's mayor reminded the sheriff that the privileges of the people of Leuven prohibited such confiscation. He thus ordered the property to be released and Yde to be treated 'with justice'. Shortly afterwards, it came to the hoped-for settlement. Yde paid fifty guilders to the sheriff – about one year's rental income from The Rose. He thereupon released Yde and her partner.

Whether this incident can ultimately be linked to Yde's 1476 promise to ban prostitution from her stew is not entirely clear. On 26 June of that year, she again went to the alderman's court, this time to solemnly swear that she would no longer harbour girls who engaged in 'indecent' practices. Henceforth, Yde literally stated, she would run the business 'as one should do in an honourable stew'. This was more than fifteen years after her clash with the sheriff, so presumably this promise was not a consequence of the 1460 case. About a month later, on the feast day of Saint Mary Magdalene, she let the stew for the first time, to a certain Liesbet Mertens. Yde inserted a clause into the lease contract stipulating that she could visit the stew as often as she wanted, free of charge. The last lease contract of Yde's stew dates from 1488. In it, she informs the tenant, Liesbet Van Sint-Truiden, that she could rent out the establishment to whomever she liked, as long as the neighbours did not complain about the activities it hosted. Did this remarkable statement refer to her confrontation with the town authorities many years before?

Presumably Yde turned her back on her old practices as a brothel keeper because by then she was a woman of a certain age. Or did she conform to the spirit of the times? After all, the days of the rich 'stew life' in the Low Countries were numbered. Although tolerance of paid sex remained high in the sixteenth century, stews managed as brothels disappeared. Street prostitution and smaller 'closed inns', 'whorehouses', or 'dance halls', as they were called, took over. It is difficult to know how far this change was due, on the one hand, to stricter sexual morality and increased patriarchal control over women by civic and ecclesiastical authorities in this period; or to more stringent hygiene on the other. Late medieval citizens clearly had a keen sense of the health dangers of air pollution, shortages of clean water, and the improper disposal of human waste. From this perspective, the imprisonment of Yde Veermans in 1460 after the bones were discovered in a bathtub bears witness to changing approaches to urban well-being. Was this also why she stopped her activities as a brothel keeper? Or did Yde decide to end an incident-rich but also successful career because she wanted to take it easy henceforth? Only Yde knows.

Jelle Haemers

2. WANTONS ON THE SCAFFOLD (1550–1830)

Elwin Hofman

It was not her first ordeal. In 1771, when Marie Anne Peccau was barely twenty-one years old, she was arrested for the eleventh time by the Brussels authorities. She was, she readily confessed, a *fille de joie*, a girl of pleasure. After her previous arrests, she had been repeatedly detained in various Brussels prisons, led out of the city, and formally exiled for three years. At her last banishment, she had even been given four shillings so that she could travel back to her hometown of Namur. Still she came to Brussels, again and again, and engaged in sex work. Just three days after her previous exile, she had been back in Brussels, rented a room under a false name and got away with it for six months. Then she had run into trouble again. Neighbours had complained about the scandal she caused and the many soldiers she hosted in her room. And so the judges again sentenced her to banishment from the city, now for six years.

If the judges thought Peccau had learned her lesson, they were mistaken. She was back in Brussels the very next day and six months later again arrested. As before, she immediately confessed: she had wandered the streets of Brussels every evening 'offering pleasure to passers-by in the street'. The judge also accused her of committing thefts, which she vehemently denied. The judges – you would think they would have realised by now that there was no point in the exercise – banished her from the city for a further ten years. Six months later, Peccau found herself once again arrested in Brussels, apprehended by patrollers who recognised her. This time, she claimed having gone to her parents in Namur, but they had simply sent her away, saying 'she has brought ruin upon herself, so she must stay there now'. Enough was enough, the judges thought: this time they not only banished Peccau, but first had her undergo a public shaming. She was put on the scaffold and flogged.

Peccau did not think she deserved this flogging. Instead of enduring her punishment with humility, she raised hell. Witnesses heard her shouting that 'the gentlemen of the magistrate were all pimps'! She made obscene hand gestures, refused to cover her breasts while being flogged, and raised her skirts above her knees. 'I'm not a thief,' she cried out. 'I'm just a whore!'

A New Order

The Peccau case reveals the changing attitudes towards prostitution in the early modern period. While many differences existed between cities and regions, we can still discern a general trend: from the sixteenth to the eighteenth century, the official attitude of the authorities in the Southern Netherlands towards prostitution gradually became stricter. New laws, more supervision, and harsher punishments were introduced. This increasingly strict policy and the growing police supervision came to a climax in Brussels in the second half of the eighteenth century.

As early as the sixteenth century, ideas about prostitution were becoming more negative, both in the Southern Netherlands and in many European countries. Increasingly, sexual self-control became the norm. The changing position of the Church played an important role in this evolution. Many leading late-medieval theologians had accepted prostitution as a necessary evil. For the theologians of the sixteenth century, however, there was no space for such moral laxity. Protestant reformers in the early sixteenth century blew the whistle. Christian faith was in a state of moral decay, Martin Luther preached. The ubiquitous toleration of fornication aroused God's wrath. 'If I were a judge,' he wrote in about 1540, 'I would torture and mangle that poisonous corrupt whore on the wheel and have her veins lacerated.' Prostitution did not protect honourable women from rape, as Augustine had argued. Only marriage did. Many in the Low Countries were attracted to Luther's and other Protestant reformers' ideas of religious renewal. In cities where Protestants came to power, government-organised brothels were shut down.

Catholics soon came to the defence: it was not they, they argued, but the Protestants who were lax in sexual matters. Consequently, Catholics too abandoned their former tolerant attitude, accepting sex only within marriage. Chastity and monogamy were to be the norm. With the so-called Counter-Reformation, the Catholic Church sought to restore its authority in the Southern Netherlands from the mid-sixteenth century onwards, tightening sexual discipline, at least on paper. Because the power of urban, provincial, and country authorities was so strongly intertwined with that of the Church, secular authorities also helped oversee sexual propriety. Sex was hence not part of private life, but a central concern of both Church and government. Unchastity undermined the social order.

Consequently, new laws, commandments, and ordinances allowing governments and fellow citizens to act against extra-marital sexual relations were introduced in the sixteenth century. In practice, however, relatively few people were prosecuted for 'fornication' and their punishment was usually limited to asking for forgiveness and paying a fine. Moreover, a countrywide ban on prostitution did not materialise, and urban authorities (together with ecclesiastical courts) remained responsible for monitoring morality. In most cities, policies remained focused on curbing prostitution and brothels rather than eradicating them. In 1580, for example, the aldermen of Brussels issued a ban on renting out premises for keeping brothels, except in some specific streets near the current Palace of Justice. In 1597, two such streets, the Rue de l'Épée and the Rue de l'Eventail, were closed off with a gate from the fancier Rue Haute, because public women all too often ventured into the Rue Haute to lure customers. Prostitution was thus allowed to exist for the sixteenth-century authorities, but had to stay out of sight of the well-to-do.

During the seventeenth century, religious authorities again felt that prostitution policies were not strict enough. Repeatedly, local parish priests and bishops sent complaints to their superiors, or even to the monarch, regarding the authorities' lax attitude. Writers also took a stand against prostitution. In 1646, for instance, the popular Antwerp playwright Willem Ogier wrote *De onkuysheydt* ('Unchastity'), a play about the ruin and misfortunes of whores and whoremongers. A stubborn punter contracts syphilis in the play, a 'lewd woman' attempts to commit suicide after becoming pregnant, and another sex worker is murdered by her own father at the play's end. The consequences of unchastity were harrowing...

At the end of the seventeenth century, in some places the moral condemnation of prostitution also led to a further tightening of legislation. In Antwerp, brothels were welcome in fewer and fewer places, and in 1679 brothel keeping was banned altogether. In Namur, too, a 1687 edict prohibited women who sold sex from operating within the city. Sex workers who did so would be chased away under drumbeats. Numerous other cities issued similar rules. Women who did not comply with regulations could, in many places, be evicted from the city or locked up for several days on a diet of bread and water. If repeatedly convicted, they could be sentenced to 'public shaming' and displayed on the scaffold as whores. Women who violated public morals excessively could also be flogged or banished for long periods of time. Brothel owners and intermedi-

Gaspar Bouttats, 'Onkuysheydt', engraving in Willem Ogier, *De seven hooft-sonden. Speels-ghewys, vermakelyck ende leersaem voor-gestelt*, Amsterdam, 1682. The image shows the fatal scenes from Ogier's moralising play: those who engage in 'whoredom' end up badly.

Elwin Hofman

aries risked fines, shaming, and eternal banishment: after all, they had incited others to sinful lives.

They *risked* these punishments. Because all in all, the number of arrests and punishments remained limited even in the seventeenth century. Authorities acted almost only when scandals arose, fights took place, or after explicit complaints from neighbours. In Antwerp, according to the preserved registers of sentences in the sixteenth and seventeenth centuries, only twelve purveyors of sex were officially convicted over a period of almost two hundred years, as were thirty brothel keepers and five intermediaries. Quite a few additional brothel keepers (some four hundred) were summoned in the seventeenth century to move to the Lepelstraat (today the Willem Lepelstraat), where prostitution was allowed until 1679. Apparently, there were never any major raids. A tolerant or at least pragmatic attitude prevailed among most town councils in the sixteenth and seventeenth centuries, just as in the Middle Ages. This is not to say that women selling sex had free rein. After all, morals were not just monitored from above. Ordinary citizens, neighbours, and neighbourhood watchmen could also help in policing the town, though we usually find few archival traces of their actions.

In the eighteenth century in particular, citizens increasingly began relying on courts and police officers to help contain prostitution. Citizens in this period expected much more from city authorities and the police, indeed holding them responsible for maintaining good order. At the same time, the taboo on sex and prostitution was on the rise. In the seventeenth century, Willem Ogier could still include 'whores' in a popular moralising play, but by the mid-eighteenth century such a thing became inappropriate. It is hence understandable that precisely in the eighteenth century – the age of the Enlightenment – the most extreme and humiliating laws around prostitution were enacted.

In Mechelen in 1736, aldermen ruled that convicted public women would be publicly displayed for an hour while sitting backwards on a large wooden horse with a sharp seat. A few years earlier, the Brussels officer of justice had put forward an equally extreme proposal. Despite frantic efforts, he wrote in 1732, he had failed to curb prostitution in the capital. The women he chased out of the city through one city gate would simply return through another. He therefore proposed that, henceforth, such indecent women be publicly displayed, for a few hours, in a revolving cage. Such a humiliation would teach them! His proposal failed – policymakers feared that all the spinning would lead to vomiting, resulting in an unpalatable spectacle – but an exhibition on the scaffold for a few hours became possible for incorrigible sellers of sex.

This did not end the problems in Brussels. In practice, most sellers of sex and brothel keepers remained out of harm's way if they did not cause a public scandal. Throughout the eighteenth century, citizens, parish priests, and the city authorities themselves complained that they could no longer keep the expanding sex trade under control. Exiled women simply continued to re-enter the city. In 1778, therefore, at the urging of the governor of the Southern Netherlands, the Brussels authorities started a special register for investigations into 'public women'. They could thus keep track of who had already been convicted and why. According to that register, from 1778 to 1794, about thirty women on average were arrested each year on suspicion of prostitution. A total of 337 different women were entered in the register, quite a few on multiple occasions. Some were released shortly after their arrest; others were expelled from the city or locked up for short or longer periods. Even with that relatively more intensive intervention by the municipal authorities, police practice remained focused on keeping prostitution in check, not on eradicating it.

All in all, despite the climate of moral reawakening and the turgid rhetoric concerning the evils emanating from prostitution, official arrest rates remained limited throughout the early modern era. There are several explanations for this. Perhaps authorities turned a blind eye because they did not want to lose the economic and social benefits of prostitution. After all, lots of men were looking for sex, especially in ports or garrison towns, and commercial sex brought in money for merchants and landlords. Moreover, the clout of urban authorities remained limited, being too understaffed to consistently monitor women who sold sex. Finally, not all surveillance translated into official arrests and reports. Police officers could also monitor public women and brothels more informally, probably evicting sex workers from the city, or locking them up briefly, all without leaving a written trace.

Occasionally, legal documents do provide a glimpse of informal policing practices. In Antwerp in the eighteenth century, women who sold sex were hardly ever officially prosecuted. But the 1767 trial of Pieter Dieles, a clerk at the Antwerp criminal court, reveals that Antwerp aldermen did in fact monitor brothels and public women. Dieles had told an acquaintance that he could put him in touch with a young sex worker. The acquaintance had then asked, 'How did he do that with those kinds of women, when the gentlemen of the magistrate do the rounds?' Apparently, the aldermen – the magistrate – sometimes made rounds to check suspicious houses and inns for the presence of lewd women. But Dieles had found a solution to this problem: as a court clerk, he had advance warning of such raids. When a raid was coming, he would notify friendly pimps and brothel owners (perhaps for a fee), who would then have their girls moved to other houses until the inspection was over. The case illustrates how prostitution was indeed supervised, but also how that supervision could be circumvented.

Elwin Hofman

Although Pieter Dieles was caught, he was not the only official to profit by the business of pleasure. In the 1750s, for instance, it emerged that several brothel keepers paid the Brussels officer of justice not to harass them, and to release arrested sex workers without trial. Moreover, several of the spies he employed were themselves active pimps or brothel keepers. He left them alone in exchange for information. This again demonstrates how formal prosecutions alone say little about the extent to which sex workers, pimps, and brothel keepers were harassed by the authorities. Thus, while there was clearly a space for commercial sex in early modern cities, that space was rarely taken for granted by those involved, and the authorities could often make their lives difficult.

Women at Work

Paid sex in the early modern era was not a trade like any other. The contemporary view that commercial sex constitutes 'sex work' was alien to the period. Even many of the women involved presented selling sex as a means of earning money akin to begging, not as proper work. Women usually presented themselves as seamstresses, weavers, or day labourers, even if their main source of income was selling sex. For most of the early modern period, moreover, paid sex remained a vague category, not sharply demarcated from other forms of 'whoring' or from ordinary pre-marital courtship. Emerging terms such as 'public women' and 'women of pleasure', however, pointed increasingly to women who were mainly 'gaining money with their bodies'. During the eighteenth century, the term 'prostitute' emerged as a term that specifically referred to sellers of sex.

It is not easy to reconstruct the backgrounds of early modern women who earned a living, occasionally or in the long term, by trading in sex. We only know about the women who in some way ran up against the authorities. Even with that limitation, they clearly formed an incredibly diverse group. Many sex workers were skilled in textile production, as were most other women in the Southern Netherlands. Many came from poor families, while some were of higher social standing. Most sex workers who had to deal with the authorities were not significantly poorer than their contemporaries. They were, however, almost always relatively young, the vast majority from twenty to twenty-four years old.

For many women, prostitution was a temporary occupation, not only in the sense that they stopped working the trade when they got older, but also in the sense that it was not always their main activity. Some women engaged in the trade to supplement other income, or sold sex when temporarily unemployed. Marie Joseph Galleij, for example, stated in Kortrijk in 1750 that she earned a living in summer by travelling through various villages with a revolving board (perhaps with some kind of spectacle). In winter, however, she made her living 'by letting herself be carnally known by diverse men'. Similarly, in a larger city like Brussels, quite a few women indicated that for them prostitution was only a supplement to the income they earned elsewhere. 'When she finds work, she works,' Jeanne Joseph Denis declared to the Brussels magistrates in 1771, 'and when she does not, she surrenders herself to John and all as a public woman'. Confirming this pattern, a neighbour testified in 1791 that Therese Van Meerbeeck spun cotton during the day, but occasionally left the house in the evening to walk the streets.

Some women, to be sure, sold sex very regularly or even full time. In Bruges in the eighteenth century, their share of the trade was particularly large. For several years, some derived most of their income from commercial sex. Still, a life outside prostitution often awaited them afterwards. Having gained money by selling sex for a while, many women went on to work in the textile industry, married, and had children. The later life of former sex workers was often not so different from that of other women with a similar social background.

Making money with sex work was not self-evident and involved many risks, such as moral repudiation, social exclusion and arrest, public shaming, and imprisonment. Moreover, some women carried the consequences of sex work with them for the rest of their lives. From the sixteenth century onwards, venereal diseases spread rapidly. Syphilis in particular – which was not yet endemic in the Middle Ages – had serious consequences for infected women and men and could, often after several years, lead to death. An effective medical treatment was only developed in 1910. Moreover, the sexual contacts of sex workers regularly led to unwanted pregnancies. Condoms (made from animal intestines) did exist, but they were expensive, impractical, and virtually unused. Women had to make do with herbal mixtures ('we take pills for that', said a woman in 1787 when asked if she was not afraid of becoming pregnant) and vaginal showers. Both methods were not always effective. Consequently, many sex workers bore children out of wedlock, which they had to raise on their own or were sometimes able to place with relatives.

So why did women go into prostitution despite these risks? In the early modern era, many contemporaries believed that sex workers were women with an insatiable sexual appetite. At the same time, these women were deemed so devious as to ask men for money to satisfy their own lust. This squared with general perceptions: the idea that women were less prone than men to seek sex only began to gain ground during the eighteenth century. The women in question themselves, however, rarely recorded such ideas.

Elwin Hofman

Another popular perception was that women ended up selling sex through deception or abuse. In 1695, the Dutch writer Nicolaas Heinsius wrote in his picaresque novel *Den vermakelyken avanturier* ('The Amusing Adventurer') about an eighteen-year-old woman from Antwerp who was impregnated against her will by a guest from her father's inn. As a result, she lost all hope for a good marriage and ended up in prostitution. Women appearing in court sometimes also told such stories. Joanne Maron from Ghent, for example, claimed in 1781 that she had been seduced by 'a certain young man's flattering persuasion'. Having become pregnant, the young man then abandoned her, and so she ended up selling sex.

In keeping with that idea, some women claimed they had come to the city in search of work but had then 'accidentally' ended up in prostitution. While this may have happened sometimes, it was also a way to elicit pity from the judges. In 1785, for example, Isabelle Boddin told her judges that she had come to Bruges to look for a job as a maid. She was hired as a maid in an inn, which soon turned out to be a brothel popular among soldiers. Under her mistress's instructions, she 'let herself be used by all those savages, though against her own will'. The ensuing investigation revealed, however, that Boddin had already been active in prostitution for two years. She strategically played on the stereotype of deception and abuse in the hope of a lighter sentence.

It seems, therefore, that many women deliberately chose to make money selling sex. Of course, this does not mean that they always enjoyed doing so, or that they were aware of the risks. Many women sold sex out of financial need. This too was already well-known in the early modern era. Playwright Willem Ogier had a public woman declare in 1646: 'oh poverty, oh poverty, it chases people there, where one would become a whore'. In court, sex workers often pointed to their dire poverty. Having lost their parents, spouse, or work, they were forced to sell sex, just 'in order to exist'.

Here too, of course, strategy was involved, and sex workers sought leniency from the judges, especially in the late eighteenth century, when elites became more sympathetic to the plight of the poor. Many women did not sell sex out of destitution, but because they hoped to make better money. The earnings of sex workers varied widely, but on average they earned more from one customer than from working a whole day as a maid or textile worker. The extravagant attire of some sex workers exuded a luxurious lifestyle, and some brothel keepers or intermediaries did not hesitate to confirm such fantasies. 'My dear', a Ghent brothel keeper enticed a young woman at the end of the eighteenth century, 'would you be in a fellowship with a gentleman seven or eight? You shall eat cakes, drink wine, and get money as much as you want!'

Women who took up selling sex often had overly rosy views of what awaited them. Yet many were not completely unfamiliar with what prostitution entailed. During their initiation into sex work, friends or relatives who sold sex often played an important role. The example of Maria Waterschot from 1787 is indicative of the ambiguous ways in which women entered prostitution. Sex worker Catharina Van Laer told a group of friends who did not work in prostitution that a gentleman had promised her two crowns if she could set him up with a girl who was still a virgin. The friends responded 'while laughing' 'that they would like to go out in the evening wearing a white apron to find someone and pass themselves off as virgins'. But eighteen-year-old Waterschot was not joking. She urged Van Laer to be allowed to join her 'tour' and earn substantial money. Van Laer initially held off: she did not want people to say she was leading other girls astray. But after some insistence ('that Waterschot constantly pursued her and drove her crazy to be allowed to go on the tour in the evening'), she took Waterschot in tow while she went streetwalking.

The first time went well and Waterschot had sex with a customer. She told a friend afterwards that she wanted to do it more often, if it helped her get out of poverty. After a few more successful rounds of soliciting, however, things went wrong. Waterschot was dragged to a ship by two boatsmen, who sexually abused her several times. Waterschot's father filed a complaint, but since several witnesses could confirm that Waterschot had sold sex before, the men were acquitted: a 'whore' could not be raped under early modern law. The Waterschot case reveals the fine line between free choice, necessity, and coercion in the decision to sell sex.

There are hardly any traces of men who sold sex to women in the early modern Southern Netherlands. Men who sold sex to other men do turn up from time to time. For the authorities, they belonged to a very different category from women who sold sex: the problem there was not that they received money for sex, but that they committed 'sodomy'. Sodomy – sex with someone of the same sex – was a serious crime punishable by death.

Thanks to sodomy trials, we get a glimpse into the world of men who sought sex from other men. Some wealthier men, the files reveal, were willing to pay good money for sex with a lad in his twenties. Forty-year-old cobbler Peter Stocker promised a young man from Antwerp in 1781 that he would put him in touch with 'gentlemen whom you will gain much money from' if he allowed himself to be 'used'. The twenty-year-old perfume dealer Jean François Le Febure, from Paris, also occasionally earned a little extra by selling sex. One of his clients in Brussels was George Beauclerk, Duke of Saint Albans. At one point, however, things went wrong, and the authorities launched an investiga-

Elwin Hofman

tion. Beauclerk claimed that he had only given Le Febure alms out of charity. While investigators clearly suspected that more was going on, Beauclerk's high status saved him from a conviction. Le Febure was sent back to his homeland after a few weeks of incarceration.

The number of known cases of male prostitution is very small. It is therefore difficult to draw hard conclusions. As for female sex workers, prostitution could be an interesting secondary or even main income for some men. As for women, there were many risks involved. The chance of pregnancy was usually limited, but if caught, the potential penalties were enormous. Moreover, the taboo on sodomy was even greater than that on sex work. While even sodomites were usually left alone – if discreet –, they had few people to turn to if something went wrong.

Delightful and Renowned

Sex was sold in all cities in the early modern Southern Netherlands. But there were certainly differences as to the extent and visibility of commercial sex. Some neighbourhoods were renowned throughout the country or even abroad. The Lepelstraat in Antwerp was notorious from the sixteenth to the eighteenth centuries, even after prostitution had been officially banned. The Brussels neighbourhood of Bovendael, near today's Palace of Justice, was also infamous. Both neighbourhoods figured in Willem Ogier's seventeenth-century play, *De onkuysheydt*, where a wanton living in the Lepelstraat travels through Brussels especially 'to see the delightful and renowned Bovendael'.

Of course, concentrations of brothels also existed outside those famous neighbourhoods. In the seventeenth century, for instance, there were no less than 160 brothels in Antwerp outside the Lepelstraat. Brothels abounded mainly in neighbourhoods with many potential customers. This was often in the city centre, near theatres and other entertainment venues, and in sailors' and soldiers' quarters. In Brussels, the Rue des Fleurs and the Rue Vander Elst, both near today's Place de Brouckère, were hotspots for prostitution in the late eighteenth century.

The concentrations of brothels did not mean that most sex workers stayed within their own neighbourhood or city. Working in prostitution meant a mobile life for many women. Women from outside the city constituted a significant portion of sex workers in all major cities. Most consciously sought out the city to practise their trade, often coming from neighbouring towns or villages. Many travelled between their hometowns and cities such as Antwerp, Mechelen, Brussels, Ghent, and Bruges. Eventually, some ended up farther afield. A small minority of the known sex workers in the Southern Netherlands came from abroad, usually from France or the Dutch Republic.

Women working in brothels, in particular, circulated. A brothel owner in Bruges indicated that customers 'used the same girl only 2 or 3 times at most', so after a few weeks, some brothel keepers were already looking for new women. Some scouted for sex workers in other cities, while others wrote letters to their colleagues or relied on intermediaries. For the women themselves, a new brothel or a new city meant an opportunity to earn a little better. Some women had a fixed base but occasionally went to other cities to work for a few weeks. In the 1770s, for instance, Marie Joseph Blo mainly worked in Brussels brothels (including that of her parents), but occasionally spent a few weeks in a different brothel in Ghent.

The high mobility of sellers of sex was not only a consequence of the constant demand for new girls. Some sex workers travelled between different cities to avoid the authorities. It was for this reason that Maria Bielen travelled throughout the country. Originally from Tienen, she had moved to Brussels in 1774 at the age of twenty, earning money by selling sex. After an arrest, she was banished and went to a brothel in Mechelen. A few months later, arrested there and banished, she returned to Brussels. After some time, she was warned that the authorities would seize her, so she moved to Antwerp, where she was again arrested, a year later, in a brothel. Even later, she stated in Brussels that she had travelled back and forth between Antwerp, Mechelen, and Brussels, 'according to how the police in those places persecuted her'. After being imprisoned in a correctional facility for four years in 1777 (at her own request, hoping that afterwards 'her wanton years would be over'), she disappeared from the Brabant registers. Nonetheless, in 1783 she appeared in Bruges, still active in the sex trade. Travelling was an inherent part of her existence.

Walking the Streets

The diverse social origins of sex workers also translated into varying interpretations of sex work. Women from poorer backgrounds were more likely to be active as streetwalkers, usually earned relatively little, and were most at risk of arrest. For some women, streetwalking was therefore a last resort. According to neighbours in eighteenth-century Bruges, the forty-five-year-old widow Marie Bosan was 'deformed' and not only begged but also provided sexual services to anyone who showed the slightest interest. Scandalised witnesses stated that she 'even solicits children of ten to twelve years old'! Other women working the streets were better off. Walking the streets allowed them to operate relatively independently – with or without colleagues – and to choose which customers they had sex with.

In the early modern Southern Netherlands, soliciting was called 'going on the tour'. Streetwalkers often went out in search of clients with colleagues, or with an intermediary. They mainly scoured busier streets in search of interested parties, whom they would then take to a quiet spot (such as an alley, an alcove, or a graveyard), or to their own room. Barbara Vander Musschen in 1768, for example, walked the streets of Brussels, usually with one or two other women. When she passed by potential clients, she looked deeply into their eyes and addressed them with 'bon soir monsieur'. Some nights she was unsuccessful. But if someone was interested, they went into an alley while a colleague kept watch. If people or patrols arrived, the colleague would sound the alarm so that Vander Musschen could flee in time.

Customers usually paid streetwalkers only after sex. The woman who had stood guard sometimes also got a share of the money. The price was not always agreed in advance, which could lead to conflicts. Some sex workers who feared they would not be paid or would be underpaid, robbed their clients. Hendrik Weemals, for instance, in 1775 noticed after 'amusing himself' with two women in a Brussels alley, 'with discourses and otherwise', that his watch had disappeared.

Brothels were generally more comfortable for both clients and sex workers but brought other risks, and differences between brothels were great. At the top of the segment, one had discreet luxury brothels where only exclusive courtesans worked. In Antwerp, at the end of the seventeenth century, Sint-Arnoldus was a luxury brothel with corresponding prices: an evening with the so-called 'High German whore' cost the equivalent of half a month's wage of a skilled labourer. At Neptunus in Bruges in the late eighteenth century, ladies dressed in 'bows and plumes' and were affectionately called 'peacocks'. Only well-to-do guests came here. At the other end of the spectrum, overcrowded 'whorehouses' in musty cellars had several women working in rooms barely separated from one another. They earned less, but customers also got less in return. In between luxury brothels and miserable little rooms, there were many brothels in inns, where interested customers could 'go upstairs'.

In some brothels, sex workers lived in; in others, women came only to work. Quite a few brothels facilitated both options: there would be one or two resident women (and possibly the madam would also sell sex herself) and an errand boy would go and collect more sex workers if there were many clients. In Marie Joseph De Wilde and Joannes Baur's inn in Brussels in the 1770s, for example, one or two women usually lived in. In addition, both customers and sex workers were mainly brought in by middlemen, mostly teenage boys and young men. The middlemen would spot interested customers near the Comédie theatre (now the Beursschouwburg), bring them to the brothel, and then quickly run to get the required number of women, either at their homes or at other brothels. At the inn, interested customers were first given something to drink and could make acquaintance with the women present, after which they could go to a separate room with one or more girls of their choice.

The women who were fetched had to hand over part of their earnings to De Wilde as rent for the room but were otherwise relatively autonomous. The resident women, however, sometimes complained about their bosses' intransigence: they had to and would sell sex, even on days when they did not feel like it. The resident women and some regular sex workers were given nice clothes by the landlady, 'so that they could better attract people'. They then had to pay these clothes off with a share of their earnings. Mutual distrust was sometimes high: if the sex workers claimed that a client had underpaid, De Wilde sometimes examined them to make sure they were not hiding anything. Yet they were not kept in the brothel by force, or at least not all of them: one woman testified that she had quit after lingering conflicts (and simply returned her clothes).

The situation in Baur and De Wilde's brothel exemplifies the ambiguous relationship between intermediaries of prostitution and women who sold sex. That relationship has often been seen as hierarchical, regularly involving coercion. In practice, while there were indeed harrowing situations, this was not the rule. Women who did not live in the brothel were relatively free and could choose not to frequent certain brothels if they were not treated well. For resident sex workers, this was more difficult. Women who started working in brothels often had to take on debts with the brothel keepers, for nice clothes, board, drinks, and lodging. Until they had paid off these debts, they could not simply leave. Some women had to pay a fixed amount for board and lodging, but then kept their own earnings. Others had to hand over part (usually half) of what they received from a customer to the brothel keeper.

Sex workers and brothel keepers depended on each other for income. Some brothel keepers therefore threatened women that they would no longer be welcome if they did not do what was asked of them. In 1776, for example, the landlady of Het Vuilhemde in Antwerp wanted Maria Bielen to come by every evening. If she refused, the landlady threatened that she would look for another girl: 'she just has to write a note to have as many as she desired'.

Yet relationships between resident sex workers and brothel keepers, often women, some of whom had worked in prostitution themselves, could also be

Elwin Hofman

amicable and even supportive. A brothel offered shelter to women who could not find it elsewhere. The brothel keepers helped them find customers and protected them from violent clients and from the authorities. They sometimes bribed court officers or helped women hide with neighbours or in gardens if a raid was imminent. For women who had lost or had no contact with their families, the brothel could be a substitute home.

Whether they worked in the streets or in a brothel, sex workers who wanted to be successful had to possess several skills and qualities. First, their looks mattered. Maria Bielen's Antwerp madam was very enthusiastic when she signed up: 'you'll gain quite a bit of money here, you're such a nice thing'. Bielen was well aware of this, sneering at another woman 'that she was too ugly to play the whore'. Sophisticated and extravagant clothing was also important. Before Maria Waterschot went to the streets in 1787, a housemate watched her getting ready. 'Now I'll dress up like the whores do,' Waterschot said as she pushed her breasts up so that they rose above her jacket. That way, potential customers would 'see that she has big tits'.

Yet beauty and dress alone did not suffice. To seduce men, women had to appear self-assured. When Henriette Noldus was unsuccessful walking the streets in 1767, a colleague told her she was too shy: 'You have to look all men frankly in their face.' Women had to make clear that they had sex on offer. In Antwerp's Lepelstraat, according to seventeenth-century texts and numerous prohibitions, women were often seen calling out to men, tugging on their hats so they had to follow them, or lifting their skirts to seduce them. Once customers had entered an inn, it came down to persuading them to follow a woman to a room. At Het Vlaschblomken in Kortrijk, a woman nicknamed 'Marianne with the big boobs' allowed herself to be touched for this purpose in 1778. When someone stirred up the fire, the funniest regular asked, 'Marianne, would you like to be stirred up as well?' 'Yes,' she replied according to a bystander who later testified in court, 'the more the merrier.' Self-confidence, assertiveness, and bawdiness increased the chances of finding clients.

The extant records of early modern commercial sex contain little explicit information about sex. Women were recorded as saying that they had 'carnally conversed' or that they were 'known'. Witness statements and reports from police officers who caught sex workers in the act indicate that vaginal sex was most common. Anal and, different from today, oral sex were rare (or at least remained well-hidden). The latter also seems to have been exceptional in homosexual relations. Flagellation was somewhat more common (in Amsterdam there were even specialised brothels for this) but it remained rather exceptional in the Southern Netherlands. Masturbation was mainly foreplay. It did happen that a sex worker satisfied several clients at the same time, or that a client had sex with several women at the same time. Apparently, many sex workers and clients in the early modern era did not remove all their clothes during sex. Instead, they removed their outer garments and pushed their undergarments aside, but simply kept them on.

Clients who demanded exceptional sexual practices sometimes received a taste of their own medicine. Most sex workers refused to indulge in what they considered to be 'filth'. In 1788, for instance, Anna Veul refused to allow a Dutchman to use her 'in an even less permitted way' and therefore only fondled his genitals, before running off with his purse. Another woman, Maria Theresia Du Pont, got into a row with a stable hand after she refused to go with him, for he had wanted to use a colleague 'in an unnatural way' a few days before. The stable hand was furious and kicked her three times, but Du Pont was not one to be pushed around. She took the lid off the stove and delivered a heavy blow to his head. The incident shows not only that many sex workers had quite conventional norms about what was natural and what was not, but also that they could sometimes set clear boundaries.

Whores and Burghers

If the government acted against prostitution, it was mainly in response to pressure from below, from neighbours or other citizens. After all, a strong stigma was attached to commercial sex in the early modern era. Some sex workers were called 'whore' on the street, especially by children. When landlords discovered that a woman was selling sex, some did not hesitate to evict them. Neighbours and relatives regularly acted against sellers of sex. This was not only because they felt that paid sex was scandalous, but also because they needed to uphold their own reputation. Parents, spouses, or close neighbours who did not act against visible lewdness were themselves seen as morally lax or powerless.

Consequently, some neighbours filed complaints and worked together to expel sex workers. In 1788, residents of the Kasteelplein in Antwerp testified about Annotje, who kept an 'indecent house' and 'never worked', much to the annoyance of the women who made their living with 'the small gains of cotton spinning'. 'Is it not to be feared that such an example will be followed?' Annotje ended up in a house of correction, a sort of prison, for two years. In 1771, Jacques Blo's neighbours in Brussels were also fed up. His brothel was a constant source of noise and violence; through the windows some neighbours even saw lewd scenes. One particularly noisy night, a neighbour came out into the street shouting that it was 'not permissible to hold such a brothel in the street!' Sometimes neighbours themselves tried to set sex workers straight: Susanna De Bruyn stated in Antwerp that she had admonished her neighbour Bellotje to 'desist from this damnable trade', but that the latter had replied 'that she had no other means to gain money than to play the whore'. Filing a complaint with the court was often a last resort for these neighbours.

Family members were held more directly responsible for the behaviour of their daughters or wives. Many sex workers were unmarried, but if a husband allowed his wife to sell sex, it was considered dishonourable. The same applied to parents who allowed their daughters to sell sex. Some parents, like Marie Anne Peccau's, wanted to break all bonds. Others tried to retrieve their daughters from the brothel where they lodged. Jean Baptiste Delwaerd, for example, went to the Brussels brothel where his daughter worked in 1778, hoping to convince her to return home. If they failed to get their daughter in line, some parents petitioned the court to have her locked up. The public scandal, they explained to the judges, had just become too great.

Yet this stigmatisation did not mean that sex workers were completely excluded from respectable society. If they were reasonably discreet, did not make a fuss or cause a scandal, they often got along quite well with neighbours, friends, and relatives. Many women who worked in prostitution had previously earned money in other ways and would do so again afterwards. They retained many of the networks they already had. They could sometimes even receive financial support. Only when they advertised their trade too openly, causing a public scandal, did neighbours file a complaint or testify against them in court. After all, then their own reputation was at stake.

By no means all sex workers broke with their parents. Many women were still living with their parents when they entered prostitution, and sometimes parents tolerated their nightly activities. Some women sold sex to support their families. In fact, some parents, like Jacques Blo and Marie Magdaleine La Motte in Brussels in the 1770s, encouraged their daughter to engage in sex work to contribute to the family income. Conversely, some children also took up the cause of their parents, who had sold sex or kept brothels. In 1766, the six children of Jan Baptist De Coene requested a pardon for their parents, who had been convicted of keeping a brothel. They even attached statements from neighbours and customers at their inn, confirming that their parents were well-behaved.

Nor did neighbours always side against sex workers or brothels. A case in Kortrijk from the 1750s reveals the ambiguous relations between sex workers, brothel keepers, and their neighbours. The Kortrijk judges had expelled Therese Tibergijn and her daughters from the city because they kept a brothel and sold sex. Tibergijn, however, appealed against her expulsion, a very unusual event, as she was one of the only early modern sex workers to appeal against a verdict. Sixteen locals signed a declaration that her inn, Duynkerke, was an honest house, and that they had never noticed anything improper there.

Shortly thereafter, however, the parish priest visited those neighbours and some withdrew their declaration, saying they had been drunk, or that they had signed without the declaration being read out to them. Several informed the priest that they had seen mother and daughters 'let themselves be dishonoured'. But not everyone abandoned Tibergijn. One neighbour refused to sign a statement that he had seen lewd behaviour, even after being threatened by an official that he would then have to go to Ghent to testify (he replied wittily 'that he liked going to Ghent'). Eventually, the Tibergijns were also convicted on appeal and their property was sold publicly to cover the costs of the trial. Still, at least some of their neighbours had continued to support them.

The moral views of many sex workers did not differ that much from those of other citizens. We already met some sex workers who drew a clear line between regular prostitution and unacceptable practices, such as 'unnatural' sex, theft, or inciting others to prostitution. Several brothel keepers stressed that they did not employ girls who had not already lost their virginity. In 1777, Maria Bielen came into conflict with a brothel keeper, Manke Mie ('who had a limp and a very fat stature'), because she let a young girl 'play the whore'. Streetwalkers sometimes robbed their clients, but even so, as Marie Anne Peccau pointed out in the introduction, they drew a sharp line between sex work and theft.

Sex workers, therefore, did not stand completely outside the rest of society. Yet they often also sought refuge with their own. There were no professional associations of sex workers or brothel keepers, guilds, or crafts as there were for other professions. Such associations were sometimes mentioned, but only in the context of literary imagination. Willem Ogier, for instance, wrote about 'the girls of the guild' when discussing the sex workers in Antwerp's Lepelstraat. There may be no traces of such guilds in real life, but sex workers did often travel together, for instance to stand guard. They formed friendships and shared their earnings. Brothel owners maintained contacts with colleagues inside and outside their cities, to better organise exchanges. When things went bad, for instance because a woman had been abandoned by a long-term partner, or had been arrested, they offered each other support. After Barbara Du Chesne was arrested and exiled from Brussels in 1762, but (naturally) returned immediately, several brothel keepers helped her find temporary accommodation, even though she was not working.

Elwin Hofman

The Coming of the Regulations

When the Revolution broke out in France in 1789, many citizens perceived the state of criminal law as arbitrary and unjust. Soon after the National Assembly seized power, therefore, it abolished the existing criminal laws and replaced them by new codes, courts, and procedures. In 1790 and 1791, the foundations of many of today's legal principles and institutions were laid. While prostitution did not appear as a crime in these codes, public indecency was punishable with a fine and short imprisonment, and the police were assigned the task of supervising brothels. When the French Republic annexed the Southern Netherlands in 1795, they introduced the new laws and institutions.

Lawmakers did not intend to leave sex workers alone. Especially not, many complained, because commercial sex seemed to soar in several cities. In Brussels and Antwerp in the 1790s, complaints about the increase in streetwalkers and brothels were ubiquitous. It is difficult to estimate to what extent this alarmism was based on real conditions, but the disruptions brought about by the revolutions and military conquests, together with laxer regulations, could certainly have pushed more women to try to earn their living through sex work. Even in the first decades of the nineteenth century, complaints about increased prostitution continued to pour in. 'The fact is indisputable', wrote the Brussels prosecutor in 1828, 'that there have never been more lewd girls walking the streets of this city to entice passers-by to fornication.'

Local police and town councils were tasked with supervising brothels and their workers, just as before the annexation to France. Now, however, the objective became less to eradicate or deter prostitution, and more to regulate it. Several larger cities began issuing regulations concerning prostitution. Antwerp and Brussels issued the first police regulations in 1803; Ghent (in 1809) and Liège (in 1811) soon followed. The police issued cards to women with permission to sell sex. These women had to report regularly for medical examinations, which were noted on the card. Those who engaged in commercial sex without a card, or who did not submit to the check-ups often enough, risked arrest, a fine, and a brief imprisonment. Prostitution would no longer proliferate clandestinely, the reformers hoped, but be regulated under government control.

This new approach, often called the 'French system', stemmed from several important developments. By the end of the eighteenth century, the late medieval view that paid sex was a necessary evil had regained many supporters. According to several authors, prostitution was necessary to prevent the rapes of honourable women and same-sex relations, especially in places where there were many single

Pierre Goetsbloets, watercolour from *Tijdsgebeurtenissen* (Brussels, Royal Library, ms. II 1492, vol. 2, 81). Antwerp nobleman Pierre Goetsbloets disliked the French revolutionaries and extensively documented their pernicious impact on the city. Here we see Antwerp sex workers welcoming the French, and some eager French soldiers.

men. A Namur madam said in 1803 that 'a whore's life was a shabby one', but 'they must be there, for otherwise honest women would be assaulted in the streets'. Many policemen, judges, and policymakers agreed. Women might increasingly be seen as naturally chaste, but the male libido seemed hard to curb around 1800.

Many commentors, moreover, no longer saw prostitution solely as a moral problem, but primarily as a medical one. In the eyes of many authorities, the main risk was no longer God's wrath, but sexually transmitted diseases. Ever since the rise of syphilis in the sixteenth century, moralists lamented the spread of venereal diseases through prostitution. 'It's ill-done, that one with money pleasure buys', wrote Willem Ogier in 1646, 'and with the miserable pox pays.' But those 'miserable pox' – different venereal diseases were not usually distinguished – did not become the main concern of many governments, sex workers, and customers until the eighteenth century. This was partly due to the greater spread of venereal diseases by that period. More importantly, the rise of modern, standing armies with professional soldiers increased the authorities' concern with soldiers' health. In fact, in this respect, healthy sex workers were crucial for the country's security. Moreover, governments in general tried to be more vigilant about the health of their citizens. In 1778, the governor of the Southern Netherlands argued that prostitution was 'the cause of the ruin of the citizen's health', and he felt it was his duty to address this problem.

The new prostitution regulations therefore focused on the medical aspect. The first Antwerp prostitution regulation of 1803 explicitly aimed 'to prevent the disastrous consequences of the scourge of venereal disease'. Women working in brothels were to be subjected to a medical examination every week. Those diagnosed with venereal disease would be hospitalised. There was, however, no proper treatment for most venereal diseases. Hospitalisation therefore mainly served to prevent women from having sex during their illness. The regulations of other cities were similar in intent: frequent medical check-ups sought to reduce the spread of venereal diseases.

For women, the mandatory medical inspections and hospitalisations were intimidating and humiliating. Moreover, brothel keepers or the women themselves had to contribute to their costs. Consequently, many brothel owners helped sex workers hide during medical inspections. If they did get hospitalised, some complained of ill-treatment. In 1828, some patients at a hospital in Brussels climbed onto a table and a chair to shout 'the most outrageous words' through a window looking out onto the street. For many women, so-called medical treatment was no improvement over the earlier moral repudiation.

Yet the rise of prostitution regulations was not only a consequence of a medicalised view of prostitution as a necessary evil, but was also linked to growing compassion for sex workers. The late eighteenth century was generally characterised by a greater appreciation of feeling, and a belief in the natural goodness of human beings. In novels, sensitive heroes showed their pity for the destitute: beggars, orphans, madmen, and sometimes also sellers of sex. Citizens who adhered to the new views saw women as naturally chaste, domestic, and romantic. Prostitution was therefore no longer a logical consequence of unbridled female lust. Women in prostitution had to have been deceived and exploited by men and brothel keepers. They were victims deserving of pity. In that respect, the scandals, corporal punishment, and banishment they risked in the eighteenth century were incomprehensible. Regulation, advocates argued, would not only prevent disease, but also permit a more dignified existence for the sellers of sex who complied.

In practice, there was little dignified about the way sex work was regulated in the early nineteenth century, and many sex workers and brothel keepers refused to submit to the new control mechanisms. Urban authorities often remained insufficiently empowered to act effectively. Although in Antwerp in the 1820s dozens of police reports were issued each year for non-compliance with prostitution regulations, clandestine prostitution was still rampant. Consequently, many of the patterns characteristic of the early modern era simply continued into the early nineteenth century.

Sex workers who came up against the police sometimes continued to present themselves as victims of poverty, deception, or brutal abuse. In some cases, they did indeed receive pity from the authorities, but more often they met with scepticism. As with many neighbours and relatives, past practices of stigmatisation and rejection continued to reign when the authorities dealt with sex workers, even if formulated in the new language of pity and victimisation.

Nevertheless, pitying sellers of sex in the early nineteenth century made way for new interventions. After all, the police wanted not only to curb prostitution, but also to *rescue* women from prostitution. Thus, while in 1803 a Brussels police commissioner wanted to be particularly tough, he at the same time stressed how sad the fate of many women was. Young girls were tricked by selfish brothel keepers and locked up in brothels without their parents' knowledge, he complained. Pimps secretly led the girls from one brothel to another, purely to make more profit. That was what he wanted to deal with.

In practice, this did not always prove easy either. In 1817, a Maastricht police officer contacted his counterparts in Brussels. The adoptive parents of seventeen-year-old Annette César had complained that a Brussels brothel keeper was holding their daughter against her will. They substantiated this with a note from Annette (full of spelling mistakes) to her 'dear beeloved paretns', stating that she wanted to return home, but that she had an outstanding debt of 480 francs and so could not simply leave the brothel. The Brussels police commissioner acted immediately and interrogated both Annette and the brothel owner. This investigation revealed that Annette did not want to return home at all, because, according to her statement, her parents treated her badly. The police commissioner concluded that Annette was not as strictly incarcerated as her adoptive parents had suggested. The fight against forced prostitution proved less straightforward than hoped.

Elwin Hofman

Attempts to rescue women from prostitution were accompanied by the establishment of new shelters, just as they had existed in the late Middle Ages, where women could 'better their lives'. In 1818, such a shelter was created in Brussels, and a decade later in Antwerp. At its head were philanthropists – a man and a woman in Brussels, a woman in Antwerp – who would train women who wanted to leave prostitution in a profession. In this way, they would 'bring and keep them on the right path'. Women only came there voluntarily and had to leave the house after three years at the latest.

The system of regulation remained in place even after the French finally left the Southern Netherlands in 1815. Moreover, some cities soon wanted to go further and began to regulate additional aspects of prostitution: brothel opening hours, the number of sex workers per brothel, whether or not public signs were allowed, and neighbourhoods in which soliciting was permissible. The regulations laid down the procedures for acquiring permission to open or close a brothel, what the associated costs were, and how the costs of medical check-ups and hospitalisations were distributed. Almost every larger town or city drew up prostitution regulations in the 1820s. Increasingly, these regulations not only targeted venereal diseases, but also aimed to control sex workers and to keep them separate from honourable citizens. Prostitution might be a necessary evil, but it had to remain a *hidden* evil. Yet all these regulations never succeeded in bringing sex workers under complete control. Like Marie Anne Peccau at the beginning of this chapter, many women in prostitution demonstrated astonishing resilience.

3. THE TYRANNY OF RULES (1830–1918)

Pieter Vanhees

Jan-Baptist Saegaert's mother was livid. She had found out that her son had spent the night with a girl named Marie-Henriette, and that he had paid her 10 francs. So off she went to the police! Marie-Henriette was secretly indulging in immoral behaviour. Were such women not supposed to be registered according to the Antwerp prostitution regulations? His mother dragged Jan-Baptist to the police as a witness against Marie-Henriette. 'It is true that I slept with Marie-Henriette four weeks ago and that I paid her 10 francs for it,' Jan-Baptist declared to the police commissioner on 8 June 1899. 'She also sleeps with other men,' he added. Marie-Henriette was arrested and countered the allegations, claiming that Jean-Baptist's mother had acted out of revenge because she, Marie-Henriette, had not responded to her son's overtures. This defence, however, did not save her from being entered in the prostitution register. After an extensive investigation, the police decided she would be 'listed as a street girl' and should immediately report to the health service for an examination.

For Marie-Henriette, this was a heavy blow. In 1885, aged seventeen, she had moved to Antwerp from her native town sixty kilometres away, to become a servant for a lieutenant in the Belgian army. After a few months, she was sent packing – according to the police report, because she was 'not behaving well'. She then worked for nine other employers and did a one-year stint in Lille, in northern France. On average, she had about three employers a year in Antwerp. A conflict with either an employer, or a colleague, for whatever reason, was enough to get the sack. Her employers gradually became less and less well-off. Consequently, she increasingly worked in what the police called 'suspicious houses'. These were often pubs with rooms rented out as lodgings on the upper floors. Marie-Henriette's working addresses were scattered throughout the inner city of Antwerp.

In many of her jobs, Marie-Henriette barely earned enough to support herself, her monthly salary often roughly covering no more than the rent of a room where she worked. Many pub owners therefore occasionally allowed their female staff to 'go upstairs' with a regular customer and earn some extra money. Usually, the owners would only permit this after the customer had drunk his fill in the taproom. The maids' role in pubs, therefore, consisted not only in serving customers: they also had to encourage them to drink a lot. Once customers had spent enough, they were allowed to go upstairs with a server. In return, the customer either paid the bar tenant (who then gave a portion to the maid) or directly to the maid, who in turn had to hand over part of those earnings to her boss. Unsurprisingly, this informal system led to many conflicts.

Some young women were also able to supplement their income by entering into relationships with one or more suitors. Charles Westerlinck, a boat carpenter in the Port of Antwerp, was one of Marie-Henriette's sweethearts. He earned 110 francs a month, disproportionately much compared to a maid's salary, and could therefore give her money so that she, too, could make ends meet. Often these relationships did not last long: arguments ensued, sailors were regularly absent, and soldiers were only temporarily quartered nearby. According to her file, Marie-Henriette had several lovers, which eventually got her in trouble. The vice police discovered that, in addition to Jan-Baptist and Charles, she also had relations with a Swedish sailor (to whom she was even engaged for a while), with 'a tall French sailor', and with 'a Finnish man'.

After registering as a 'public woman', Marie-Henriette did everything she could to avoid the consequences. She feigned a return to her hometown, had herself expunged from the population register, and did not show up for the medical examinations – hated like the plague by women who gained money with sex. The weekly inspection of their genitalia with a speculum for traces of syphilis or gonorrhoea made them feel ashamed of their profession. Other citizens knew very well why these women were going to the health service every week. In addition, the mandatory examinations did not make finding a 'good' job easy. How could you explain to your employer that you would be absent at a fixed time every week without revealing the reasons? So, after her return to Antwerp, Marie-Henriette did everything she could to avoid the police. Whenever the neighbourhood police officer came to remind her to report to the population service, she could not be found. Only when she fell ill and was admitted to the Saint Elisabeth hospital for a time to recover from a venereal disease did she begin to comply with the prostitution regulations.

One of the last documents concerning Marie-Henriette's fate as a registered 'prostitute' is an 1891 letter drafted in her name. The writer explained that she requested the city council to be exempted from the mandatory examination: 'As she does not indulge in immoral behaviour, it is very painful to have to submit to

Pieter Vanhees

this examination every week.' The request was denied. It is not clear from her file what happened next. What does become clear is that young women who entered the prostitution register ended up in a revolving door of regulations imposed by police officers and doctors. All these rules and regulations, however, could hardly encompass the complex and diverse world of nineteenth-century prostitution.

Hyperregulation

During the nineteenth century, the regulation of prostitution flourished. From the 1850s on, in particular, government officials, backed by doctors, police, and the military, believed that the only good approach to commercial sex was one in which tolerance and control were central. Under pressure from these 'regulationists', several city councils began to organise the periodic medical examinations of sex workers, register women in prostitution, distribute prostitution booklets (which served as passports) and grant licences to brothel keepers. This so-called 'French system' was based on the regulation of the selling of sex in Paris, an important inspiration for many cities in Belgium and beyond. By about 1850, the regulatory nexus to which the sex industry was supposed to conform became so extensive that contemporaries spoke of 'hyperregulation'.

Major Belgian cities such as Brussels and Antwerp introduced the first regulations at the very beginning of the nineteenth century, when the territory was part of the French empire and, from 1815 to 1830, of the United Kingdom of the Netherlands. The succession of French, Dutch, and Belgian rulers believed that they could steer society in the right direction through the regulation of 'undesirable' social phenomena. So-called 'hygienists', a diverse group including doctors and engineers, who presented themselves as experts in public health, believed it was possible to elevate the working classes through better and healthier housing, the construction of sewers, public toilets, sidewalks, and streetlights. The campaign against begging, immorality, and an unregulated sex trade also figured prominently in their policies.

Later in the nineteenth century, the French example continued to lead the way. The work of the French physician Alexandre Parent-Duchâtelet, a member of the Paris Health Council, played an important role in this. In 1836 he published a magisterial study on prostitution in Paris. Parent-Duchâtelet not only developed a typology of sex workers, but also formulated policy recommendations. He advocated segregating sex workers from the rest of society in a system that the government, represented by law enforcement officers and doctors, could always oversee. Sellers of sex were to offer their services in secluded and hidden *maisons closes* or 'closed brothels'. In addition, authorities were required to set up dedicated hospitals, prisons, and 'correctional institutions'. Police forces in large cities were required to create specialised vice departments. One of the main reasons Parent-Duchâtelet wanted to refine the existing Parisian system was that public women's careers in the sex trade were often short-lived. By watching over their health and behaviour, authorities could prevent former sex workers from spreading their 'pernicious' influence to the rest of society.

By mid-century, belief in the effectiveness of regulation, combined with moral and sanitary motives, led Belgian city councils (empowered by the Municipal Law of 1836) to introduce particularly detailed regulations. No detail was overlooked and rules were drawn up for each person involved. Brussels took the lead in 1844 by introducing regulations based on the Parisian model and served as an example for the rest of the country. Ghent issued detailed regulations in 1850, and Antwerp followed in 1852, implementing the regulations still in use during Marie-Henriette's time. Many smaller cities also adopted prostitution regulations. Sint-Niklaas, for example, did so in 1855. In terms of content, they all illustrated the popularity of French thought.

Tolerance did not mean a free pass for women who sold sex. Nor did the element of control make the profession easier. Take the Antwerp regulations of 1852, that began with a definition of public women: 'Are considered public women, all daughters or women who habitually or publicly indulge in immoral behaviour.' The regulation divided them into two classes: the 'house girls', who lived in a brothel, and the 'secluded girls', who lived independently.

The focus on the second group was new. In past regulations, the municipal administration had sought to concentrate commercial sex in specific neighbourhoods. The Rietdijk, epicentre of regulated prostitution in Antwerp, was the most famous example. The city council soon realized, however, that it was impossible to accommodate the entire sector in brothels in specific districts. Regulated brothels were feasible for the limited group of professional sex workers who moved from city to city and obeyed the rules. Yet this group was only the tip of the iceberg. Many more women, 'who habitually indulged in immoral behaviour', sold sex as a survival strategy or to earn an additional income from 'illegal houses' – usually a pub – or on the street. Therefore, the 1852 regulations stipulated that these 'secluded' women also had to be registered.

Women who wanted to sell sex legally – there was no mention of men – had to report to City Hall. They would then be entered in a register of public women and receive a booklet recording the results of their weekly medical examination. For many, 'being on the register' soon turned out to be a form of imprisonment, for even women who only occasionally indulged in prostitution came under

The Antwerp prostitution regulations of 1852 (Antwerp, FelixArchives, 731#365). These regulations are a paragon of nineteenth-century hyperregulation.

the control of the vice police and were required to see a doctor weekly. As the example of Marie-Henriette suggests, it was not easy to be removed from the register. While the regulations did specify how to have one's name expunged, the many files in the Antwerp municipal archives reveal that police cooperation was crucial. The power of police officers over women who sold sex was particularly strong, not seldom resulting in abuses. Yet the regulations also provided a minimal form of protection for women in the profession. Brothel owners who, for example, attempted to detain women, risked severe penalties.

The regulations also stipulated in which establishments prostitution was permissible. The first type consisted of brothels where sex workers had a permanent residence. They lived and worked there under the authority of a brothel owner or keeper. In the second type, the so-called *maisons de rendez-vous* ('meeting houses'), women could rent rooms to receive clients, discretion being essential for the houses and patrons in question. Signs on the street were forbidden and thick curtains had to conceal from the view of passers-by what went on inside. The occupants had to be discreet as well. They were not allowed to be drunk or appear on the street in 'indecent' clothes; to stand in the doorway or at the window; to hold obscene conversations in groups; or to make signs to men on the street. Some places were explicitly off limits, i.e. the Groenplaats, the docks, parks, and fortifications. In theatres and at racetracks, they would be assigned discreet seats.

Lastly, the Antwerp regulations also stipulated the medical examination's modus operandi. In theory, this mandatory examination occurred five times a month, and doctors examined women working in official brothels on the spot. Women working from *maisons de rendez-vous* had to report to the city's health service for an invasive and not very delicate examination. Speculum in hand, the city doctor checked their genitals for signs of venereal disease. Sick women had to present themselves for care in a dedicated ward at the Saint Elisabeth hospital, and lost their income. Their madam was also affected financially. Consequently, many cosmetic practices were applied to hide symptoms of venereal disease from the doctor's eye, as evident in regulations targeting this deceit. 'The use of any deception or trickery by a public woman to deceive the doctors about her state of health' would be punished with the severest police penalty possible.

Regulations undeniably made the profession ever more difficult. They were, of course, by no means strictly followed. A large part of the police archives consists of official reports establishing non-compliance with a provision of the prostitution regulations. The changing numbers of registered sex workers also shows how practice deviated from theory. In Brussels, the number of registered women decreased continuously from the introduction of the regulations in 1844. Fewer women were registered and the proportion of registered women in public houses continued to decrease. More and more sellers of sex tried to work outside the system. Faith in the possibility of regulating the prostitution sector gradually declined, both among the police and policymakers. Finally, several scandals in the last quarter of the nineteenth century greatly diminished confidence in regulation.

'White Slavery'

On 13 December 1880, a court case in Brussels against twelve brothel keepers commenced. Among other things, they were accused of kidnapping underage women and inciting them to prostitution. The controversial trial was part of a highly mediatised international scandal. The 'white slavery scandal' had tentacles in almost all neighbouring countries and placed Brussels and Belgium in the spotlight – and not in a good way. For critics of regulated sex work, the trial proved that the police and courts were not protecting young women. The scandal was a symptom of outdated regulations out of touch with reality.

Pieter Vanhees

A British journalist, Alfred Dyer, blew the whistle. On 3 January 1880, he published an article in the *London Standard* about the alleged trafficking of underage (meaning under twenty-one, at the time) British women and girls to regulated brothels in continental Europe. He did this after hearing Ellen Newland's story. This twenty-year-old Londoner had met businessman Frédéric Schults in 1879, forging a friendship that soon became a relationship. After a few weeks Schults proposed that she accompany him to Calais, where it transpired that he had to return to London on urgent business. Not wanting to interrupt Ellen's trip, he allowed her, accompanied by a friend, to travel on to Brussels. This 'friend' turned out to be a brothel owner, who promptly took Newland to his establishment in the Rue Saint-Laurent, the following day escorting her to the vice police to register as a public woman. The bureaucratic process was hindered by the duty inspector's lack of English, but Newland was eventually registered, under a false name and birth year. According to the registry, she was already twenty-one, thus of legal age to work in a brothel.

Ellen later testified that this was when her nightmare really began. Under pressure from physical threats, days of confinement in a dirty little room, and relentless reminders of her travel debts, she was forced to sell sex. After only a few weeks she had to be admitted to the hospital with venereal disease. This, however, would be her salvation. In the infirmary she met a Swiss pastor, Anet, and confided in him. He informed Ellen's parents and was able to convince her to make a statement to the British proconsul in Brussels. At that point, Dyer also got wind of the affair.

The story of Ellen Newland is just one of many hundreds of stories of young women allegedly held against their will in brothels during this period. To what extent all these stories reflected a historical reality is difficult to say. Some brothels undoubtedly exploited women. Brothel owners took advantage of the weaknesses of illiterate women with limited job opportunities. Moreover, as the scandal unfolded, it became clear that allegations of overly close ties between the authorities, police, and brothel keepers were not unfounded. Thus, Inspector Pierre Schroeder, head of the vice police, regularly visited the brothel in the Rue Saint-Laurent, where he had an affair with a certain Niniche Flore. Superintendent Lenaers of the Brussels police was sidelined in 1881 after it became clear that, through his son, he was supplying liquor to many of Brussels' regulated brothels. That same year, Mayor Félix Vanderstraeten was forced to resign after it was revealed that he had sold his parents' tavern to a brothel keeper.

Stories such as these were often uncovered by opponents of regulation, who always portrayed women in prostitution as the naive victims of shrewd brothel owners, pimps, and human traffickers. Extensive research into the Brussels scandal, however, has shown that the issues were much more complex. Some of the underage women enrolled in tolerated brothels were not novices. Many already had experience with sex work before entering legal brothels. For some, migration and commercial sex was a conscious strategy in their search for better living conditions.

Belgian opponents of regulated prostitution during this period drew inspiration from the British feminist and social reformer Josephine Butler. Close to evangelical Protestantism, Butler assembled a diverse group of supporters in her struggle against regulation in British port and garrison towns, situating her struggle against government interference in what she considered to be sexual slavery in line with the movement for the abolition of slavery. Soon, therefore, they were called 'abolitionists'.

While the abolitionist movement is often associated with women's rights, supporters also had other motives, e.g. they fought against moral decay and worked to protect individual liberties from the arbitrariness of the police, courts, and authorities. For many abolitionists, the sale of sex was not a necessary evil, as it was for the followers of Parent-Duchâtelet, but something that could and should disappear. What united them was the view that it was not for the authorities to create a framework within which the sector could flourish. Such a system encouraged corruption, and the Brussels scandal only confirmed that trafficking and corruption were not an illusion.

After a strong start for abolitionism in the British Isles, Butler tried to gain a foothold on the continent, where regulation was more firmly established than in her homeland. In 1875, the British and Continental Federation for the Abolition of Prostitution was founded in Geneva. Belgium, the reputed epitome of regulation, soon caught the organisation's attention. Initially, the Belgian abolitionist movement remained limited in scope. Butler quickly established contacts in academic and Protestant circles, primarily in Liège and Brussels. In 1879, she convened a conference in Belgium, attended by well-known abolitionists from neighbouring countries. One of the key attendees was Alfred Dyer. Participants there explicitly linked the struggle against abolishing the 'trade in white slaves' to the struggle against the prostitution regulations of the big cities.

Some months after the conference, the group brought the Brussels scandal to light. This became a turning point, sparking a broader debate about regulation, which in turn led to the foundation, in 1880, by the young lawyer Alexis Splingard and the industrialist Jules Pagny, of the Société pour l'affranchisement des blanches ('Association for the Liberation of White Slaves'). Not much later, in 1881, Belgian abolitionists united to form the Société de moralité publique, the 'Society of Public Morality', which remained in existence until 1908, and became

Pieter Vanhees

the most important abolitionist association in Belgium. The association devoted itself to the prohibition of human trafficking, the protection of minors under the age of twenty-one, the punishment of incitement to immoral behaviour, and the struggle against the regulation system. It boasted many influential members, including lawyers, doctors, pastors, politicians, philanthropists, and academics.

Abolitionists, however, were not alone in considering policy reforms. Proponents of municipal regulations did not lose their conviction but were increasingly aware that uncontrolled clandestine sex work and venereal diseases did not disappear with strict regulations. Time and again, policymakers, doctors, and police forces came up against their limited efficacy. Brussels commissioner Lenaers had, already several years before the white slavery scandal broke, been calling for a reform of the 1844 regulations, in an attempt to make them more effective in the fight against clandestine prostitution. A new regulation, part of a broader reform, was adopted in 1877. Aimed at convincing women to choose the industry's legal track, it granted some freedoms to registered sex workers. Thus, working from home became possible, and women only had to undergo one medical examination a week instead of two. Still, some difficult-to-enforce measures, such as the ban on soliciting sex along busy thoroughfares, were retained. In addition to new rules, efforts were also made to professionalise the vice police. These were problematical, since the police forces in Belgium's major cities, and their vice departments, were understaffed. Furthermore, the personnel proved to be quite susceptible to corruption.

Belief in hyperregulation, subsequently, was fading in both camps. It was a sign of fundamental changes in attitudes about extra-marital sexuality, seduction, nightlife, and unwanted pregnancies. During the first half of the century, local governments had placed much emphasis on regulation, hoping to protect the nation from venereal disease, while at the same time accommodating unavoidable sex work as discreetly as possible. In the second half of the century, however, they became aware of the impossibility of such a project. Abolitionists led the resistance against the excesses of regulation and medical control. Yet it was not until after the Second World War that regulationism would be prohibited by law in Belgium.

A Snapshot

The realities of the sex trade in the nineteenth century were miles away from Parent-Duchâtelet's ideals. Women who sold sex were also daughters, mothers, sisters, colleagues, and neighbours. They could not be completely isolated from the rest of society. Nor were all these women the passive victims of vicious tricksters or playthings of an unhappy fate. Reality was infinitely more varied, each person's story unique. The trade was a diverse industry. There were posh regulated houses, which sometimes specialised in 'exotic' women or in specific sexual practices such as orgies, bondage, or sadomasochism. At the same time, there were also harrowing forms of survival prostitution. We know much about what went on in the field in Antwerp, partly because of well-preserved archives and a unique source from François-Jean Matthyssens, a contemporary physician. Therefore, in what follows, the port city often takes centre stage. At the same time, similar evolutions took place in many other Belgian cities.

In 1845, Matthyssens drew a picture of the diversity of the industry based on his own observations in Antwerp. Befitting his profession, convinced of the need for rules, he was commissioned by the minister of the interior to study prostitution 'in detail' but also 'in general', through the lenses of both morals and public health. In his report, he made clear from the outset that regulation was a necessity: 'It is important to say that [...] you will always find prostitutes when many people live around the same place, and also that, given the corrupt human heart, their existence contributes to the preservation of good morals in the family.'

Tolerated sex work in Antwerp was highly concentrated in two neighbourhoods. The most important and notorious – boasting twenty-four tolerated brothels – was around the Rietdijk, today located between the Burchtgracht and Koolkaai, close to the Scheldt quays. In addition, there were a dozen brothels in the now-vanished Papenstraat, on the site of today's Stadsschouwburg theatre, near the Old Arsenal and the city walls. Finally, a few scattered brothels existed near the Antwerp citadel. In total, during this period, 150 to 170 women resided in these brothels, an average of about four per brothel.

Few of the women who worked in the tolerated brothels were from Antwerp. While most came from other places in Belgium, quite a few were foreign, mainly from neighbouring countries, the bulk of German origin. Their presence in the sex sector in Antwerp became increasingly important as the century progressed. Many Germans were attracted by all the activities around the developing port, and selling sex was one of them. The recent railway network and the good connection between the Ruhr region, the Rhineland, and Antwerp contributed to the attraction. The brothels had a high turnover, women moving from brothel to brothel, neighbourhood to neighbourhood, and city to city. Migration, like today, was always an important factor in the profession, going hand-in-hand with the desire of clients for new sex workers, and of sex workers for the best possible earnings.

Matthyssens may have been a regulationist, but he was also aware of the limitations of overly strict rules. The fact that almost all tolerated public houses

Félicien Rops, *Prostitution and Madness Dominate the World*, 1886 (Namur, Félicien Rops Museum). Images and stories about sex work were rarely as important in the artistic imagination as at the end of the nineteenth century, when the sex worker was at the crossroads of several social and scientific debates. For the Belgian artist Félicien Rops (1833–1898), sex work was a frequent topic.

in Antwerp also served as pubs was a good thing for him, preventing customers from turning to clandestine establishments where drinks and sex work merged. He thought it a poor choice that the city council had in previous years closed brothels outside the main areas of prostitution. Clients like married men, who wanted to uphold their reputation, were, unlike sailors and soldiers, less keen to visit the Rietdijk. In crowded neighbourhoods, one always risked bumping into an acquaintance. Clandestine sex work and brothels now flourished without police and health officials being able to exercise control. Moreover, according to Matthyssens, it led to better-off men more often attempting to seduce maids and female day labourers to have sex.

In 1845, Antwerp had only four recognised rendez-vous houses, establishments where you could rent a room for a short time. These houses were frequented by sex workers who did not reside in a brothel. They found their customers in taverns and on the streets. Servants and other workers also sometimes met their sweethearts there, as did adulterous couples. In contemporary police documents, it is often extremely difficult to tell whether sex for money was involved. Often a loose, pre-marital, or extra-marital sexual affair was as decisively dubbed 'immoral behaviour' as an encounter including a monetary transaction.

Finally, Matthyssens also mentioned the existence of a refuge for sex workers, maintained by Helena Van Celst in Antwerp. It had existed since 1824 and by 1845 had taken in a total of 457 women. Women ended up there for all kinds of reasons, and some made the transition to a life outside prostitution. Others returned to commercial sex when they left the house. In this refuge, religious duties were linked to work and meals, but the women who ran it were not themselves religious. Such establishments were in fact part of a long tradition of conversion institutions. They existed in other Belgian cities as well, e.g. in Ghent, where a similar refuge was founded in 1844.

Changing Times

In the decades following Matthyssens' description, the situation in and around the brothels changed profoundly, the entrepreneurial spirit of brothel owners and young women playing a major role in the transformation. As early as 1847, the Antwerp mayor received a message from his police force complaining of an uncontrolled exodus from the Papenstraat brothels. The resident women were moving in large numbers to the Rietdijk, which offered more customers and thus potentially better earnings.

The Rietdijk was home to successful entrepreneurs who prospered in the neighbourhood, running large brothels. The Francophone Antwerp writer Georges Eekhoud described these entrepreneurs several decades later, in *La Nouvelle Carthage*, published in 1888. Brothels outdid one another in terms of fame and luxury, he wrote, and each had its peculiarities. 'Madame Charles was recommended by the cosmopolitanism of its staff, impeccable service and, above all, ease of payment; the Crystal Palace monopolised the delicious and new English women; at the Palais des Fleurs, the ardent southerners and even the temple dancers of the Far East flourished.' Fancy establishments on one street stood in contrast with cheap brothels in another. In opposition to the sustained erotic illusion of the famous brothels, these cheap establishments were, at least in Eekhoud's literary account, places where sailors and soldiers could indulge without much fuss.

Important brothel keepers possessed political clout in the city and used it to help their businesses flourish. Well-run brothels were the cornerstone of an orderly sex industry. This became clear, for instance, when the introduction in 1852 of the new regulations threatened to jeopardise their business model. An active lobby sprang into action, maintaining that these regulations were too advantageous for the women employees. Their introduction, with the vice authorities repeating on every visit that no woman should be held against her will, had prompted a high turnover of women seeking better working conditions. Brothel keepers argued that it cost them much money to keep renewing their workforce. They were, consequently, in the habit of 'reselling' women, along with their debt, to other brothel keepers. The constant need for new women stimulated the development of (international) networks of middlemen, who offered their services for a fee. So-called 'placers' helped young women find employment as maids, but sometimes led them to pubs where sex was for sale.

Such hard-to-eradicate practices contributed to rumours of sexual slavery and forced sex work. By the latter part of the century, accounts fitting in the abolitionist discourse around human trafficking appear more frequently in the archives. Terms with negative connotations, such as *proxenete* or *souteneur* (for pimp) and *makerelle* (for brothel operator), were increasingly used. While stories of human trafficking clearly fitted the Zeitgeist, the archives show that some women were indeed outsourced to other brothels for payment. Until women could repay their debts for new clothes, jewellery, travel, or accommodation, the new employer often had to pay compensation to his predecessor. Women in the trade thus carried their debts with them, from brothel to brothel.

In 1886, for instance, a German inhabitant of Antwerp denounced a certain Thonessen to the police. He, allegedly, 'had delivered 2 women in Rotterdam, to a certain lady Zander, who keeps a brothel; for one he received 20 guilders, for the other nothing'. Later in the police report, however, it becomes clear that the witness himself also placed maids in brothels. One of the women, ostensibly to have been placed in Rotterdam, was found to have refused this 'transfer'. Police reports containing interrogations of persons involved in the sex sector are full of contradictions and quarrels. Women who left an employer out of discontent or due to inadequate payment could retaliate with a testimony alleging coercion and violence, which could then lead to the closure of clandestine brothels. Conversely, gossip and slander could also tarnish women's reputations.

Men looking for sex helped determine the industry's transformations through their changing desires. As the nineteenth century progressed, clients' interest in officially tolerated brothels waned. They preferred more informal forms of commercial sex, where brothel keepers and policemen exercised less influence. The illusion that the sex was something 'real', that seduction was involved, gained in importance, too. Besides married men, sailors, soldiers, and many bachelors also called on the services of purveyors of sex. It was often hard for numerous lower-middle-class men to raise the money needed to start their own family. An 1869 letter from commissioner Maillard to the Antwerp mayor lists the men who frequented a clandestine brothel in the Paulusstraat: they included a station clerk, a sergeant, a warehouseman, and a messenger at the docks. Given the sometimes-blurred line between sex for pay, gifts, and relationships, both in practice and in the sources, it is often difficult to work out what kinds of relationships were involved.

Despite the desire for more informal sex work, the stigma attached to the profession made it harder for clients to establish real relationships with women in prostitution. It sometimes happened that a young man would write to the mayor or police, asking them to provide his partner with the necessary documents without mentioning her former profession or address (an address on the Rietdijk left little to the imagination). An 'immoral' past could jeopardise a couple's future. The stigma linked to the trade meant that women who wanted to quit often faced obstacles.

Speaking about brothel visits and relations with sex workers was impossible for clients in many contexts. An example from Leuven in 1877 makes this clear. In that year, the mayor received an anonymous letter from a man who had contracted a venereal disease in the Chateaux-de-fleurs, a pub on the corner of the Burgemeesterstraat. Obviously, as a married man, he could not speak to his wife about it, but he did want to spare other men such suffering. 'A small blonde' from that pub was responsible for his misfortune, so he asked the mayor to make the necessary arrests.

Not just staff and customers, also neighbours determined where the industry could flourish. Neighbourhood protest had a major impact on geographical shifts of paid sex in the city. Local authorities were bombarded with complaints and petitions from locals agitating against noisy bars, bawdy songs, or ill-concealed sex in back alleys. In 1857, the Antwerp city council received a letter from some homeowners in the Kloosterstraat. They felt wronged because they had to rent out their premises for a reduced price after an establishment nearby was recognised as a brothel. Disgruntled neighbours who felt unheard by politicians also took recourse to the fast-growing press. In 1852, a telling report appeared in *Le Messager de Gand*. A reader's letter on the front page reproached the Ghent city council, despite all its promises, for not paying the slightest attention to the rampant selling of sex in the parishes of Sint-Baafs and Sint-Niklaas.

New streets, the demolition of fortifications and of the Citadel, adjusted municipal boundaries, the expansion of the port to the north: the grand urban development projects in nineteenth-century Antwerp naturally also affected the dynamics of the sex sector. Domestic and foreign public women found their way to the railway stations and to the newly opened public parks. Yet the major construction and infrastructure works not only created new opportunities for sex workers, but also new restrictions. A police commissioner reported in 1857, for example, that Rosalie Dobbelaers wanted to take over a public house in Antwerp's Cellebroedersstraat. He advised the city council not to grant this request, as the house in question was located in a street that had recently become a thoroughfare; and because a new gateway had been created to better connect the city centre with the recently opened train station, the house was no longer in a discreet corner. This was reason enough for the police commissioner to declare not only this establishment unfit, but also the other active brothels in the street.

Administrative boundaries also determined where sex could be sold and bought. Women in prostitution often used boundaries, such as those of police zones and municipalities, to their advantage. Many Antwerp sex workers in the nineteenth century, for instance, settled in the then independent municipality of Borgerhout, which had no strict prostitution policy. By living in Borgerhout but working in Antwerp, a sex worker could avoid medical controls. Similarly, in Brussels, many women settled in working-class suburbs like Saint-Josse-ten-Noode, Schaerbeek, Uccle, and Molenbeek-Saint-Jean. The understaffed police force was powerless to prevent this.

At the end of the century, the police started to pay more attention to 'new disguised' forms of 'immoral behaviour' emanating from the large pubs established on the trendy De Keyserlei. This connecting road between Antwerp Central Station and the historic centre became a veritable entertainment district.

Notorious bars such as the Palais Indien and the Eden attracted a well-to-do clientele. Some of the women who frequented such bars regularly returned home with a man. Extra-marital sex, mostly involving payment or gifts, was an important element of fashionable nightlife. Some of these demimondaines, living off the money and gifts they received from one or more lovers, did not meet the criteria used by the police to define public women.

Of course, more traditional forms of (clandestine) commercial sex also continued to exist around 1900. The ever-expanding port meant that prostitution aimed at seamen moved northwards. Many women who made their living through sex settled around the new docks and trading houses. Although the historical inner city was also in demand, much sex work disappeared there after the straightening of the Scheldt quays began in 1875. The Rietdijk was partly demolished. It was towards the end of the nineteenth century that the still familiar term Schipperskwartier or 'Sailors' Quarter', came into vogue.

In other places, too, the urban fabric underwent similar transformations, all of which affected the sex industry. Infamous working-class neighbourhoods north of the Brussels city centre had to make way for large bourgeois houses along beautiful avenues. Brothel owners, especially those of a low social standing, found it increasingly difficult to obtain a new licence. As a result, both labourers and bourgeois men increasingly had to take their pick from women working out of pubs, cafés, and restaurants. The Saint-Roch neighbourhood also had to make way for an elegant connection between the commercial heart of Brussels around the Grand Place, Stock Exchange, Saint-Hubert Galleries (downtown), and the government district around the royal palace and royal parc (uptown). In this neighbourhood, among others, a gay scene had developed in which commercial sex played a major role. There were pubs frequented by men who sought sex with other men; there was also cruising in the streets, galleries, and urinals. Many of the ensuing encounters involved the exchange of money, especially when older men met younger men, or when rich men slept with poorer men. By 1900, this neighbourhood was also demolished.

The Great War

At the beginning of the twentieth century, supply and demand clashed with the straitjacket of regulations to such an extent that few continued to believe in the potential of a tightly organised system. Moreover, the voice of the opposition grew stronger: several Catholics, feminists, liberals, and socialists found one another under the umbrella of abolitionism, in what appeared to be an unnatural coalition. In 1900, Catholic Minister of Justice Jules Lejeune undertook an attempt to criminalise the sex trade, but met resistance from defenders of municipal autonomy. For the time being, it remained up to the municipalities to decide what was tolerated and what was not, in terms of paid sex.

Still, the system was stalling. In 1914, only a handful of tolerated brothels and registered sex workers remained. Virtually all sex work took place outside these brothels, clandestinely, but not necessarily hidden. Nevertheless, the proponents of regulation kept the upper hand. In this period, doctors and army officers propagated degeneration theories, arguing that 'hereditary diseases' like alcoholism, venereal diseases, and tuberculosis were linked. Inaction, they claimed, contributed to the weakening of the nation, even the entire 'race'. According to many, only tight medical control of women in sex work could ameliorate the state of affairs. This line of thought was fully upheld during the First World War.

On 20 August 1914, German troops occupied Brussels. Mayor Adolphe Max and his College of Aldermen negotiated the surrender with officials of the German army. Just before the Belgian government's withdrawal to Antwerp, the local authorities had been instructed to continue their work under the occupation. Mayors were required to continue with the monitoring of public order and security in their municipalities. The principle of cooperation with the occupying forces was put into practice by the vice police from the outset. Although many policemen served as soldiers in the Belgian army, the Brussels police was responsible for the safety of German troops travelling through the capital. The operation of the vice police was hardly disturbed by the outbreak of war. Joseph Broché, in service since 1886, remained in charge of the Brussels branch for the duration.

From the summer of 1914, however, Brussels was overrun by German officials and soldiers. By August 1916, there were about 9,200 German soldiers in Greater Brussels and 21,000 in the Brabant province. This created a sharp demand for paid sex. Although the vice police continued to function, sex work caused tensions between the city authorities, the Brussels population, and the occupiers. It was not long before the latter expressed discontent with the local approach to commercial sex, described as too lax.

Henceforth, the German military police actively interfered with soldiers visiting sellers of sex. Whenever a soldier fell ill, they informed the Brussels police so that a medical examination could be carried out. Soon, however, German interference expanded. In November and December 1914, the last tolerated brothels were placed under the authority of the German Kommandantur, and restricted to use by German soldiers alone. In this way, follow-up medical inspections were easier to monitor, and brothel rows between Belgians and Germans were avoided. A similar process took place elsewhere. In occupied

Bruges, for instance, the supervision of brothels was also transferred to the local Kommandantur in July 1915.

Obviously, the main problem with this approach was that the bulk of paid sex did not take place in official brothels. In early 1915, the Brussels prostitution register contained only about one hundred women. There was a sharp increase in clandestine prostitution and the number of syphilis infections. In February 1915, the German administrators therefore decided to introduce new regulations and set up their own vice police, the Sittenpolizei. According to German contemporaries, this form of 'relaxation' could not be denied to soldiers on furlough from the front for a few days. Needless to say, interest in the circumstances in which sex workers in Brussels or elsewhere had to provide relaxation, was much less pronounced.

The German vice police was placed directly under the jurisdiction of the German civil authorities in Belgium and was responsible for Brussels and several peripheral municipalities. Since the staffing of the Sittenpolizei remained limited throughout the war, cooperation with the Belgian forces remained necessary. With the new regulations, the new vice police focused mainly on medical matters. Any woman selling sex professionally was subject to medical supervision at the Saint-Gilles hospital, and examinations were mandatory. The emphasis on health rather than morality was in line with the army command's observation that prostitution and military presence always went hand-in-hand. The main danger lay in the rapid spread of venereal diseases, which could compromise the functioning of the army.

The war situation put pressure on existing family ties, social rules, and ideas about sexuality. It also pushed local women into the profession. In the chaos of war, it became easier for young women and adolescents to leave their homes when tensions rose. Once on their own, however, there were few employment options. Commercial sex often appeared to be the obvious choice. Initiation into the trade could then take place through friends already working in the sex industry. For these young women, it was afterwards often difficult to turn back, and the lack of alternatives made them heavily dependent on pimps and brothel keepers.

Moreover, more married women than before also ended up in the sex sector, for the dire economic situation obliged many to seek out alternative forms of income. Wartime conditions often led to new groups entering the sector out of sheer necessity. At a time when food prices rose at alarming rates, a piece of meat or chunk of bread sometimes became a means of payment. The profiles of these women, who soon accounted for a significant share of the sex sector, did not make it easy for the vice police to determine who exactly should be medically examined. This was not only the case in occupied Belgian cities. Achiel Van Wallegem, vicar of Dikkebus near Ypres in the western part of Belgium, described in his war diary similar scenes in unoccupied territory: 'Is it then to be wondered at that much physical and moral misery arises from this degrading situation? This explains why many women start craving the soldiers' food and soldiers' money. And unfortunately, there are enough bad fellows in the army who exploit that need of our unfortunate population for the satisfaction of their animal urges.'

Brussels, as the largest occupied city in Western Europe, was a hotspot of leisure and entertainment for stationed German officials and soldiers, and for those in transit. As soon as they arrived at the North Station, they were accosted by pimps and streetwalkers, the latter easily recognisable. Because, according to the period's bourgeois code, the female body had to be hidden from view as much as possible, visible cleavage and loose hair signalled sexual availability. By smoking, wearing light clothing, and loitering in the streets and near the doorways of their homes, these women did just about everything unbefitting bourgeois women. Once a woman and a customer had found each other, they retreated to a room where the exchange of money for sex took place. Clients and sellers of sex often undressed separately. The actual sex often lasted no more than fifteen minutes, after which the client departed.

For many soldiers at the front, buying sex was a part of leisure activities, on both the German and Allied sides. It was a way to leave the war behind, even if only for a moment. In De Panne, Veurne, and Poperinge, in the West Flanders province, nightlife boomed as never before. There were cinemas, restaurants, inns, coffee houses, hotels, and cabarets galore. Close contacts between young men and women were an integral part of that nightlife. In such local centres, as well as in the small villages beyond the Yser river, relationships, marriages, and children sometimes resulted. Often, these contacts leaned towards various forms of sex work. The Belgian army, unlike most other armies, did not set up brothels itself. In some coffee houses, however, there was more to buy than just coffee and tea.

To counter the high spread of venereal diseases, regulatory initiatives soon emerged at the front too, both on the initiative of the West Flanders governor and the army command, as well as on that of local administrators. In Catholic and Flemish circles, associations were set up and articles published to dissuade young men from getting involved in paid sex. Thus, they might advise soldiers against spending their leaves in Paris, suggesting a pilgrimage to Lourdes as an alternative. By appealing to their conscience, these organisations and publicists tried to win soldiers over. Unsurprisingly, the impact of these initiatives proved limited. Indeed, the selling of sex flourished during the war years.

4. WORLDS APART (CONGO, 1885–1960)

Amandine Lauro

In late 1945, as the Second World War was coming to a close, a young African named Etienne Ngandu published an article in the Congolese press. Its hard-hitting title screamed: 'Prostitution is devouring the Congo.' 'It is a plague', wrote Ngandu, 'a merciless gnawer on the Congolese family'. As a new practice that did not exist 'before the arrival of the Europeans', it left Congolese people distraught. To be sure, continued Ngandu, our ancestors 'waged wars on each other, but they were unaware of frivolity and prostitution'.

This article was the first of many. Throughout the 1940s and 1950s, numerous pieces on prostitution and women's immorality appeared in the columns of *La Voix du Congolais*, the official magazine of the so-called *évolués*, the literate Congolese elite who would lead the country to independence in 1960. There are several reasons for the great interest in this issue. First, there was the censorship of the colonial press and – more broadly – of political discourse in Belgian colonial territories. Since more explicitly political subjects (such as racial discrimination or civil liberties) were difficult to tackle in newspapers, *évolués* were particularly invested in more 'societal' debates such as that on prostitution. Second, the importance of gender and sexuality issues in colonial contexts also played a role. Colonial authorities had made the improvement of Congolese women's status a priority of the 'civilising mission' and used sexual and conjugal morality as a criterion of 'civilisation'. For the Congolese elite, these issues therefore constituted strong identity markers. To be recognised as an *évolué* worthy of the name, they had to be able to demonstrate their adherence to the European ideal of the nuclear, bourgeois, and Christian family – and their abandonment of traditional African norms.

However, as the content of Ngandu's article suggests, this process was less unequivocal than it seemed. Admittedly, the condemnatory discourse of *évolués* about the evils of prostitution and the perversions of the 'modern' city echoed the sermons of missionaries and colonial authorities. Yet it was not devoid of

La prostitution ronge le Congo.

La prostitution sévèrement condamnée par nos traditions ancestrales était très rare voire même inconnue dans beaucoup de tribus congolaises. Aujourd'hui c'est un fléau, un impitoyable rongeur de la famille congolaise, et une des principales causes de la dépopulation.

Des rapports officiels et médicaux sur l'état démographique du Congo parlent de dénatalité, et ce problème je l'avoue, est au dessus de notre formation. Mais de l'aveu de nos vieillards, beaucoup de grands villages, même des tribus entières ont diminué et même disparu. C'est une preuve de dénatalité.

D'un côté nos ancêtres étaient très malheureux, ils se vendaient, ils se faisaient des guerres, mais n'oublions pas qu'ils ignoraient la frivolité et la prostitution de nos jours. Malgré leur barbarie, nudité et indigence, la natalité était si élevée qu'elle suffisait à combler les vides sans cesse causés par les interminables guerres, les grandes épidémies et la traite des Nègres. Chez les Balubas par exemple, les pères répétaient aux fils et les mères aux filles, que le but de la vie humaine n'était que de perpétuer sa race, qu'on devait se marier, faire les enfants qui remplaceront les morts et lutter ainsi contre la mort pour que le nom de sa famille puisse survivre à tout jamais. Ce souci traditionnel d'avoir beaucoup d'enfants fut avec l'héritage une des principales causes de la polygamie. A dix ans, les petits Balubas savaient déjà qu'ils avaient envers la famille le devoir de la perpétuer. Cette tradition de faire tout, même le mal, pour avoir des enfants avait tellement pénétré les Balubas que pour beaucoup, les liens coutumiers et religieux n'avaient aucune valeur pour rompre une union sans enfants. Nos missionnaires au Kasaï savent combien les Balubas tenaient à cette tradition et plus d'une fois, ils ont regretté la rupture de bonnes unions chrétiennes simplement parce qu'un enfant n'est pas venu égayer la famille. Que le chrétien en renvoyant sa femme ait agi par lui-même ou qu'il ait agi sous l'influence de sa famille, le motif de la dislocation du mariage était presque toujours le même : « Que cette stérile ne fasse pas disparaître le nom de no-

tre famille sur la liste des vivants ». Je n'approuve pas tout ce que faisaient nos pères pour avoir beaucoup d'enfants, je vous dis ce qui était mais pas toujours ce qui aurait dû être. J'ai voulu vous montrer l'importance que certaines tribus attachaient à la natalité.

Mais aujourd'hui, le souci de se marier, désir instinctif et divin de se multiplier, perpétuer sa race et sa famille, s'est éteint chez beaucoup de jeunes congolais. Beaucoup de chos s ont changé en bien, mais d'autres en mal. L'indigène doit savoir que si nous avons l'habitude de dire qu'avant l'arrivée des Européens tout était triste, cela ne signifie pas qu'aujourd'hui tout est heureux, évolue vers le mieux et qu'il faut tout, tout imiter.

Tout ce que je viens de dire peut porter à se demander si l'occupation européenne qui nous a fait tant de bien en sauvant notre pays en nous apportant le christianisme a en même temps été en d'autres choses la cause de notre perversion ? Je réponds sincèrement non. L'occupation européenne en elle même n'y est pour rien, mais dans son administration, les germes des vices que portait notre propre âme, nos propres passions se sont déchaînées et ont trouvé le moyen de se développer démesurément. C'est aux Evolués maintenant de prêcher d'exemple que la liberté que nous avons retrouvée dans l'administration européenne, l'égalité que la congolaise jouit grâce au christianisme ne sont pas pour nous le moyen de relâcher nos mœurs, mais de nous permettre d'employer librement notre vie à l'accomplissement de nos devoirs et à l'exercice de nos droits, c'est-à-dire à faire le bien pour lequel nous avons été créés et éviter le mal. Notre responsabilité à ce point de vue est effrayante. Si notre exemple va à l'encontre de l'éducation de la masse et entrave la civilisation chrétienne dans notre pays, quel terrible mal aurons-nous fait à notre race ! !

J'ai dit plus haut que la prostitution ronge le Congo, je vais maintenant vous exposer brièvement sa part dans la dénatalité, son poids sur l'économie du pays et son influence sur l'éducation de notre jeunesse.

209

Etienne Ngandu, 'La prostitution ronge le Congo', in *La Voix du Congolais*, 1945. Congolese women's commercial sex and 'vice' in general were popular topics in *La Voix du Congolais*, the official magazine of the Congolese elites after the Second World War.

Amandine Lauro

criticism, even if veiled, of Belgian colonial rule. Stressing that prostitution did not exist in the Congo before the arrival of the colonisers did not put European conquerors in a good light. Pointing out that ancestors were unaware of 'frivolity' – read *sexual* frivolity – was also a way of countering the racist rhetoric of alleged African hypersexuality and 'natural' lasciviousness. Above all, acknowledging the existence of this 'plague' also meant acknowledging the failure of colonial policies to control prostitution. In 1945, the criticism was faint, but over the years it would become more outspoken. By the end of the 1950s, the *évolués* were asking more openly why the colonial authorities were unable to control prostitution. Were they really the best-placed to solve this problem?

In the midst of these political confrontations, the women most directly concerned had little opportunity to speak out. African women who made their living from sex work remained mere *objects* of the many debates led by the colonisers and the colonised elites. In Belgian as in Congolese media, their own voices remained inaudible. While this observation echoed the contemporary situation in metropolitan Belgium, the silencing was even more absolute in the colonial context. Being colonised was an additional burden on top of being a woman and a sex worker, reinforcing the exclusion of these women from public speech. To reconstruct their experiences is therefore a particularly difficult task. Thus, the portrayal of their history in our current state of knowledge remains fragmentary.

Little Prostitution, Many Laws

In their travel accounts, European explorers and conquerors in Central Africa wrote about sexuality far more than we imagine today. Westerners at the end of the nineteenth century were fascinated by the conception of sexuality they encountered in African societies, precisely because it seemed so different from the moral constraints of bourgeois society in fin-de-siècle Europe. They wrote about polygamy, ritual initiations, and, above all, the social acceptance of pre- and extra-marital sex in some Congolese societies. Generally, their observations either constituted moralising judgments, or were saucy accounts designed to titillate the reader under the guise of ethnographic description.

These visions were imbued with evolutionism and primitivism, the two main prisms through which Europe looked at Africa at the time, and the sexuality of African peoples depicted as being closer to nature and less inhibited by the moral standards of 'civilised' societies. Described as more 'animalistic', African sexualities were purported to reflect a more 'primitive' stage in the history of humanity. References to sexuality in European accounts served to define and assert racial hierarchies. European supremacy was also equated to the superiority of those capable of policing their sexuality over those who remain governed by their instincts. In the same period, this racial framework was also being applied to sellers of sex in Europe: some experts presented sex workers as women who were more primitive than others, and their alleged propensity for unbridled sexuality as the relic of an archaic form of femininity.

The question of whether a form of sex work existed prior to colonialism is often raised in debates on colonial prostitution, well beyond the case of the Belgian empire. To what extent did colonisation build on existing practices? As such, this question is not irrelevant, but it is often brought up in a simplistic fashion. In some colonial territories, barter sex existed before the conquest but, in most cases, colonialism brought changes both in terms of its extent and nature. Colonisers tended to bring along their own ideas about prostitution, and to create the conditions for a sex market with new contours. As such, they gave rise to a new marginalised and reprobated social group – that of 'prostitutes'. We must also be cautious about tales of alleged cultural or folkloric traditions that might have predisposed certain categories of women or certain population groups to prostitution. This was, after all, an argument used by colonial authorities to shield themselves from their own responsibilities in the development of a sex trade. Moreover, these traditions, where they existed, also followed very specific social codes, which we cannot generalise to a whole social group.

In the case of Central Africa, and of the Congo in particular, there was no commercial sex trade prior to colonisation. Sexuality and gender transactions not only obeyed very different rules to those that prevailed in Europe in the same period, but they also varied greatly within the Congo itself. The second-largest country in Africa, seventy-five times the size of metropolitan Belgium, the Congo is, from a cultural and social point of view, one of the more diverse territories of the continent. Kinship systems, conjugal models, and the norms governing intimacy and procreation vary from region to region. The social acceptance of extra-marital sexual engagements for women that prevailed in some areas of the country particularly caught the imagination of colonisers. The transactions that governed these practices, and more generally the exchange of material goods that played a key role in marriage, led many foreign observers to conclude not only that local societies were lascivious, but also that women were considered mere commodities. The widespread practice of bridewealth, by which unions are sealed by a payment (in varied forms) made by the groom or his kin to the bride's family, played a significant role in this view. Bridewealth implies social and symbolic dynamics of alliance that are of course far more complex than 'buying a woman'. But in the minds of colonisers, this practice constituted additional proof that relations between men and women were primarily governed by material transactions.

The development of prostitution in the Congo was closely linked to the colony's urbanisation. Under the regime of the Congo Free State (1885–1908), when the colony was managed by King Leopold II as his personal property, cities were still non-existent. Even the capital, Boma, resembled a small market town rather than a real urban centre. Furthermore, the armed forces, which in many other colonial contexts were a hotbed for the development of prostitution, were organised differently in the Congo: military camps and columns included many women who were the soldiers' companions and carried out logistical work (such as the preparation of meals) for the army.

It was not until the 1910s and after Leopold II's Congo Free State became a full-fledged Belgian colony that urban growth took off. The emergence of cities was largely the product of economic exploitation: towns developed around production and trading hubs where labour forces gradually settled. Up until the 1920s, urban centres were home to an essentially male population of migrant workers, i.e. young, single men recruited from rural areas who came to the city on temporary contracts, at the end of which they were expected to return to their region of origin. The first centres were designed more as workers' camps than as real towns. This was reflected in their demography: there were far more male than female urban dwellers. In the early 1920s, for example, when Leopoldville (present-day Kinshasa) took over from Boma as the capital, there were almost three men for every woman in the city's African districts. This is an essential factor to better understand the development of commercial sex in the Belgian colony. Although this gender imbalance would diminish in the following decades, it persisted in Congolese cities until independence in 1960.

Furthermore, the mobility of women was more tightly controlled than that of men. Both the colonial authorities and traditional chiefs tried to keep women in rural areas, as they provided the bulk of labour input in agriculture and subsistence. Despite these obstacles, women travelled to the cities. A small number migrated illegally from the 1910s, in search of new opportunities or in the hope of escaping unfavourable family circumstances. Their urban presence grew from the 1920s onwards, but it was not until the early 1930s that they were officially recognised by the colonial bureaucracy as urbanites in their own right. At the same time, Belgian authorities also realised that many male workers had no intention of returning to their villages at the end of their contract: city dwellers were there to stay. This realisation also led to changes in the way colonial authorities dealt with sex work.

Belgian colonial territories were quite unique in that they had legislation on prostitution *before* the sex trade developed. The first ordinance on the subject was issued in early 1909, barely six months after the take-over of the Congo Free State by Belgium, when the colony's urbanisation was still in its infancy. These first measures were part of a strategy of prevention, as the new Belgian authorities tried to present themselves as exemplary colonial rulers. The sombre reputation of Leopold II's Congo played a decisive role here: the new administration wanted to demonstrate to the world that it was committed to the duties of the 'civilising mission' and to the moralisation of the colony, and that the era of ruthless economic exploitation without social care was now over.

In terms of content, there is nothing to suggest that these measures were specifically intended for the Congo. The 1909 ordinance is a simplified 'copy–paste' version of the legislation in force in Belgium, and follows the tradition of nineteenth-century European regulationism. While the creation of brothels or red-light districts was not on the agenda, the text provided for the registration of women who 'notoriously or habitually' engaged in prostitution, police surveillance, regular medical examinations, and imprisonment in the event of venereal contamination or contravention of the above-mentioned requirements. No thought was given to how such a regulatory programme could be adapted to local practices. Nevertheless, in 1913 colonial authorities confirmed these measures in a new decree, in what was to remain the only official legislation on prostitution until the end of the colonial period.

As was often the case in colonial contexts, the terms of the law and the reality on the ground were two very different things. By the colonial authorities' own admission, legislation on prostitution always remained unheeded. During the interwar period, they attempted to implement the 1913 decree in several cities (in Boma, in Leopoldville, in the mining towns of Katanga and in Stanleyville, among others), but all these attempts ended in failure. In some places, urban authorities managed to register a few women and at best to monitor them for a few months. But these experiments only involved a ridiculously small number of women and were never sustainable in the long term. Colonial authorities simply did not have the means to convert their ambitions into reality.

Nevertheless, from the end of the 1910s, and even more so in the interwar years, the expanding sex trade in the colony's first urban centres became a real cause for concern. As cities grew, colonial leaders became more anxious about the moral, sexual, and sanitary consequences of the migrant labour system. These concerns reached the top level of the colonial hierarchy. In 1917, the official Annual Report presented by the Minister of Colonies to the Belgian Parliament identified this 'problem' as a major challenge: 'It is becoming urgent to combat the immorality that reigns among the natives grouped around the large centres; the number of people without confession who languish there and find in prostitution the resources they disdain to gain from work is constantly increasing. Having left their environment, where their vices were kept in check by strict customary regulations, they indulge in all manner of excesses.'

Many colonial commentators described Congolese towns as riddled with 'immorality'. They saw the low number of women and the overwhelming number of single men as conducive to rampant prostitution, itself described as the cause of an unprecedented spread of sexually transmitted diseases. Syphilis and gonorrhoea were indeed wreaking havoc. Colonial authorities worried not only about the threat these diseases posed to the workforce's health, but also about their consequences on birth rates. As in the metropole, demographic decline and falling birth rates were important political concerns and fed moral panics. The corrupting effects of 'detribalisation' were perceived as particularly strong on women. Female urban migrants were viewed as women 'on the loose' whose only interest was to get free from the moral constraints of traditional environments. Once settled in the city, the alleged idle existence and easy money of urban life would further debauch them.

The reality of the social landscape of Congolese towns and of the lives of the women who settled there was, however, quite different from this stereotypical portrayal. Ironically, the discrepancy between the moralising rules of the colonial powers and the urban reality largely explains the failure of measures to control prostitution.

'Theoretically Living Alone'

Prostitution practices can only be understood as part of the manifold new conjugal configurations that emerged in Congolese cities during the period. The first women to settle in Congolese urban areas did so either independently or by following a partner. Many embarked on informal economic activities (petty trade, food production, sexual or domestic services) and were able to acquire some economic autonomy. Together with the gender imbalance that placed women in an unprecedented social position, these new roles contributed to the development of new types of sexual, domestic, and conjugal relationships – and of new ways of negotiating those arrangements. These relationships transgressed both European gender and moral norms, as well as traditional African patriarchal rules. It was precisely these transgressions that worried colonial authorities.

When it came to commercial sex, Congolese practices had little in common with what was understood in Europe as 'prostitution'. No pimps, no brothels, no mass soliciting in public space: until the early 1950s, these defining character-istics of commercial sex in Europe were practically absent in the Congo and in the mandate territory of Rwanda-Burundi (1919–1962), which Belgium gained control of after the First World War.

Commercial sex in the Congo was not limited to providing sexual services in a strict sense. The services that 'sex workers' provided were often also of a domestic nature. They included, i.a., the provision of food, preparation of meals and drinks, and all kinds of domestic tasks – in other words, a measure of the 'comforts of home'. In practical terms, relationships with customers took the form of more or less long-term cohabitations, ranging from 'temporary mar-riages' to concubinage (for a few days, a few months, sometimes more) with var-ying degrees of exclusivity. Some women made a career out of these exchanges, moving from one man to another, while others engaged in them only occa-sionally or combined them with other activities, such as market gardening or petty trade. The concept of 'transactional sex', developed by anthropologists and referring to a broad spectrum of exchanges or relationships including affection as well as financial and non-financial compensations, is useful when consider-ing the practices described by colonial observers in the Congo as 'prostitution'.

The gender imbalance in urban centres played an important role in this his-tory. Not only did it make prostitution a potentially lucrative activity, following the principle of supply and demand, it also led to an increase in bride prices. In the interwar period, bride dowries already amounted to huge sums of money, often several months' pay for an average worker. This meant that many young men could not afford to marry. It also explains the proliferation of new forms of domestic arrangements such as extended engagements, or concubinage based on more or less formal, long-term relationships, and on more or less substan-tial transactions. A whole new moral and material economy of sexuality and gender relations emerged in the cities. The uncertainties of rural flight and of wage labour in colonial companies, the lowering of the age of marriage, the new dynamics of compensation that governed marital arrangements in the city: all led to new conceptions of married life, to more opportunities for pre- and extra-marital relationships, and of course to more transactional sex.

In many respects, colonial legislation, inspired by provisions drawn up in Europe, was ill-suited to control these practices. Congolese 'prostitution' raised difficult classification issues for colonial authorities. The very basis of these measures, i.e. the identification of 'public women', proved problematic from the outset. In the context of relationships of varying duration, involving multiple

Amandine Lauro

degrees of commitment and transaction, how could one clearly identify what defined a 'sex worker' as against a 'respectable' woman? Where did concubinage begin and prostitution end? Should every unmarried urban woman be considered a public woman? At the end of the 1920s, colonial authorities in the capital Leopoldville seriously wondered: 'Who do we call a prostitute here?' They fully realised that answering that question with 'a woman without any means of existence other than those she gains from her relations with men' would mean applying the term 'prostitute' to 'legions of women'. That explains why the colonial administration struggled to fit the changing gender and sexual patterns at play in the towns into its moral and administrative categories. The task was all the more complex because colonial prostitution also challenged the limited means of control at the disposal of Belgian authorities.

The failure to control prostitution reflected an inability to control the work and mobility of women in urban centres. When attempts were made to do so, the police quickly lost track of those registered as public women. At a time when identification and civil registration services were barely developed, many women moved from one neighbourhood to another or disappeared within the city. More so than in Europe, commercial sex was not confined to specific neighbourhoods. The women went wherever men lived and worked: in the *cités indigènes* (urban native districts), in companies' workers camps, in those of the army, and even in the European quarters.

Moreover, despite official criticism of prostitution, the attitude of colonial rulers had its own ambiguities. Big businesses and industrial companies were well aware that complex domestic and subsistence realities lay behind the moralising rhetoric on prostitution. For the mining companies in particular, turning a blind eye to women's sexual and domestic work allowed for economies of scale. Recruiting single workers was cheaper than recruiting married workers, and this workforce was more flexible. The work of urban women, their activities in small-scale food production and petty trade, and the sexual and domestic services they sold, helped ensure that the hard-pressed workers were (relatively) comfortable. The companies would then not have to invest in expensive facilities like family housing, or family support measures such as extra food rations. Between the wars, many companies tolerated the presence of officially single women in their workers' camps.

This (relative) tolerance did not, however, mean relinquishing the ambition to achieve tighter control over these women. By the 1920s, it was clear that regulatory measures had failed. Colonial authorities began to consider other strategies. One policy quickly came to the fore. Introduced in 1929 in Leopoldville, and subsequently adopted in all the major cities of Congo, Rwanda, and Burundi, it was an original measure with no equivalent in Europe or elsewhere in the colonial world: a system of taxation for 'women theoretically living alone' – a euphemistic formulation for which the Belgian colonial authorities had a unique talent.

As its name suggests, the tax was to be paid by all adult unmarried African women residing in the city (with a few exceptions). The law was therefore not aimed solely at women earning a proven income from commercial sex, but at all women living outside the bounds of nuclear family: independent traders, concubines, dependent female relatives, young unmarried girls and, from the end of the 1940s, 'additional' wives of polygamists, whom colonial legislation now refused to recognise. On the part of Belgians and Africans alike, nobody was fooled about the tax's real target, i.e. prostitution and 'immoral' urban women. Some critics took offence at this measure, as it stigmatised all single women and conflated women of 'loose morals' with 'respectable' women. This was all the more problematic because the status of 'woman theoretically living alone' imposed gynaecological surveillance: all women registered as such had to undergo regular medical examinations to detect venereal diseases. Another major ambiguity pointed out by several observers was that, although officially intended to curb the rural exodus of independent women, the tax nonetheless signified the recognition – and to some extent acceptance – of their presence in the city.

Free Women

The tax coincided with the emergence of a new social category of independent women in the cities, and of a new term to describe them: *femmes libres* or 'free women'. In the 1920s, the economic boom in the Congo drove more and more women to urban centres. After the stock market crash of 1929 and during the economic crisis of the 1930s, their presence in cities increased. While many male workers, now redundant, were forced to return to their villages, women remained and positioned themselves on the margins of the formal economy. In these difficult economic times, their income was particularly valuable, helping support families who had stayed in rural areas. In Leopoldville, for example, while the male population halved from 1929 to 1935, the female population increased by 8 per cent. The expression 'free women' gradually came to designate urban women who led independent lives or earned a large part of their income from their relationships with men. African populations quickly adopted this expression initially forged by colonial authorities. There were also regional variations. In the towns of Lower Congo, for example, people spoke of *ndumba*, a term that originally referred to young unmarried girls in Lingala; in

Amandine Lauro

Swahili-speaking areas, the term *malaya* referred more clearly to independent women who made a living from prostitution.

The 1940s and 1950s saw the rise of a certain category of free women, renowned for their independence, beauty, and power over men. These women became key figures in urban culture. They played an important role in the development of a new entertainment economy in Congolese cities. In the capital in particular, a few free women ran high-profile bars and dance halls. These were essential venues in Congolese towns, as they were the only places away from colonial surveillance where Congolese people could socialise. Free women notably played a significant role on the music scene – even if the orchestras remained male bastions. It is not by chance that these women are celebrated in many popular songs of the time. For rumba artists, free women were muses, inspiring them with the transgression of gender norms they embodied. Free women were indeed a far cry from the model of the docile *évolué* housewife extolled by missionary propaganda. Numerous songs described these independent young women as bewitchingly beautiful, wealthy, and as social butterflies breaking the hearts of their many suitors.

Free women were also at the origin of new forms of women's associations, known as *sociétés d'élégance*. These 'elegance societies' sprang up in several Congolese cities in the 1930s. They began as mutual aid and collective savings associations, set up by independent women, shopkeepers, and others who had acquired some financial autonomy. Within this associative landscape, the elegance societies placed particular emphasis on fashion, aesthetics, and new urban entertainments; above all, they brought together free women who openly made a living from prostitution. The names of these associations are evocative: La Lumière ('The Light'), La Beauté ('The Beauty'), La Fille Gentille ('The Nice Girl'), La Plus Belle Toilette ('The Most Beautiful Outfit'), Au Chic ('At the Style'), and so on. One of the most famous was the Diamant ('Diamond') association, founded in Leopoldville in 1933 by shopkeepers, but dominated by free women from the 1940s on and suspected by the colonial administration of fronting a prostitution ring.

Another association in the capital, La Reconnaissance ('The Recognition'), was set up in the 1940s on the initiative of a bar owner who hoped to attract a new male clientele to his establishment. Once a week, members of the association (often pretty young women) were invited to meet at the bar in exchange for gifts, and to entertain clients – 'and more if they wished'. Like many other elegance societies, La Reconnaissance also led young women to entertain wealthy men, who could ask for sex and paid generously. Many of these associations were also based on generational ties, as they brought together both young single and older women (known in the capital as *mama mikonzi*, that is, women who had already 'made a life for themselves'), in a dynamic of apprenticeship.

Some free women were therefore quite wealthy. The income they earned through commercial sex allowed them to purchase luxury consumer goods and, in some cases, become houseowners. The financial success of some of these women should not, however, mask the harsh reality of the lives of many free women and their precarious condition. Interviewed in the early 2000s, Marie A., a free woman who had been active in the 1950s, recalled how 'during the period of the occasional marriage break-up, the free woman led a life of misery'. Other sources remind us that many free women did not choose this life, but were often driven into it by personal circumstances, such as widowhood or divorce, combined with the difficulty of earning a living through other job opportunities. African women were largely excluded from wage labour in Belgian colonial territories and therefore had no chance at employment in the formal sector. Even domestic work was monopolised by men, the so-called 'boys'.

In addition to these difficult material conditions, free women were also subjected to the constraints and hassles of the colonial administration. Every year, they had to pay the single women's tax. Although official circulars recommended that women not be sent to prison for debt, the authorities in some colonial towns did not hesitate to use this means of coercion against women who did not pay the tax. Like sex workers in Belgium, they had to undergo painful and humiliating medical examinations several times a year. In the 1950s, the Red Cross, which was responsible for examinations tracking sexually transmitted diseases in the Congolese capital, admitted that the lack of staff and cramped premises made it impossible to maintain professional confidentiality or even to respect 'mere modesty'.

Free women also had to contend with a series of other vexations at the hands of the colonial bureaucracy. They were, for example, prevented from owning property, or refused licences to operate businesses. Some rebelled, such as Anna K., a free woman from Léopoldville who was denied a bar licence in the early 1950s. She protested, stating that she had 'worked a lot for my own benefit over the past twenty-five years'. To that she added that she had always paid the single women tax on time, that she had 'grown up here in Leo[poldville] and I don't want to steal anything that belongs to someone else'. Her efforts were to no avail.

Yet the introduction of the single women tax had paradoxical consequences, i.e. offering the women concerned unintended grounds for protest. Stigmatising or not, the official status of 'woman living theoretically alone' marked the entry of urban women into full legality. In other words, it gave them rights. While some women did not hesitate to challenge the legal loopholes of the sta-

Amandine Lauro

tus, others filed official complaints with colonial authorities when they felt they had been wronged.

When we think of resistance by the colonised, we often think of spectacular revolts or informal manoeuvres away from colonial institutions. Yet protest sometimes took very official routes. Africans were, more than we imagine today, aware of the inner workings of the colonial bureaucracy, and of the opportunities for protest that colonial institutions could unwittingly offer them. 'Women theoretically living alone' were no exception. At the end of the 1930s, several took their cases to the courts in Leopoldville to claim repayment of the taxes they had paid. Their argument: they were not living from prostitution and were even able to provide evidence of the respectability of their means of subsistence, such as small-scale food trade or property income. Even though these plaintiffs did not always win their cases, their complaints helped persuade colonial authorities to broaden the conditions for exemption from the tax at the end of the 1930s, notably in favour of young girls living with their parents, and elderly women.

In addition to these legal protests, other forms of opposition to the single women tax existed, despite the coercive apparatus deployed by the administration. Historical sources only offer snippets in this regard: fluctuating incomes from one year to the next, recurring calls from colonial officials to tighten the surveillance of free women, and the various camouflage tactics such as using a friend to pose as a woman's husband or fiancé.

Protests also took more collective forms. At the end of the 1940s, for example, the free women of Inongo, a small administrative and port centre located several hundred kilometres north-east of Leopoldville, organised a demonstration outside the local administration's buildings. Some seventy women protested the conditions under which the medical examinations were conducted and voiced their refusal to submit to them. The nun who examined them was brutal and insulted them with classic racist invectives from the repertoire of Belgian colonisation: *macaques* ('monkeys'), *chèvres* ('goats'), and so on. They did not see a doctor, even when it was decided to lock them up in hospital. The town authorities were quick to write them up without taking their grievances seriously. But the free women of Inongo were aware of the tensions within the colonial bureaucracy. Thus, after their demonstration, they approached the local magistrate, who opened a judicial investigation that confirmed the veracity of their complaints.

Sometimes free women set their sights even higher in their challenges to colonial power. In 1955, several courageous women from Bujumbura, the capital of Burundi, chose to address King Baudouin himself. The Belgian monarch was touring the colonies at the time, and a group of free women took advantage of the visit to air their grievances about the single women tax. As the royal carriage passed through their quarters to the cheers of the crowd, a small delegation of women threw the many letters they had prepared into the convoy of convertibles. It is not certain that the king read them, but we do know that Bujumbura authorities were summoned to explain themselves, and that free women paid the price. In retaliation, city authorities rounded up all the free women who had not paid their bills, in the process increasing the tax by 50 francs. In the Swahili district of Buyenzi, which was the most affected by this movement of collective mobilisation (and by its repression), free women did not stop there. They called for a boycott of the tax, with some success, since while 90% of women had paid the tax in 1955, only 68% did so the following year.

Racial Segregation

It is no coincidence that we have so far only discussed commercial sex between Africans. The racial segregation introduced by the colonial powers weighed heavily on the organisation of the sex trade, making some types of encounters impossible.

From the outset, legislation on prostitution was designed to apply only to African sex workers. For the colonial authorities, tolerance of European sellers of sex in the Congo was out of the question. In fact, this was one of the colonial power's few successes in regulating prostitution, for until independence, Belgian authorities managed to enforce this ban. There were several reasons for this, starting with the repugnance with which Europeans viewed the idea of white women selling sex to an African clientele.

Colonial powers were obsessed by the prospect of sexual relations – consensual or otherwise – between white women and black men. In a way, it represented a sacrilege, as if the colonised were symbolically accessing the privilege of the coloniser. This concern triggered deep-seated anxieties about preserving white supremacy. Commercial sex, in particular, threatened the so-called prestige of the colonisers and with it a certain idea of their superiority. The Belgian colonial administration therefore ensured that such encounters remained impossible. White immigration to colonial territories was tightly controlled. Not everybody could enter Congolese territory, and immigration records reveal the extent to which Belgian authorities were wary of 'suspect' female profiles, such as single women or cabaret singers on tour. The small number of white women in the colony allowed the authorities to keep them under close surveillance. Security services were vigilant towards even vaguely ambiguous behaviour. At the very beginning of the 1930s, for example, a simple article published in the newspaper *La Gazette de Bruxelles* casting aspersions on white women working as waitresses ('and possibly more…') in bars for Africans in Leopoldville triggered a meticulous investigation on the orders of the minister of Colonies. The investigation revealed that this trivial rumour was entirely unfounded.

A few months later, a Belgian woman living in the Congolese capital became the subject of a wide-ranging investigation led by State Security. The inquiry was the result of a simple letter of denunciation accusing the woman in question of 'misbehaving as a real prostitute' with Portuguese men and of 'easily offering the hospitality of her room to friends passing through'. Although there was no question of an African clientele, the prospect was worrying enough to scrutinise the woman's alleged actions with a fine-tooth comb. A tail was set up. The Leopoldville police intendant even summoned several of the young woman's neighbours to hear their views on her behaviour. Once again, the case turned out to be a pure hoax, in this case involving a rejected fiancé. It is, however, a good illustration of the extent of the sensitivities aroused by the mere prospect of such behaviour. It also shows the close surveillance that colonial authorities were prepared to deploy to ensure that it remained impossible. Here again, white prestige and the fear of damaging the superior image of the coloniser were at stake.

Similar concerns can be found in another context: the travel of colonised people to the Belgian metropole. Throughout the colonial period, Belgium sought to limit as much as possible the presence of its African subjects on its home soil. Again, the spectre of interracial sexual intercourse played a significant role. Even during the First World War, when Belgian authorities considered bringing troops from the Congo as reinforcements to the Yser trenches, decision-makers cited this threat as a reason for rejecting the project. Exposing African soldiers to relations – remunerated or not – with white women was a potential threat to the prestige and security of the colonial community in Africa: how would these soldiers, once back in the Congo, still respect 'white superiority' and submit to the racial deference expected of them?

Right up until the end of the colonial period, the interracial encounters of Congolese sailors working on ships sailing between Matadi and Antwerp were also a cause for concern. Everything was done to discourage them from frequenting the brothels in the port of Antwerp. During the 1958 World Fair in Brussels, Congolese soldiers' meetings with Belgian women and their visits to the 'women's cafés' in the northern districts of the capital were only reluctantly tolerated, and the soldiers systematically tailed.

The racial segregation enforced in the sex trade also had consequences for white men seeking relationships with black women. Since the first years of

'Groupe de ménagères de Blancs à Luluabourg', in *L'Illustration congolaise*, n°72 (1 September 1927), p. 1,587. This kind of picture often appeared in travel reports on Belgian Congo in about 1900, but the publication of this photo in the official propaganda magazine of the Belgian authorities is surprising. We see five young women explicitly identified as 'housewives for whites'. The picture shows the continuing appeal of exoticising fantasies about interracial relations among colonialists.

colonial rule, the predominant form of interracial relationships had been that of concubinage with a companion euphemistically called *ménagère* ('house-wife'). The status of these relationships is difficult to define, for they were at the

Amandine Lauro

intersection of conjugal arrangements, domesticity, and transactional intimacy. They raise the question of consent within what was a doubly unequal relationship, between man and woman, and between coloniser and colonised. Most of these 'housewives' lived in the home of their white partner for the duration of his posting, for several months or several years. Marriages *à la mode du pays* ('in the way of the land') were sometimes concluded, but had no value in the eyes of Europeans. Legally recognised marriages were the exception, not the rule, and most of these women were abandoned as soon as the European returned to the old continent. Not surprisingly, fathers very rarely recognised the children born of these liaisons. If such relationships were tolerated by colonial society in the early years of colonial rule, it was notably because they offered several advantages over prostitution. In a context where white women were largely absent and the colonisers were single men in the prime of their lives, colonial authorities felt that a long-term relationship with a regular African female companion was a lesser evil compared to multiple short-lived sexual encounters, which fostered sexually transmitted diseases and did nothing to improve the morale of lonely colonisers. As the number of white women in the colony increased after the Second World War, the practice of interracial concubinage decreased.

Still, the widespread practice of these relationships did not prevent prostitution in urban areas, though interracial prostitution was never common. As was the case for Congolese customers, towns in the Congo offered neither red-light districts nor brothels catering to European customers. Although colonial authorities were less meticulous than when these encounters involved white women, they ensured that the affairs of European men with African women did not cross certain thresholds of visibility. Racial segregation laws also affected colonisers: it was not just the Congolese who were excluded from the city's white areas, but also Europeans who were banned from African neighbourhoods at night.

Many Europeans, of course, flaunted the ban, and individuals were regularly caught at night in the native districts. The authorities discovered several meetings arranged with the help of taxi drivers or messenger boys. In Elisabethville (present-day Lubumbashi) in the early 1950s, a Congolese passer-by told the police: 'At around 11 o'clock at night, a car driven by a native in which four Europeans were lying, the fifth sitting at the window of the door, stopped in front of my house. As I happened to be standing outside, the European called out to me and asked if I knew of any place where there were "girls" to amuse themselves. I told him it was too late to look for any more women. He promised me 100 francs if I would drive him. I refused, so he said good night and the car drove off.' Underground bars frequented by a clientele 'warmly in favour of the policy of "non-discrimination", as an official report from the 1950s ironically put it, also periodically emerged on the fringes of white neighbourhoods. Still, from a quantitative point of view, these practices remained marginal.

'Even if Prostitution Doesn't Exist in the Congo...'

In the 1950s, the exponential urban growth of Congolese cities changed the landscape of prostitution. Between the end of the Second World War and independence in 1960, the population of Leopoldville, for example, increased tenfold. Colonial police were less and less able to keep the close watch over free women they dreamed of. The influx of migrants also created a new market for commercial sex, and while no figures are available, the archives of the colonial administration mention street prostitution more often, even if the phenomenon seems to have remained relatively marginal.

In the Congo, as in many other colonial contexts, prostitution reveals the contradictions of the colonial project. Despite the moralising condemnations of Belgian authorities, it was the political economy of colonial exploitation and in particular the system of migrant labour that created a new market for commercial sex. Regulating these practices was an important ambition, connected as it was to the control of urbanisation and of women's mobility. At the same time, prostitution did not necessarily contradict the racialised and gendered conceptions that colonial authorities had of African populations, such as hypersexuality. It therefore appeared – even more than in metropolitan Belgium – as a 'necessary evil'. Prostitution highlights the coercive power of the colonial administration, as well as its limitations in the face of the challenges and ever-renewed protests of the colonised – in this case, colonised women. Finally, while commercial sex was segregated, the opportunities for contact that it offered raised major anxieties throughout the colonial period. As soon as it involved Europeans, prostitution undermined the image of moral and sexual superiority the colonisers prided themselves on.

In 1948, Belgium abolished the regulation system. This was not the case in the Congo, where regulatory provisions such as the tax on women theoretically living alone were maintained. A year later, the United Nations General Assembly adopted the Convention for the Suppression of the Traffic in Persons and of the Exploitation of the Prostitution of Others. Belgium, without much explanation, refused ratification, claiming that it was 'unsuited' to the Congolese situation. Colonial exceptionalism was therefore more topical than ever. Behind the scenes, some people were concerned about this strategy: 'Even if

Amandine Lauro

prostitution doesn't exist in the Congo – what a happy country – wouldn't it be in our interest to declare in theory that we will not support the pimps [*soutenir les souteneurs*]?' queried the Ministry of Colonies in 1949. Yet this argument was not new: since the 1920s, in the face of international pressure to abolish the traffic in women, Belgium's strategy had always been to deny the existence of prostitution in its African territories, and to argue that there was no need to abolish something that did not exist. The absence of trafficking, pimps, and brothels – all elements that Westerners considered to be part of the sex trade – rendered this argument sustainable. In a way, free women and colonial prostitution challenged the definition of commercial sex that existed in metropolitan Belgium.

5. PLEASE TURN OFF THE LIGHTS (1918–1970)

Magaly Rodríguez García

In late November 1924, the American Paul Kinsie visited Antwerp and Brussels. First, he met Abie, a pimp from Buenos Aires who was briefly in Antwerp to smuggle diamonds to Argentina. They went together to the New York bar on the Saucierstraat near the Sailors' Quarter ('Schipperskwartier'), Antwerp's famous red-light district around the harbour. There they hoped to find 'a girl' for Kinsie through the pub owner, a 'burly' Belgian who spoke excellent English. He assured Kinsie and Abie that there were 'plenty of girls who would be glad to go where there is real money, but they all have comrades [pimps] and it is pretty hard to get them loose'. Antwerp was no longer the prostitution paradise of yesteryear. According to the publican, only 'old grandmothers' who 'ain't worthwhile' or young women 'with no money or boy' to go elsewhere, stayed in Antwerp. There were a few on the street who were no longer that young, but still good-looking; he knew everyone in the neighbourhood would gladly lend Kinsie a hand. A handsome American guy like Kinsie would have no trouble recruiting someone quickly.

Armed with business cards from his friends, Kinsie continued prospecting in the Sailors' Quarter and other prostitution neighbourhoods, finding quite a few registered brothels employing young women close to the Antwerp Central Train Station. They were all Belgian girls, but not underage. The same was true of clandestine brothels, although many foreign women worked in the streets, cabarets, taverns, bars, and hotels. Most hailed from France and the Nether-lands. Judging by their appearance and impertinent behaviour, it was clear that they hardly earned anything. Kinsie also noticed this in the red-light districts of Brussels, where he stayed until early December. Jean, Georg, and Yankel – three pimps in Antwerp and Brussels – told him that 'at the first opportunity, women and their men go abroad'. While Kinsie knew that Alexandria, Cairo, Istanbul, Montevideo, and Rio de Janeiro were popular among European sex workers and pimps, those places apparently did not appeal to the Belgians. Their favour-ite destinations were Buenos Aires, Havana, and Mexico City.

In his quest for more detailed information, Kinsie told his friends how he had found his first girl. Yankel then confided to him that 'his Suzie' was only twenty years old. He had met her after the war in Liège; she had worked in a store selling butter and eggs. In early 1924, Yankel brought Suzie to Brussels and lived from her earnings in commercial sex. They planned to go to Mexico together as soon as she had earned enough to pay for the trip. Considering Suzie's good height (about 1.65m or 5.4 feet), light skin, fashionable blonde hair (short bob hairstyle), blue eyes, and beautiful white teeth, Kinsie thought they would soon succeed at their plan.

Kinsie himself was between twenty-five and thirty years old when he visited Belgium. Good looking and charming, he knew a lot about the world. Before ending up in Antwerp, he travelled around South and Central America. From Cuba, he sailed to England and continued to France and the Netherlands. After Belgium, he moved around in the rest of Europe, the Middle East, and North America. Wherever he went, he met all sorts of people from the prostitution milieu who provided him with golden tips to recruit women, evade the authorities, and find the best working places.

But Kinsie was not a pimp. Nor was he looking for a girl, as he claimed in Antwerp. Furthermore, contrary to what he told Yankel in Brussels, he had no girl working for him. Kinsie was a secret agent commissioned from 1924 to 1926 by the League of Nations (the forerunner of the United Nations) to investigate international human trafficking. After his brief stint in Belgium, he concluded that there was no trace of forced migration for prostitution. If there was migration, it was in the form of an exodus from Belgium, he wrote in his reports (now preserved at the League's archives in Geneva). It is noteworthy that he worked on behalf of the organisation precisely during the interwar period, a time when prostitution was increasingly becoming an international issue. The ideas on commercial sex that developed during that period influenced the prostitution policies of many countries during the twentieth century. Belgium is no exception. But as we shall see, the international views on prostitution did not always coincide with local policies, identities, and sexual interactions on the ground. The sale of sex was never what it seemed.

Lobbying Avant la Lettre

The trauma of the First World War and the revolutionary situation in Russia after 1917 convinced political elites of the need for an international body to prevent future conflicts. In the Treaty of Versailles, they approved US President

Magaly Rodríguez García

Woodrow Wilson's proposal leading to the foundation of the League of Nations in January 1919. Headquartered in the chic Palais des Nations in Geneva, the organisation was the first of its kind, for it aimed at becoming truly universal, not only in terms of geography but also as an institution that welcomed governmental representatives and a broad range of non-governmental actors. Nonetheless, many history books describe the League as a complete failure. After all, just twenty years after its creation, the world witnessed another horrific war. The League of Nations was certainly responsible for not being able to prevent the spread of fascism and Nazism, but the organisation was not only concerned with diplomatic issues. Article 23 of its founding charter also made it responsible for social and humanitarian issues. According to the League's founders, world peace needed to go hand in hand with social justice, the promotion of culture and education, the 'prevention and control of [sexually transmitted] disease', and the fight against international crime. In so doing, the Geneva organisation laid the foundation for several initiatives that would emerge after the Second World War under the umbrella of the UN and European institutions.

One of the League's key concerns was trafficking, i.e. the drugs trade and the coerced recruitment and movement of women and children for the sex industry. As chapter three describes, Brussels had at the end of the nineteenth century become the centre of attention due to a media scandal that decried the police's involvement in the international trade in 'white slaves'. The British spoke of 'the Belgian traffic' and recounted in great detail the shocking discovery of underage girls in brothels, in Brussels and elsewhere. That proved, according to feminist and abolitionist activists, the 'obvious' link between the regulation system and trafficking, as well as the urgent need to continue the fight against regulationist countries. They called Brussels 'the citadel of regulation' and Antwerp 'the most immoral city of the universe' and, by the late 1800s, joined hands with women and men abroad who sought to protect 'innocent women' and the 'sanctity' of the family. Their efforts coincided with the outcry produced by Jack the Ripper and the murder of five women in London, which engendered much public support. After the war and with full conviction, the women's and abolitionist movements continued their activities to gain access to the League of Nations. Together with social hygiene and eugenicist organisations that fought 'venereal danger' and 'degeneration', they formed a cast-iron international network that lobbied in Geneva to put the regulation of prostitution on the agenda. To do so, however, they needed to take a detour. And they did so in an extraordinarily original way.

Since the League of Nations's jurisdiction was restricted to supranational matters and the regulation of prostitution belonged to the national realm, the issue needed to be 'internationalised'. The League established a Committee

The Body of Experts of the League of Nations, with Belgian representative Isidore Maus in the left chair, ca. 1924–1927 (Geneva, United Nations Archives). No photographs of Paul Kinsie have so far been found. Information on his age and appearance comes from comments in the correspondence of members of the Body of Experts.

against the Trafficking of Women and Children, which included both state and non-state representatives. Belgium sent Isidore Maus, legal adviser, president of the Belgian National Committee for the Defence against Trafficking in Women and Children, and a leading partner of Belgian and French feminist organisations. Unlike his British and French colleagues, Maus was not a show-off, but enjoyed respect because of his knowledge of the white slavery scandal and the 'diabolical' consequences of the regulatory system.

Belgium and France were the only countries in Europe where the regulation of prostitution still existed. When the Americans proposed an international inquiry about trafficking in 1923, Maus agreed to join the newly created Body of Experts, to coordinate the study. They deemed such an inquiry necessary, as the white slave story had resulted in many sensationalist media reports. The

Magaly Rodríguez García

League wanted to know the 'real facts'. Therefore, the Body of Experts hired secret agents to infiltrate the world of prostitution and find concrete evidence of forced prostitution. Paul Kinsie was the most prolific agent. Disguised as a pimp, he visited some forty cities over two years and talked to thousands of people from the 'underworld'.

Kinsie's unpublished reports contain all sorts of details about the (in)efficiency of the vice and immigration police; the profiles of pimps, sex workers, brothel madams, and other middlemen; the production of false papers; migratory movements; places of prostitution and women's seduction strategies. But they do not say much about his main mission: proof of trafficking. Even though he permanently looked for minors and adult women forced into prostitution, he did not really find any. While there were many minors in the red-light districts he visited, their stories did not match the black and white picture of the 'innocent victim' lured into prostitution by perverted men. He therefore concluded that there was no such thing as a well-organised international network of traffickers. That did not prevent the League of Nations from drawing other conclusions. The Body of Experts published a summary of the reports and indicated that not only did a trade of 'considerable proportions' exist, but that regulated brothels were the breeding grounds of that 'international plague'. This opened the door to the League's interference in national prostitution policies.

The League's publication became wildly popular and was eagerly used in anti-prostitution campaigns worldwide. Once the link between trafficking and the regulation system was 'exposed' by the renowned experts from Geneva, the League was from the late 1920s onward able to fully advocate for abolitionism. This made the abolitionist camp in Belgium more combative, although it would take until 1948 for the regulation of prostitution to be banned.

Meanwhile, Maus continued his work within the League. As the organisation's mandate was continually expanded, it could deal with prostitution in its entirety. During the 1930s, three follow-up studies were conducted after the initial inquiry into the international traffic in women and children, and Belgium contributed significantly to the new studies. While the focus of the 1920s was on the intermediaries of prostitution – brothel owners, pimps, and traffickers – in the following decade the focus shifted to the sex worker herself. This shift coincided with the growing tendency inside and outside the League of Nations to pathologise prostitution. Commercial sex, in other words, was presented as a disease.

Indeed, once everyone in Geneva agreed to the closure of regulated brothels, the question arose of what to do with the 'ex-prostitutes'. Therefore, the League organised an international survey on rehabilitation programmes. Since the study revealed that many sex workers refused to take advantage of rehabilitation opportunities, the League initiated a follow-up research on the social pro-files of women in prostitution, in the hope that the resulting insights would lead to better programmes and help identify 'girls at risk'. Doctors and psychiatrists who introduced controversial ideas about the 'mental state of prostitutes' and about 'exemplary' youth programmes in Nazi Germany, played a key role in the League's work of the 1930s. Its conclusions on the prevention of prostitution appeared in a final publication by the end of the decade, but the start of the Second World War precluded it from becoming a bestseller.

Nevertheless, Maus and his abolitionist partners in Belgium and elsewhere agreed that 'debauched women and girls' did not deserve oppression, but rather compassion and moral education. In their view, the culprits of female 'degen-eration' were malevolent men and regulationists who allowed the continuation of the 'evil trade'. That is why abolitionists advocated for the termination of the system of regulation instead of outright prohibition of prostitution, in place in, among others, the United States and the Soviet Union. The international public shaming brought about by the League's publications slowly but surely contrib-uted to the transition to abolitionism in Belgium, France, and other regulation-ist countries outside of Europe. But for that to happen, Belgian abolitionists still had to fight a fierce battle with the proponents of regulation on the home front.

To Regulate or Not to Regulate

Despite the efforts of the abolitionist movement, the regulation system remained in place in Belgian cities and towns after the First World War. Owners of 'for-nication houses' were required to apply for a licence and sellers of sex were registered in the 'list of prostitutes' and were given a booklet in which medical check-ups were recorded. But the supporters of regulation, the system itself, and ideas on 'the prostitute' changed in those first decades of the twentieth century. Like in the revolutionary period of the 1790s and early 1800s, the main goal was to protect the male population from sexually transmitted diseases (STDs). So, the war against STDs waged from 1914 to 1918 continued in the post-war period, both at the national and international levels.

The authorities perceived two major dangers. First, demobilised soldiers who were infected during the war would become 'sources of contagion' upon their return home. Second, the 'deviancy' of girls and women who had engaged in 'illicit sex' or plain prostitution during and after the war years would cause the moral and physical deterioration of the 'Belgian race' and maybe even 'depopulation'. These fears led to the first national policy for the voluntary treatment of STDs for the

Magaly Rodríguez García

whole population and to the continuation of compulsory medical checks for sex workers. As stipulated by the ministerial decree of 1920, municipalities of more than 5,000 inhabitants were required to take measures against the spread of infections. This was accompanied by a morality offensive targeting 'suspicious girls', especially from the working class. This broad offensive prevailed during the interwar period and started to undermine the support for the regulation of prostitution.

Soon after the war, however, the regulation system in many Belgian cities just continued, with the familiar argument: regulated prostitution was the best way to prevent disease and to contain the so-called 'uncontrollable' male sex drive. Prostitution had, after all, increased during the wartime occupation and only began to decline in about 1920 Indeed, the replacement of German troops by the Allies' armies after the November 1918 ceasefire, and the miserable post-war living conditions, worsened by the Spanish flu affecting the whole of Europe, drove many into commercial sex. The Brussels authorities therefore retained the intercommunal medical structures that the German occupiers had installed for the testing of sex workers. When an outbreak was discovered, the infected women were interned in a hospital in Saint-Gilles, a municipality located in the southern part of the Brussels region. Other large cities, i.e. Antwerp, Ghent, and Liège, as well as smaller towns also opted for the continuation of the system.

Bruges, for example, adopted a new 'vice policy' in 1920. Since local governments could no longer prohibit 'public women' from settling in certain streets or neighbourhoods, the Bruges City Council sought a way out of the restriction by targeting owners of private properties. If a registered sex worker rented a house or room, the owner was expected to prevent 'the movement of men' in his or her property – on pain of a fine. The freedom of sellers of sex was further limited by a whole series of provisions. They were required, for example, to ask for permission to live with other women. They were not allowed to stand for too long by the window, in front of their house or in the street. Furthermore, they were ordered not to 'leave their house when they are dressed in an immodest manner or in such a way as to cause annoyance'. Finally, as expected, the weekly medical checks became harsher.

At the same time, during the 1920s, the number of Belgian municipalities enforcing the regulation system diminished. According to Kinsie, some thirty municipalities maintained specific prostitution policies, the registration of brothels, and 'lists of prostitutes'. Other towns chose to focus on the treatment of STDs. La Louvière in Wallonia, for example, had neither registered houses of prostitution nor registered sex workers throughout the interwar period.

Brussels, too, remained convinced of the need to maintain the control of STDs, but was persuaded to carry out an abolitionist experiment in 1925. The city council took the initiative, along with Maus' Committee against the Trafficking of Women and Children and members of the newly founded (1922) League to Combat Venereal Danger. All agreed that the spread of syphilis and gonorrhoea could only be stopped with strict medical controls and the suppression of 'sexual misconduct' in the whole population. As in the pre-war period, they remained convinced of the immorality and inefficiency of the system of regulation, as its double standard only targeted women. After six months, however, the Brussels authorities decided to put a halt to the experiment. Local politicians and the medical community were not sure about the advantages and disadvantages of abolitionism. The Brussels press and residents also protested vehemently against the abolition of regulation, for the experiment had created a pull effect. Indeed, as soon as Brussels abolished the system, many women from surrounding municipalities and elsewhere suddenly moved to the Belgian capital to profit from the new laissez-faire policy. Needless to say, that was not what the authorities had intended. Hence, the regulation system was reintroduced. But the abolitionist movement did not capitulate.

The Bumpy Road to Abolition

The traditional abolitionist core in Belgium and abroad was not, as some may think, filled with pious individuals and women's organisations. The international abolitionist movement consisted of Catholic, Protestant, and Jewish actors, as well as prominent leaders from liberal and social democratic parties. In Belgium, it also opened its ranks to the labour movement and, like in other countries, received the full support of doctors, psychiatrists, and criminological anthropologists. During the interwar period, only military doctors continued defending regulation. As in the League of Nations, prostitution in Belgium became increasingly medicalised and interpreted as 'abnormal'. Moreover, commercial sex was placed within the broader framework of moral degeneration. According to Armand Meyers – attorney general at the Court of Appeal in Liège – prostitution, syphilis, pornography, contraception, abortion, and crime in general would drag the family and the nation 'from one degradation to another' and to 'total decay'. Such views were motivated by the economic revival and vibrant urban life that the Roaring Twenties offered to youngsters, in particular women.

For that reason, the idea of 'the prostitute' as a helpless victim of evil seducers, brothel exploiters, and ruthless traffickers was weakened and became replaced with the old image of the frivolous woman. But unlike past views of

Magaly Rodríguez García

'fallen women', interwar abolitionists no longer relied on moral and religious doctrines alone, now being supported by scientists who claimed to have discovered the 'real' causes of prostitution. While these did include low wages in the conventional labour market, physical and above all mental traits were in their view the most important pull factors to commercial sex and promiscuity in general. Abolitionists believed that sex workers could be 'cured', that prostitution could be prevented, and that sexual regulation would lead to a healthy nation. New rehabilitation and prevention programmes acquired a scientific cachet and contributed to the promotion of abolitionism and broad moral reform. Self-control became the key word. Sexual discipline was not, according to these social reformers, a renewed prudery but just a symbol of modernity.

In their view, modernity implied that the double standard had to disappear for good. Unlike animals, women and men could learn to control their impulses. Extra-marital sex was therefore frowned upon, and clients of prostitution were increasingly problematised. The League, in its publication on prevention, even devoted an entire chapter to the 'demand side' of the sex industry. Education, cultural activities, early marriage, and sports ('especially swimming') would protect men and women from immorality. Maus spread these ideas widely throughout Belgium. Belgian reformers, for their part, used international forums like the League to promote their own handling of 'problematic' minors.

Indeed, since the turn of the century, Belgium had pioneered the 'scientific observation' of young people who did not conform to social norms. The first observation centre was established in 1913 in Mol, near the Dutch border. After the First World War, public and private institutions for the treatment of boys and girls, mostly from working-class backgrounds, sprang up throughout the country. The system was particularly harsh on women. Delinquency in girls was not only equated with prostitution, promiscuity, pre-marital sexual activity, or simply 'loose behaviour' but also linked to theories of heredity. Their so-called degeneration would be transmitted to their offspring and constituted a danger to the entire population.

Young working-class women were also targeted, particularly those who worked in 'suspicious places' like cinemas, bars, gambling dens, hotels, and theatres. In fact, all working women were seen as potential threats to society. As female employment increased and diversified, young women entered the public sphere and worked less often as servants in protected domestic settings. Female factory workers, office clerks, or store helpers like Suzie (Yankel's girlfriend) had more free time and better wages to spend on what Belgian moral crusaders called 'inappropriate' clothes, 'indecent' dance halls, 'obscene' cinemas, or 'bad' literature. In the reformers' view, all these things would sooner or later lead to prostitution.

Other countries and international organisations followed the same logic. Thus, at the end of the 1930s, the League invited the International Labour Organization (ILO) to write a chapter for its publication on the prevention of prostitution. According to the League and the ILO, the 'moral protection of young women' during and after working hours would contribute to a healthy relationship between the two sexes. This implied the regulation of leisure-time and far-reaching youth control. Despite the organisations' staunch anti-communism, the authors of that chapter referred to the Soviet Union as a model of good youth policy. Nazi Germany was also considered a good example when it came to disciplining young people.

Indeed, the Nazis had a clear vision of 'deviant sexuality', although their approach was not consistent with that of the abolitionist camp. At first, Germans focused on the promotion of abstinence and condom use among their soldiers, but soon after the invasion of Belgium in May 1940, they opted for strict surveillance of prostitution. Since military mobilisation had caused a rapid increase in commercial sex, the system of regulation was considered necessary to prevent STDs and espionage activities. The German occupiers also reinforced the nineteenth-century idea that regulated prostitution would help eliminate the 'danger' of homosexuality.

While the new measures were determined at the national level by the Ministry of Health and Food Supply, they were not very different from traditional local regulations. Yet important changes impacted the nature and targets of medical check-ups, as well as the level of police surveillance. Sex workers had to undergo biweekly controls, plus annual bacteriological and X-ray examinations to detect tuberculosis. In addition, individuals in the immediate environment of the women in question also had to be checked for possible infections. It is not clear to which extent this measure was actually applied, but in theory husbands, lovers, brothel owners, and even landlords were all required to undergo the humiliating examinations. For their part, municipal authorities and the local police were required to send monthly reports to the Nazi Kommandantur. Rapporteurs such as Félix Van Bellinghen, in charge of the vice police in La Louvière, provided a gold mine of information about both the increased controls and the comings and goings of all actors of the sex industry during the Second World War.

Increasing prostitution and the strict German rules provided sufficient ammunition to the abolitionist movement. During the war, alarming stories of 'countless' minors and young adults who destroyed their lives selling and buying sex spread through newspapers, magazines, and rallies. Abolitionists emphasised victimhood in prostitution, thereby helping create a broad political coalition and obtain public support. They insisted that the misery of the war years, outright coercion, and the legitimisation of the trade (thanks to the system of regulation) were the main cause of women's 'sexual slavery'. The parliamentary lobbying that had gained momentum during the 1930s continued with full vigour in the immediate post-war period. At the international level, Belgian reformers remained equally active and supported the continuation of the League's activities by the future UN. Their campaign was rewarded on both fronts.

In 1946, a bill to abolish the regulation system was introduced in the Parliament by the socialist Isabelle Blume, the Christian democrat Margarite De Riemaecker-Legot, and the communist Suzanne Grégoire. While easily passed by the Belgian Parliament, the turbulent post-war period delayed the law's enforcement until 1948. Two years later, the UN adopted the Convention for the Suppression of the Traffic in Persons and of the Exploitation of the Prostitution of Others. The treaty was pretty much a copy of an abolitionist proposal that the League had prepared in the late 1930s, but did not get approved due to the outbreak of war. Belgium, however, did not ratify the UN treaty until 1965, because it allegedly did not suit the Congolese situation. The mother country, they claimed, was ready for the abolition of regulated prostitution, the African colony was not.

Yet when it came to the regulation of commercial sex, nobody really cared about what was going on in the colonial world. What mattered was that Belgium had finally joined other 'enlightened' countries that no longer wished to tolerate the 'shameful trade'. Abolitionism thus triumphed both nationally and internationally. Prostitution was henceforth associated with fundamental suffering, something that was 'done' to women. Because commercial sex, according to the new legislation, violated human dignity, no one would voluntarily choose it. But unlike incitement to immorality, brothel keeping, and pimping, prostitution itself was not criminalised. Abolitionism targeted the organisation of the sex industry in the hope that, in the long run, prostitution would disappear. That was, at least, the theory.

'The Whore Business'

In practice, it proved extremely difficult to successfully implement all the measures designed to put sex workers and other young women on the 'right path'. Paid sex could easily take place underground, and local control mechanisms were often ineffective. Since it was not always clear to the authorities when a monetary transaction had taken place, they did not know exactly how many women were selling sex. Still, local governments and the abolitionist movement drew on a whole range of numbers. These figures were inflated by both groups.

Regulationists used them to demonstrate the so-called efficiency of the system, whereas abolitionists claimed that the huge numbers only proved the system's immorality and weakness. The high number of registered women, they argued, demonstrated the extent of human trafficking; and the many clandestine places of prostitution symbolised the reach of pimps and other 'evil' intermediaries.

According to opponents of regulation, Brussels in the early 1920s numbered 15,000 to 20,000 unregistered women. However, Abraham Flexner – an American social reformer – estimated in 1914 that Brussels had about 150 enrolled and 3,000 clandestine sex workers. It is unlikely that the illicit sector increased by more than 500 per cent in six years. Brussels' hospital registers may offer a more reliable view of the real extent of commercial sex during the post-war period. In 1919, there were forty-seven registered and two hundred clandestine sex workers admitted for treatment of STDs. Kinsie did not provide statistics in his reports on Antwerp and Brussels, but the League wrote in its publication on human trafficking that the number of registered women in Antwerp had increased significantly since the First World War, i.e. from 215 in 1915, to 652 in 1924.

There was also talk of an 'unseen debauchery' among young women, who would sooner or later end up in prostitution. That, too, seems to have been grossly exaggerated. Young people of the interwar period ventured into pre-marital sex, but the difference with previous generations was not great. As in earlier periods, about half of teenage men and women were sexually active during the first half of the twentieth century. The number of girls formally brought before juvenile courts on charges of 'sexual deviancy' was also low. But this says nothing about the actual extent of underage commercial sex, which is partly explained by the difficulty of distinguishing between commercial sex and fleeting love affairs; and partly by the differing local attitudes to law enforcement on prostitution and (in)tolerance of 'lewd behaviour'. Most police departments were understaffed and had other priorities. They did their best to keep regulated brothel keepers and sex workers in check, but did not really interfere in clandestine prostitution as long as it did not disturb public order.

Despite the uncertainty about the number of people who sold sex full time or occasionally, the underground sector was clearly much more extensive than the legal market. Sex was exchanged in any place where there was a concentration of men, i.e. in the vicinity of ports and factories, around train stations, parks, or other spaces where one could easily hide. Since military mobilisation resumed soon after the First World War, for example, many people sold sex close to barracks. Prostitution also existed in poorer parts of cities or on roads connecting to the countryside, albeit without the decor of the urban sex scene. This more discreet form of prostitution foreshadowed the many semi-rural brothels and *Chaussées d'amour* ('Highway of love') that characterise modern Belgium. The same goes for brothels that moved to the vicinity of residential areas in the 1920s, such as Sint-Mariaburg – colloquially called 'Hoerenburg' or 'Whore town' – in the north of the Antwerp province.

In the same period, there were about twenty recognised brothels, as well as a variety of clandestine rendez-vous houses hidden in the many small streets and alleys of Antwerp's Sailors' Quarter. According to Kinsie, some twenty women worked in the luxurious but 'infamous' Crystal Palace, depicted on this book's cover. Many other women, however, took their clients to dingy hotel rooms, lodging houses, and inns, as well as into the backrooms of stores, or rooms above pubs and taverns in the winding and dark streets of the harbour district and Antwerp Central Train Station. In Brussels too, most of the prostitution venues were located in the side streets of the central avenues, around the North and South train stations and near the Bourse and Saint-Hubert galleries. The numerous *caberdouches* (bars with a rough reputation) in the popular districts of old Brussels, theatres, and cinemas, but also parks and tobacco or grocery stores with hidden rooms or sofas, attracted many sex workers and (potential) clients.

The same was true for other large, medium-sized, and small towns, from Ostend to La Louvière. The tourist and textile industries in the (present) Flemish region and the mining industry in Wallonia were poles of attraction for young men and women from neighbouring areas and Brussels, but also from France, Germany, or the Netherlands. La Louvière itself listed no official brothels during the interwar period. The available archival material, however, reveals twenty-three addresses where prostitution most probably took place. Moreover, to the north of the city centre some eighteen pubs renting rooms to couples existed, while to the east there were five clandestine brothels. During the Second World War, the German occupiers demanded a prompt solution to this chaos.

Belgian authorities did what they could to prevent illegal prostitution, but the strict regulation advocated by the Germans changed little. Hotels, taverns, and inns multiplied, and fleeting contacts between soldiers and the civilian population increased. Inspector Félix Van Bellinghen of La Louvière became extremely frustrated with the cat-and-mouse game. Unable to extract confessions from suspicious women, he ironically commented in one of his reports that they were not far from swearing to God that 'they were all still virgins'.

In war-time Bruges, a double system was used: sellers of sex needed to be registered by the city council, and two brothels were set up specifically for the German Wehrmacht – the Nazi armed forces. Other official brothels existed, open only to civil occupiers, and closed to women of the 'wrong race'. Soldiers, in turn, had to have their genitals checked in the *Sanierstuben,* or health centres, located in the immediate vicinity of brothels, identifiable by a small blue lamp with a red cross on it. Brothel rules stipulated that only 'light country wine, beer, mineral water and fruit juice' could be served. The entrance fee (2 to 5 Reichsmark) was also higher than in clandestine establishments, but a condom was included in the price. Unsurprisingly, the strict conditions drove many German soldiers to what one contemporary observer called 'the whore business'.

Like in the nineteenth and early twentieth century, the detailed sources of the interwar period, and definitely those of the war years, reveal much about the various commercial sex venues and the people who frequented them. But who were the sex workers and what drove them into such a stigmatised profession?

Greed, Despair, and Desire

The profile of sex workers did not change significantly between 1918 and the 1970s. As Kinsie reported on Antwerp and Brussels, the bulk of women in prostitution were adults and working class. In fact, the minimum age of women who first appeared in police records rose from twenty-one in the nineteenth century to about twenty-five in the aftermath of the Second World War. Moreover, journalist Carl De Poorter described in the early 1930s how 'old, toothless prostitutes' satisfied their clients orally in the Sailors' Quarter. Published and unpublished sources contain many examples of such disrespectful descriptions of women involved in sex work, highlighting that not only young women were active in the industry.

Indeed, there are many archival records of older women registered as 'prostitutes'. Of course, it may be that some women managed to evade the vice police over a long period of time. In such cases, we cannot know whether they were underage when they became engaged in commercial sex. Georgette S., for example, was twenty-five years old when she first entered the Bruges' 'register of indecent women' in 1937, although she had been exposed to the sex trade from an early age. In the early 1920s, her mother and stepfather, Elvire D. and Jan C., operated a 'secret house of fornication'. Georgette's frequent moves also suggest that she was already active as a sex worker before 1937. From 1931 to 1939, she had fifteen different addresses in Sint-Andries, Oostkamp, and Bruges – all in West Flanders, and during the war she moved at least eight times. Elisabeth D.'s migratory movements during the same period were even more impressive, but she was not registered until 1945, at the age of forty-three. Florentine V.H. – Jan C.'s second wife – and her daughter Marie-Louise, also entered the list in 1940. And in 1942, Georgette was again caught by the vice police, this time with her eighteen-year-old half-sister, Rachel D. There was an increase of younger (especially seventeen to twenty-year-old) sex workers during the war years, but the twenty to twenty-four age group remains the strongest represented in the archives. What these stories also tell us is that many interwar sellers of sex learned about the milieu through family members or friends, and that the main motivation was economic.

The booming 1920s offered young people many opportunities for both work and leisure. Wages in the traditional labour sector, however, were low while the cost of living rose. That reality motivated some women to start 'pleasing' men full-time; others combined a job as a waitress or store assistant with occasional prostitution. Such was the case with Marie-Charlotte M., a twenty-seven-year-old woman from Borgerhout, a district north of Antwerp's city centre. She left her husband because he drank too much and spent all day with his comrades instead of working. Marie-Charlotte found work through a friend at an inn near Antwerp's old stock exchange building. She earned about 70 Belgian francs a week, not enough to pay her rent, and therefore decided to take clients from the inn to a nearby hotel, where she was detained on charges of clandestine prostitution during a police raid in May 1930. Another waitress from the same inn was also caught in the hotel red-handed, but the police officers could not find proof of a financial transaction, so she was not arrested. During her interrogation, Marie-Charlotte confessed that she sold sex three to four times a week to earn some extra money. She promised not to do so again; she would henceforth take more shifts at the inn to support herself. A year later, Marie-Charlotte moved to Bruges, where the police again found her 'indulging in fornication'.

Commercial sex paid better than conventional jobs. Kinsie claimed that women involved in prostitution barely earned anything, but since he was primarily interested in finding evidence of trafficking, he focused on foreign women who probably did not know the local labour market well. Particularly those women who combined a regular job with occasional prostitution could earn good money. In 1924, Kinsie described the situation around Brussels' North Train Station, where women waited for potential clients in bars or taverns. Once a woman got talking to a man, she made him drink a lot, often in exchange for a small percentage from the pub owner, and then took him to a nearby hotel where she received between 20 and 40 francs for her services. Several sources from the 1930s and 1940s reveal that similar rates were charged and sometimes much higher, depending on the client's generosity. This means that with four clients a week at the minimum rate of 20 francs, women like Marie-Charlotte could earn more than a full-time waitress.

That extra money came in handy at a time when entertainment and the consumption of luxury goods became increasingly important, a fact that Maria

G. was well aware of. She was a single mother and worked in a bar in Ant-werp, earning 250 francs a month. When she came into contact with the vice police in April 1929, she told them that since she needed 225 francs to raise her child, she was left with only 25 francs for her own maintenance, and there-fore felt obliged to sell sex to make ends meet. The police noted, however, that 'her dress is far from that of a regular maid'. Her appearance and 'neat clothes' proved, in their view, that Maria was not really engaging in survival sex. Indeed, commercial sex allowed Maria and many other young women to participate in consumer society.

'Easy money' was therefore often used as a synonym for prostitution, though many women did not receive cash in exchange for sexual services. New clothes, jewellery, or movie tickets were also used as means of payment. The German Anna M., for example, received 'shoes, stockings and so on' from her client, and the French Lucienne-Josephine D. – work-name 'Loulou' – received clothes and drinking money from Thomas, a British sailor with whom she stayed several nights. Such women were called 'charity girls' in the United States, even if it was not really charity they were looking for. The fact that many sex workers came from the working class does not mean they were all poverty-stricken.

Yet there were situations where the line between prostitution and begging was thin, especially during the Second World War. This was the case for Yvonne, who hung out near the army barracks in Charleroi to exchange sex for food and perhaps some money. Similar cases were discovered in the previous decades. In 1924, Kinsie noted that streetwalkers in Brussels begged for 'lucky money' or a few cents from men who did not respond to their advances. Those who engaged in full-time prostitution and were not able to get more than the minimum rate from a few clients a week lived in very precarious circumstances. Passers-by took pity and occasionally gave pennies to these marginalised women.

The vice police occasionally intervened. Evidence of power abuse is difficult to detect in state archives, as the sources were produced by the police them-selves. Private sources do testify to draconian practices in medical institutions and police stations. Insulting language is, for example, very common in police reports. Older sex workers in particular were disparagingly described as 'old tart' and 'worn out'. But local policemen were not always insensitive to the suf-fering of women. In poor neighbourhoods, clandestine sex workers were often left alone and during periods of economic hardship, the police could be even more lenient. In the case of twenty-one-year-old Bertha B., for example, they revealed their best side. In December 1931, the Antwerp police had stopped Ber-tha and her client just when they wanted to book a hotel room. She cried and

Magaly Rodríguez García

explained that she only had 3 francs, which made her accept the old man's offer to have sex in exchange for 20 francs. Bertha was heavily pregnant with her second child and Alex, her German husband, couldn't find work for months. One police officer subsequently gave her a little money, another some meat.

Hunger and desperation drove Bertha to prostitution, that much is clear. What is not clear is whether she sold sex prior to her arrest, nor whether Alex was aware of this. If that was the case, it means that he lived from her earnings, so he was formally a pimp. But that does not mean he was the stereotypical aggressive and lazy man who exploited his partner through sex work. In actuality, the relationship with male intermediaries was (and still is) often complex. These relationships fit within a universal patriarchal framework where physical or psychological violence was common, but it was by no means a simplistic matter of naive victims and brutal exploiters. According to Boscom Johnson, an American social reformer who worked closely with Kinsie, it was frequently difficult to know who the recruiter was. Some women actively sought out a pimp; others embarked on lucrative love affairs with middlemen. This is clear in the story of Melanie D.R. and 'handsome Charles'. In April 1940, a client accused Melanie of giving him a disease, so she had to explain to the vice squad why she was involved in underground prostitution. To learn more about her background, the police interviewed the bar owner where Melanie worked as a waitress. Her boss said that Melanie had been 'led astray' by Charles, who was renowned for his dealings with other women.

Yet the police could not always find evidence of pimping or prostitution. Many women who hung out on the streets vehemently denied that they were looking for clients. Sometimes they were quite honest about their intentions. Magdalena B., for instance, a twenty-one-year-old from Antwerp, stated during a police interrogation in September 1929 that the man she was caught with had not handed her any money. She clarified to the police that what she did with that man 'was out of desire, not greed'. The archives from the war period are also full of stories of relationships of unclear nature. Some cases clearly involved full-time or occasional commercial sex; many others were cases of 'friends with benefits'. However, contrary to the current definition of the term, past authorities linked such cases not only to pre- or extra-marital sexual activity, but also to the financial and material advantages such friendships involved. It was that kind of 'opportunistic promiscuity' that marked the difference between commercial sex and other relationships. The police therefore invested much of their time and energy in tracking down details on transactions and working conditions – information that was necessary to suppress illicit sex commerce.

Crime and Punishment

Sellers of sex often needed extra help to pay off debts, especially from brothel or bar owners. The arrangement with third parties was often the same, in Belgium and abroad: regardless of what the customer paid, half of the amount went to the person who facilitated the encounter, the other half to the provider of sexual services. In the late 1930s, Maria Adolfina L. worked at the Mimosa bar in Antwerp and took clients to a small room behind the kitchen. They paid 30 francs, half of which went to the bar owner. At Chez Carmen, on the Rue du Marché in La Louvière, Bertha worked as a waitress during the war and received two customers – most probably Germans – in one week: one of them paid 100 francs 'for one turn', the other 50. As agreed with the proprietress, Bertha gave 50 and 25 francs respectively to Carmen. But, unlike Maria Adolfina, Bertha also received from her boss a quarter of the income from the drinks she sold to customers.

Yet brothel keepers and other intermediaries were not always reasonable. In their efforts to make workers subservient to their interests, owners of commercial sex venues could lead women to drug and alcohol addictions. Cocaine was very popular among sex workers during the interwar period, but alcoholic drinks also flowed liberally in the prostitution milieu. In her painful testimony to the Antwerp police in the mid-1930s, Maria J. recounted how she was 'induced to drink by the patron and his wife'. Moreover, they set the conditions by which Maria had to 'go upstairs with anyone'. Maria eventually left their bar, but other women remained in a vicious cycle of debt, substance dependence, and labour exploitation. In those cases, the help of 'a goodhearted person' was highly welcome.

Obviously, clients and 'friends' did not always behave. Then again, it was not always clear whether actual abuse had taken place. In late February 1940, for example, an anonymous woman who was not listed as a 'prostitute' in Bruges gave a detailed account of one such incident. During a nice winter night, she went out with her friend Estella D. and met two well-known men who accompanied them to the Louvre bar on the Philipstockstraat. After some good laughs and drinks at the pub, 'barrister Jean' and 'the baron' lured the two friends to the Saint Amand hotel, where they were treated to whisky. When the alcohol went to their heads, both women wanted to go home. But Jean and the baron hid their shoes to prevent them from leaving. The woman later explained to the police that they were 'more or less' forced to spend the night with those men: 'me with Jean, who of course used me, and the baron with Estella'. Since the situation involved two upper-class men, the authorities apparently did not deem necessary further enquiries on what really happened in that hotel room.

Magaly Rodríguez García

Indeed, when it came to abuse, sexual or otherwise, women needed to present concrete proof. Lack of protection, too, pushed many into full-time or occasional prostitution. Police reports often tell the story of women who saw in commercial sex a welcome opportunity to escape bad home situations and abuse by family members. Stephanie W., for example, left her home in 1929 and moved from Malines to Antwerp because she had a bad relationship with her mother-in-law and her husband. He drank and one day became a 'truly brutal fellow', so Stephanie decided to leave. In Antwerp, she worked as a servant and sometimes 'gave herself' to men in exchange for some money.

Stephanie had lost her parents at a young age and grew up in a Brussels orphanage. She thus belonged to the group of women who ended up selling sex because they had no one to fall back on. This was also often the case with single mothers. If the bond with parents or other family members was not broken, single mothers could leave their children with them while working elsewhere. Otherwise, children were sent to a state institution. In both cases, the women in question had to contribute to the children's expenses. The crisis of the early 1930s and the war only aggravated the situation, consequently bringing a higher percentage of married women into the prostitution registers. During the Second World War, some 40 per cent of (known) sex workers in Bruges were married and had children. Elsewhere, the situation was similar. Precarious living conditions and the departure of husbands and fathers to the front drove many single, married, or widowed women into prostitution.

Still, Félix Van Bellinghen (rapporteur of the vice police from La Louvière) could not understand their situation. In his view, their behaviour equated immorality, adultery, and anti-patriotism. He did not understand why a woman like Aline, mother of five children and wife of a husband who had left for Germany, did not take a 'normal' job. 'She prefers an easy job, and the most agreeable to her, on top of that', he wrote in one of his reports. He could show some mercy to girls who 'got back on track' but lost his patience completely with women who seemed 'incorrigible'. Yvonne was one of these. Her husband was a prisoner of war, a Belgian hero, whereas she ruined at least three marriages with her 'carnal activity'. She did not receive clients at home but worked in several brothels in La Louvière, Binche, Manage, and even Brussels. And she was clever, always thinking of ways to evade the police. Even worse, women like Aline and Yvonne had no trouble selling their services to the German occupiers. And from 1944 onwards, they switched sides and kept company with American, Canadian, English, and 'even' Indian soldiers, who as part of the British army had contributed to the Allies' victory. Such cases led Van Bellinghen to conclude that the armed conflict had simply made some women shameless.

After the war, people in the opposing camp wanted revenge. The term 'intimate collaboration' was broadly interpreted: both paid sex and love affairs with the enemy or collaborators were seen as a disgrace and a threat to the nation. They were accused of providing sex for money or even a piece of bread and of not distinguishing between army uniforms. In October 1944, the Bruges newspaper *De Koerier* incriminated 'that German-minded girl who sat on an officer's knees and now declares her love to a *Canuck*'. In about the same period, a journalist of a liberal newspaper from Antwerp, *De Nieuw Gazet*, was clear about the penalty such women ought to pay. In his view, they deserved to be subjected to 'the shave-her-head operation'. In his diary about Aalst and Dendermonde, two small towns in the west of the country, Frans De Koninck recounted that when (presumed) female collaborators were publicly shaved, they were called 'nasty whores', 'German mattresses', or 'Wehrmacht cunts'. Women accused of snitching risked even harsher punishments.

On a few occasions, public repression of female 'traitors' led to deadly casualties, as in Denise's case. Van Bellinghem started to follow her as early as 1942 because she had left her husband and child behind to work at the Stelle tavern and Hotel Bristol in La Louvière. Soon thereafter, she began passing on information to the German occupiers. She was discovered and, in all likelihood, executed by members of the resistance. In Namur, too, the lifeless bodies of two sisters were found in August 1944, each with a bullet in the head. The police suspected that this was probably also the work of the resistance.

But the repression and condemnation of 'deplorable behaviour' apparently did not deter many young women from profiting from commercial sex. Angèle B. sold sex to Germans during the war at a rate of 50 to 100 francs and admitted in 1945 that she had multiple partners. She claimed that she no longer lived off prostitution and that her relationship with an American soldier she had met at the Piccadilly bar in Brussels was a regular one. She also knew two other soldiers, but hung out with them for love and thus received nothing in return, she told the police. Her army lovers were less romantic-minded, for once they became infected with an STD they did not hesitate to report Angèle and other girls to the vice squad.

All the stories of 'widespread immorality' and the link between regulation and the German occupiers facilitated the work of abolitionists. The shame of being one of the last countries in the world where the system of regulation still existed, as well as the enthusiasm for post-war reconstruction and moral revival, motivated Belgian political elites to align themselves with the vision of prostitution propagated by the United Nations. Thus, the system of regulation was abolished in the second half of the 1940s. Predictably, little changed on the ground.

The 'Milieuke' after 1948

Perhaps the main difference between the regulation and abolitionist periods is the number of documents produced. While the regulation system was often inefficient, the vice police did systematically keep track of the personal details and comings and goings of all known actors of the sex industry. This was no longer the case after 1948, when municipalities were prohibited from regulating commercial sex. The police were only allowed to gather information and to intervene when the sale of sex became too 'scandalous'.

There is, however, sufficient evidence of local governments flouting the abolitionist law. Liège was one such case. An unofficial registration system for self-employed sex workers existed at least until the 1960s. The Liège authorities also required sellers of sex to abide by a set of rules, which closely resembled those of the regulation period, except for one detail: sex workers were not allowed to steal the clients' clothes. Why the authorities decided to include this particular clause in their rules, and the actual number of clients sent out into the streets half-naked, remains unknown. What we do know is that this kind of sex workers' agency was as old as prostitution itself. There was, in other words, much continuity in the control of, and the sale of sex itself, in the post-war period. The changes that took place were mainly linked to the new social context.

Until the 1960s, prostitution was intimately intertwined with homosexual subcultures. The Sailors' Quarter in Antwerp, or the red-light district in the centre of Brussels, were visited by gays, lesbians, and heterosexuals looking for paid and unpaid sex. Homosexuals and cross-dressers often frequented the same joints as full-time and occasional sellers of sex. During the interwar period, Antwerp's most notorious brothel, the Crystal Palace, transformed into a gay bar. In 'transvestite bars', customers – often sailors – were led to booze parties after which they woke up next to a 'lady companion'. Similarly, in the neighbourhood around the Rue des Bouchers in Brussels, there were all sorts of 'convivial bars' where gays and lesbians mingled with sex workers, pimps, and drug dealers. One of these establishments, the Chez Sergy, was operated by the wife of a police officer. Brussels lesbian activist Suzanne De Pues, better known as Suzan Daniel, in an interview recounted that La Pergola primarily attracted a female crowd, but single men or heterosexual couples 'looking for someone to fool around with' were also welcome. Men sought one another in parks and public restrooms, where young sellers of sex often solicited, but that started to change in the post-war period. Many urinals disappeared from the streets as city marketing began to play an important role. Thus, for the Expo '58, the small streets around the Brussels' Grand Place were 'cleaned'; sordid places closed their doors and streetwalkers were chased from the city centre.

Two sex workers, one of whom dressed as a man. They lived as husband (Marie) and wife (Caroline), ca. 1920–1925 (Antwerp, FelixArchives, PHOTO#50720).

Magaly Rodríguez García

A bit further afield, hetero- and homosexual prostitution quietly continued, though female sex workers were easier to recognise. As in the pre-war period, sellers of sex in the 1950s and 1960s often worked near train stations, theatres, cinemas, cafés, or dancing bars. They picked up their clients and took them to rendez-vous houses or hotel rooms. These hotels were often run by retired sex workers or pimps. In some, men could come alone and choose a woman from a photo album. The lady in question was then called up by the hotel owner. Renters of private houses also used the photo album system, sometimes sending clients to another apartment to circumvent police controls. Self-employed sex workers also operated from *rez-de-chaussées* (apartments or rooms on the ground floor) in Brussels and Liège, where they did not live themselves. In Brussels, some sex workers received clients in the woods of the Bois de la Cambre or the Sonian Forest, places that were easily accessible by both public transport and private automobile.

Cars played an increasingly important role in the lives of working people, and thus also in the sex industry. Remote brothels in 'Hoerenburg', on the road from Antwerp to Bergen op Zoom, a town in the south-west of the Netherlands, continued to exist until the 1960s. They were originally reached by tram, but in the post-war period increasingly by car. Clients with cars would pick up streetwalkers near the Porte de Namur and Avenue Louise in Brussels, and then drive together to an apartment or hotel room in the Leopold District or near the South Station. Some women solicited with their own cars. They drove slowly or parked their car with the lights on, to attract potential clients. These sex workers were seen as the crème de la crème of the prostitution scene: young, beautiful, elegant, and discreet.

The same was true of 'call girls', a new name for elite prostitution that became common in Britain after the Profumo affair. In 1963, Conservative government leader Harold Macmillan resigned after an affair between John Profumo, Secretary of State for War, and Christine Keeler surfaced. Keeler was a nineteen-year-old model and ostensibly involved with KGB agent Yevgeny Ivanov. It was the heyday of the Cold War, so the British got nervous. Belgium was spared such a political scandal until the late 1970s, but the phenomenon of call girls or escorts working for one or two wealthy clients cropped up in several sources in the early 1970s.

Window prostitution, for its part, was far from the discretion of escort work. The 'viewing carousel' became more widespread in Belgium and surrounding countries after the Second World War, but offering sexual services through windows or doors is as old as prostitution itself. Twentieth-century pictures show how women displayed their charms in front of regulated and clandestine brothels or cafés. Written sources also indicate that women gave all kinds of signs from their windows to attract customers. In the early 1930s, for example, journalist Carl De Poorter described this soliciting method in the harbour district of Antwerp: 'In the evening they turn on the light, slide the curtain away and display themselves behind their window. In fine weather they even open it, so that no one would overlook them.'

In the 1960s and 1970s, the use of red lights in commercial sex venues increased, thanks in part to the development of the fluorescent light. Consequently, where no specific regulations existed, window prostitution became conspicuous. In the Rue d'Aerschot behind the Brussels North Station, which belonged to the municipality of Schaerbeek, women waited for customers behind windows with no curtains; a little further away, on the Rue des Plantes, Rue Linné, and Rue de la Prairie, they were somewhat more discreet and sat behind curtains. Next to Schaerbeek, the municipality of Saint-Josse-ten-Noode was stricter. There, too, the abolitionist framework was ignored when the local authorities approved a municipal regulation that required bar or room owners to hang curtains in front of the windows, and service providers to sit in the dark.

Street, window, or brothel sellers of sex were known for their 'quickies', i.e. getting customers drunk and then get rid of them as soon as possible. Yet some, like Micheline, took the trade very seriously. Originally from Brussels, she moved to Antwerp by the late 1960s, walked the streets in the Sailors' Quarter, and testified that she was always respectful of her clients, 'no matter how bizarre their desires sometimes were'. For 'a prostitute is a psychologist', she argued. Sonia Verstappen, who entered the Brussels sex industry in the early 1970s, arrived at the same conclusion. As she provocatively said in countless media interviews and in her account for this book, the only difference between sex workers and social workers is the sperm.

Micheline started working when she was twenty-one and Sonia was twenty-two, but most sex workers from that period were over twenty-five; as before, there were also many women over forty. A criminologist from the Université libre de Bruxelles speculated in 1970 that mature women engaged in commercial sex when they were fired as waitresses. German and French women also crossed the border before the end of their careers to earn money through prostitution. But they were a minority: throughout the country, most (known) women involved in commercial sex were Belgian nationals.

At the end of the 1960s, the Brussels police counted some 2,000 sex workers; researchers estimated that the reality must have been at least 3,000. Many shared their profits with pimps who worked in the formal economy as cab drivers, shopkeepers, bartenders, café owners, or hotel managers. As in earlier decades, rates varied depending on the segment and the bargaining power of the woman in question. A sex worker who took three to four clients a day on Avenue Louise charged up to 2,000 francs per turn, but Sonia charged the same in the much less posh neighbourhood around the North Station. She had no pimp and received more clients per day, so she made good money selling sex. Other women had even more clients, but for shorter periods and therefore at lower rates (500 to 800 francs per session).

Jenny, who 'worked the streets' in Antwerp, received 500 francs per customer. She was interviewed by writer Jack De Graef for his 1970 book on Antwerp nightlife. During her first working week, she told De Graef, she only earned 2,000 francs. The following week she counted 7,000 francs. 'Not bad for a beginner!', she said proudly, and compared her situation to that of 'an office girl [who] has to work a month for that same amount'. That was slightly exaggerated, because in the early 1970s the gross monthly salary of a female clerk was about 15,000 francs. The fact is, however, that a young woman like Jenny earned much more with prostitution than with office work. These earnings enabled Jenny to purchase a nice flat, where she sometimes did 'crazy things', for example receiving married men and their wives, explaining that 'for such a joke, they have to pay extra, of course. Especially if the woman wants to join in, a threesome, you know!' During the interview, Jenny also mentioned a strong non-economic motivation to leave her previous job: commercial sex allowed young women like herself to get rid of obnoxious bosses who could not keep their hands off female employees' bodies.

Despite the economic boom, increased labour opportunities for women, and the sexual revolution of the 1960s, prostitution therefore continued to attract potential sex workers. For some, high and quick earnings outweighed the stigma. This explains why the occasional sale of sex remained popular among the working class and made its appearance among single, divorced, widowed, or married lower-middle-class women. Jenny, for example, quit her job when she was told she could get a pay raise if she slept with the head of the office. There is little evidence of cases of women who used commercial sex as a survival strategy. The post-war 'milieuke', as one Brussels magistrate called it, did remain populated by colourful figures, many of whom combined different activities, some more legal than others. By 1950, Rachel G. of Sint-Amandsberg in East Flanders had been convicted seventeen times for theft, extortion, beatings, insults, robbery, and disturbing public order through prostitution. In 1966, when a judge of the Brabant's Court of Assizes asked a certain Havelange why he had listed 'pimping' among his extensive catalogue of wrongdoings, he replied, 'Mr. President, do you think I can go to work as a regular labourer between one prison sentence and another?'

For sex workers and middlemen alike, commercial sex was a quick way to pay off debts or to participate in consumer society. A private car, new clothes, and household appliances like refrigerators and washing machines had become symbols of modernity. New forms of prostitution, hidden or otherwise, could help finance these things. In saunas, for example, well-to-do clients were treated to erotic massages. There, customers avoided the embarrassment of a vulgar quickie, and the masseuse avoided the 'hooker' label. Porn magazines such as *Candy* and *Chick* (on the market since the late 1960s), on the other hand, concealed nothing. They came over from the Netherlands and included advertisements where both women and men offered their services with nude photos.

Abuse also existed in the prostitution milieu, but not always in the direction one might think. In 1950, for example, the socialist newspaper *Vooruit* carried the story of a barmaid who pushed her pimp into a cesspool. Other newspapers reported on cases of sex workers and partners who exchanged fisticuffs with each other. Other stories told of (convicted) pimps abusing their wives. However, under the influence of the women's movement, female sex workers increasingly stood up for their rights. It took until the second half of the 1970s for the international sex worker movement to take shape, but in Belgium calls for humane working conditions in prostitution and for the acknowledgement of sex workers' place in society were already heard in the mid-1960s. A few years later, young sex workers like Micheline and Sonia were striving for the same goal. For them, the lights did not need to be turned off.

Magaly Rodríguez García

6. OUT OF THE TWILIGHT ZONE (1970–2024)

Maarten Loopmans and Ilias Loopmans

1992. The red lights in the Burchtgracht (the street just behind Antwerp's City Hall), that had been known to host sex work premises since at least the fourteenth century, are switched off. In the run-up to Antwerp93, the city's twelve months of fame as European Capital of Culture, mayor Bob Cools put an end to sex work in the heart of the city. The travelling cultural festival did not tolerate dingy places.

The 1990s were a turbulent decade in many Belgian cities. For the first time in many years, the police regained an interest in the stricter control of sex work and joined forces with urban planners and health workers. While sex workers tried to organise to influence policymaking, local residents also raised their voices. The latter's complaints about public nuisance led to a policy that increasingly segregated sex work in dedicated red-light districts. Meanwhile, the introduction of the Internet boosted more hidden forms of sex work, scattering brothels and escort services across the country.

The 'Antwerp model' turned out to be the most daring. The 1998 Antwerp Prostitution Policy Plan attempted to accommodate the demands of the police, sex worker activists, and residents by combining three objectives. It aimed to eliminate the nuisance caused by the sex trade and concomitant petty crime; to provide sex workers with better working conditions; and to revalue urban real estate in the red-light district's neighbourhood. Window prostitution would be restricted to a tolerance zone of only three streets. Under fierce protest from sex workers and window owners, fourteen of the seventeen streets in the Sailors' Quarter, the city's biggest red-light district, were cleared. Of the 283 windows on display in 1999, only 150 remained in 2001.

Urban development funds from regional, federal, and European institutions supported the city's 'strategic investments' in public spaces and buildings in the once infamous neighbourhood. Crime dropped abruptly and property developers took over vacated sex work premises and turned them into lofts and offices.

Trendy bars, restaurants, and cafés sprang up all over the neighbourhood. Inside the tolerance zone, stern regulations for window owners were applied, guaranteeing better working conditions. To obtain a licence, buildings needed to be renovated according to strict rules. In 2004, the conversion of a former city warehouse into the flagship brothel Villa Tinto increased the number of windows in the tolerated zone to more than 280, almost equalling the number before the operation started. Furthermore, dedicated health services and a police station were established in the area, and the revamped Sailors' Quarter was showered with urban planning awards. The Antwerp model was enthusiastically imitated in Brussels, Liège, Ghent, Ostend, and Seraing. After a long period of policy neglect, Belgian mayors entered the red-light districts with newfound fervour.

From 'Happy Hooker' to 'Social Problem'

This turnaround did not come unannounced. After all, by the end of the twentieth century much had changed in the world of paid sex. In the 1970s, the sexual revolution brought about a more liberal attitude towards sex work. Dutch ex-call girl and brothel owner Xaviera Hollander in her autobiographical bestseller proudly proclaimed herself a 'Happy Hooker', and the fame of *De Wallen* in Amsterdam made the red-light district a trendy place.

While sexual values in Belgium remained more conservative than in the Netherlands, window and street-based sex work were openly tolerated. Red-light districts expanded, taking over inner-city buildings vacated in the wake of the massive suburbanisation of Belgian cities. Real estate owners more than welcomed alternative forms of rental income. Shops, pubs, and living rooms were transformed into sex-work premises with the simple addition of a red light. Moreover, whether in Antwerp's Sailors' Quarter, near Brussels' North and South stations, or in Liège's *Carré* neighbourhood, commercial sex was integrated into a wider urban nightlife scene. Dedicated sex work premises were interspersed with dance halls, cabarets, and bawdy bars where female, male, and trans sellers of sex fished for clients. Yet sex work was not a uniquely urban experience. Suburbanisation and the increase of automobile ownership stimulated the expansion of commercial sex along certain highways between cities, in popular parlance often called *Chaussée d'amour* or 'Highway of love'. Neon signs flaunting revealing names like Daddy's Place or Pussycat coloured the Belgian automotive landscape.

But not all sex work took place in the open. A wealthier clientele preferred the discretion of call girls or escorts, private clubs, striptease bars, and posh

Maarten Loopmans and Ilias Loopmans

brothels. These too were found in both city centre and suburbs. More scattered – and without neon-lighted signboards – such establishments advertised in local magazines. In the big cities, travelling businessmen or foreign politicians were often regaled with sexual pleasure by their business partners, smoothing the deal concluded afterwards. The discretion sought-for was, however, relative. After all, sex parties did not just serve as a lubricant for successful business deals. They could also lead to blackmail.

'Leaks from the establishment' helped journalists fill their pages. Juicy stories about the *partouzes* (orgies) of the elite attracted a gleeful audience. In the late 1970s and early 1980s, Belgian newspaper readers could feast for months on stories about the *Roze Balletten* (Pink Ballets) of 'Madame Tuna' and 'Madame Claude'. The papers reported on drug and sex parties, in which high-profile individuals and minors participated. While the stories appeared in a wide range of Belgian newspapers, their factuality has never been proven. These and other stories about the sexual escapades of top international politicians and businessmen were widely reported and linked to organised crime, but did not really affect their reputation. Apparently, the then male-dominated world of business and politics didn't consider expensively paid sex out of the ordinary.

Not much later, however, the liberal decade ended abruptly. In 1983, HIV was discovered, effectively ending an era of carefree sex. At first attributed to the gay community, the virus spread fear and caused immense grief among its members. It also afflicted the community with a terrible stigma after a period of relative tolerance. When the virus turned out to be equally transmitted through hetero-sex, sex workers experienced similar reputational damage.

Globalisation cast another shadow over commercial sex. Both the high-end escort business as the window and street prostitution sector experienced rapid globalisation. In Antwerp, Liège, but especially Brussels, the number of elite clients increased. With the establishment of multinationals and, in Brussels, governmental institutions such as the North Atlantic Treaty Organization (NATO) (1967) and the European Union (EU) (permanent since 1997), the share of the global elite in the city's population grew, today constituting an estimated 10 to 15 per cent. They work and live mainly in the south-east of the city, from the green suburbs of Uccle to the buzzing neighbourhoods of Ixelles and Saint-Gilles.

Moreover, Brussels developed into a top destination for business tourists, and with an average of fourteen million delegates a year, Brussels is now the fourth largest conference city in the world. Nor do business travellers limit their local consumption to waffles and beer. Sex workers catering for travelling or resident elites used to await customers in hotel lobbies, private clubs, and striptease bars; today, an escort service is just a mouseclick away. Elite sellers of sex do not always reside permanently in Brussels, but commute to the capital from other parts of Belgium or fly in from abroad. Their workplaces are concentrated in the city's most cosmopolitan neighbourhoods. Proudly advertising their establishments as 'proximité CEE' (near to the European quarter), private clubs emphasise their accessibility. Luxury hotels in the centre and along the major arterial roads in the city's affluent east and north-west districts (including Laeken and Koekelberg) are popular workplaces among outcall escorts.

Globalisation was experienced very differently in the worlds of window and street prostitution. In public debates, these sectors were increasingly associated with migration and human trafficking. In the 1990s, the Iron Curtain fell, and Europe's internal borders were lifted. Increasing car, train, and air traffic made travel cheaper and easier. But while walls and border posts disappeared, stricter controls on settlement and residence came along, access to social services became more limited, and entry into the labour market was increasingly prevented. Smugglers took advantage of migrants' uncertain residence status and turned themselves into transnational pimps.

In the early 1990s, investigative journalist Chris De Stoop exposed human trafficking in Belgium in the Flemish weekly *Knack*. The book resulting from his research, *Ze zijn zo lief meneer* ('They are So Sweet, Sir'), turned around public opinion about sex work. Belgians suddenly looked at commercial sex in a new light: the 'happy hooker' had become a 'sex slave'. Subsequent revelations of teenage boys selling sex in Antwerp and Brussels further aroused indignation over human trafficking. As at the end of the nineteenth century, stories of forced migration for prostitution again stigmatised sex work. Yet, the public outcry did not improve sex workers' status. Sympathy for victims of trafficking soon turned into fear of migration. Chris De Stoop himself, in a later publication, decried how the human-trafficking discourse had stigmatised migrant sex workers.

Indirectly, trafficking also affected other people in the industry. Self-employed sellers of sex were pushed out of the market in favour of networks that increasingly controlled sex work premises. In some neighbourhoods, sex workers tried to resist and defend their rights. In Antwerp in 1996, Pandora was founded, an association of (ex-)sex workers that tried to support colleagues in their struggle with traffickers, pimps, and an increasingly troublesome government. In Brussels, the network Carré des dames (a reference to *carré*, the local name for a place used for window prostitution) fought against discrimination, legal insecurity, and the exploitation of sex workers in the early 2000s.

The expansion and globalisation of sex work in the traditional red-light districts caused tensions with the locals, as well. Complaints grew about nighttime noise, car traffic, street fights, and used condoms on the pavement. While

The Vanderdoncktdoorgang ('Glazen Straatje') in Ghent, a nineteenth-century shopping arcade now famous for its window prostitution, in 2006. Photo Wikimedia Commons.

residents were used to and tolerant of some nuisance and had generally maintained good contacts with local sex workers, pressure on the neighbourhoods grew. Rowdy nightlife increasingly dominated the area, and the rapid rotation of international sex workers made it difficult to build and maintain contacts with neighbours.

The neighbours themselves changed, too. Ongoing urban renewal attracted a more outspoken, more powerful, and less tolerant type of inhabitant to the red-light areas. In Antwerp's Sailors' Quarter, a 1980s urban renewal programme replaced run-down medieval houses with new social housing units. Even though social housing was meant to counter displacement, social housing companies did not always allocate locals to their stock. As candidates for social housing did not have much choice but to accept what was offered them, quite a few ended up in the red-light district against their will and started to protest against nuisance in their neighbourhood. In Brussels, the red-light zone next to the North Station bordered the Rue de Brabant, which blossomed into a thriving Moroccan and Turkish commercial street. The new middle class running businesses on the street grew increasingly disgruntled about the nearby sex-work premises. Fearing for their reputation, they started to organise and to weigh in on local politics. Closer to the city centre, in the 1970s street prostitution was common in the former industrial Alhambra district. Twenty years later, the first gentrifiers discovered the area around the renewed KVS theatre. Similarly, in Ghent gentrifiers displaced the original community around the Glazen Straatje ('Glass Street'), a nineteenth-century glass-roofed shopping arcade whose shops have been turned into sex work premises. These gentrifiers equally mobilised against sex work to protect the quality of life and the property values in their neighbourhood. As politically empowered and well-organised citizens, the new activists had a strong impact on the city government. From the second half of the 1990s, neighbourhood protests were often the trigger that put mayors to work in the red-light districts.

Step by Step towards Neo-Regulation

In the 1970s, neither municipalities nor supralocal governments showed any interest in the sex industry. Prostitution policy remained limited to occasional police interventions in street brawls and the levying of specific (but indirect) sex-work taxes. In 1948, the national parliament had abolished the regulation of prostitution. Local governments could still interfere in sex work for the sake of public order but could not introduce any other regulation beyond that scope.

Maarten Loopmans and Ilias Loopmans

National legislation did not prohibit commercial sex as such but did outlaw third-party exploitation. As a result, sex work could not be recognised as a category of labour, nor could it be taxed. Through taxes on rooms, on 'bar staff', or some other indirect phrasing that avoided indicating the real origin of the taxed income, local governments still tried to skim off some of the revenues from the sector.

For sex workers, the system felt like 'unregulated tolerance'. Exploitation by third parties may have been prohibited, but the authorities turned a blind eye so that sex workers could still informally rent premises or engage in an employment relationship with a brothel or bar owner. Such half-hearted control was particularly convenient for local governments, allowing them to collect indirect taxes on commercial sex while offering few services in return. But it also exposed sex workers to the whimsicality of local politics, as their informal status offered them little legal protection. When a mayor planned a new office tower or museum in the red-light district, sex workers were left no choice but to pack up and leave to another twilight zone. In Antwerp – where in the 1980s the red-light district stretched to just behind City Hall – successive projects had moved sex work northwards street by street. The megalomaniac 1970s Manhattan project in the Brussels North Quarter, or the subsequent urban development projects at the Brussels South Station or the Liège-Guillemins neighbourhood, equally left sex workers defenceless.

As stated above, the era of political neglect abruptly ended in the 1980s with the arrival of HIV/AIDS. Suddenly, the public health sector regained interest in the red-light district. Doctors and medical centres worked to better monitor and supervise sex work, often in collaboration with local universities. In some rare instances, sex-work activists themselves seized the initiative, in the process acquiring both legitimacy and resources from public health programmes. This was particularly the case with the sex workers' association Payoke in Antwerp, which combined sex-worker advocacy with health prevention campaigns and the mobilisation against trafficking. New social services and organisations targeting sex workers were founded in all larger cities. The underage boys' sex-work scandal triggered the establishment of organisations (Adzon – now Alias – in Brussels in 1992; and Project Antwerp Street Children – now Boysproject – in Antwerp in 1999) specialised in assistance and health care for men and boys who sell sex. Most organisations followed the pragmatic logic of harm reduction, aiming to limit the negative impact of prostitution on public health and on sellers of sex. As the fear of AIDS subsided somewhat in the 2000s, sex workers' access to regular physical and mental health care also became a focal point for these organisations. Since the stigma on commercial sex often made (and still makes) it difficult to seek help from a regular doctor, these organisations attempted to compensate for that.

The public health crisis caused a paradigm shift in sex work policies. While HIV/AIDS undermined societal tolerance, sexual health organisations opened the door to a form of neo-regulation – the first step in a more general move away from the unregulated tolerance regime of the 1970s and 1980s. Although national legislation maintained its abolitionist stance, city governments gradually tried to get a better grip on sex work. The pioneering health organisations played a vital role in the local regulation of sex work, although limited financing and logistical issues limited their area of operations to the traditional red-light districts where sex work was concentrated and happened out in the open; hidden, more dispersed forms of sex work remained largely inaccessible to them.

The outcry over human trafficking also triggered a renewed and tense moral debate about sex work. Social workers and activists operating under the harm reduction framework advocated for decriminalisation or even legalisation, to guarantee basic rights and services to sex workers. Despite their close collaboration with sex workers, they were increasingly challenged by Catholic (e.g. Mouvement du Nid, a conservative French organisation) and radical feminist (e.g. Conseil des Femmes or 'Women's council') organisations that advocated a stricter form of abolitionism. In the twenty-first century, the latter started campaigning for the so-called Swedish model, which criminalises not only pimps and traffickers, but also clients of prostitution.

Under the impetus of the late King Baudouin, Belgium introduced innovative laws against human trafficking. The 1995 law, with its main focus on the relationship between sex work and migration, represented a second step towards neo-regulation. Victims of human trafficking were given protection through residence status and accommodation in specialised centres. Thus, the law made it easier to punish human trafficking and linked migration control to the governance of sex work. The federal police also became increasingly involved in the growing regulatory network. The implementation of the new law succeeded in suppressing violent trafficking gangs but made traffickers turn to more subtle forms of coercion. Sexual exploitation of male minors also decreased dramatically in the late 1990s. Later, as the law tightened in 2005, it was successfully used against massage parlours offering 'happy endings'.

The final blow to the regime of unregulated tolerance came from the field of urban development. Gentrification was encouraged by city governments from the late 1990s onwards in a bid to eradicate urban dilapidation and areas of concentrated poverty. In the Sailors' Quarter, Antwerp had demonstrated that sex work could go hand-in-hand with profitable urban development, on the

Maarten Loopmans and Ilias Loopmans

Where sex work disappears, urban development and gentrification take over.
Photo Maarten Loopmans, ca. 2005.

condition that commercial sex be strictly regulated through urban planning and police enforcement. This successful Antwerp experiment stimulated other Belgian cities to seek a cohabitation between sex work and gentrification.

In 2008, pressured by residents' protests against street sex work in the trendy Alhambra neighbourhood, the Brussels Region developed a similar plan, but failed to implement it due to the resistance of francophone feminists and some local municipalities. Other Brussels municipalities, however, picked up the pieces and set up their own neo-regulationist policies, often in competition with one another. In Liège, window prostitution had to make way for urban development. In 2009, most of the buildings around the new Liège-Guillemins station were demolished. All brothels were cleared in the alleys around the Rue de la Cathédrale, but streetwalking remained prominent, and the cleared buildings long remained unused. The crackdown on window sex work in Liège provoked a shift of window prostitution to Seraing. In the Rue Marnix – a secluded, dead-end street – sex workers found refuge. However, following the Antwerp model, Seraing introduced an exploitation permit for sex work premises and announced the development of an urban 'Eros centre', to be operated by a non-profit association linked to the local government. In 2019, however, radical feminists of the Conseil des Femmes pressured the authorities to abandon the plan.

In Charleroi's Triangle red-light district, a 2002 local regulation enforcing the permanent closure of bars where trafficking victims had been working engendered a shift from window to street sex work. When, in 2007, the local government planned the upgrading of the area around Triangle, including the establishment of a large shopping centre, the authorities promised the real estate developer to eradicate sex work from the area. Since 2014, they explicitly forbade streetwalking in its entire territory. In recent years, Charleroi has vacillated between repression and a search for an alternative tolerance zone.

At the beginning of the twenty-first century, using zoning regulations, Ghent tried to restrict sex work to the Glazen Straatje and an adjacent street. Over the past decade, residents of the gentrifying nearby South neighbourhood have campaigned against this tolerance zone, which resulted in the Ghent authorities installing stricter regulations, to include in 2015 a permit and control system for sex work premises. In response, brothel owners established the organisation Glastra to represent their interests with the government.

The Hazegras neighbourhood near the train station was Ostend's red-light district. Since the late 1990s, the district housing and warehouses have been gradually demolished and replaced by luxury high-rise condominiums. The neighbourhood gentrification, now nearly completed, pushed out traditional residents, as well as sex workers. In return, Ostend has promised a tolerance

Maarten Loopmans and Ilias Loopmans

zone in the port area. Hangar 1, a protected early twentieth-century harbour warehouse, was turned over to the developer on condition that part of the warehouse would become a mini-Villa Tinto – like in Antwerp – with thirty rooms. While most sex workers have already been displaced from Hazegras, the warehouse has yet to be refurbished.

Belgium long retained an abolitionist stance in its official sex work policies. Most North-Western European countries drastically reformed their prostitution legislation: some countries legalised sex work, while others criminalised the buying of sex. Belgium, however, failed to reform its existing abolitionist legislation. Sharp ideological divisions and institutional fragmentation prevented the development of a coherent national policy around a multifaceted social issue like sex work. As a result, local governments took the initiative to respond to emerging challenges. Each city developed its own form of neo-regulation, mixing three recurring ingredients: social work, police, and urban development. While Belgium thus, inadvertently, moved back towards a regime of local regulation, one striking difference with the classic system of regulation remained: a disinterest in hidden forms of sex work. Curiously, these more hidden forms had recently started to flourish.

From Offline to Online Sex Work

Sex work is an important economic sector, although it remains difficult to know how many people are involved and how much money is moving around in it. Most estimates are based on a combination of data from police reports, workplaces, and advertisements. Publicly visible forms of commercial sex such as window and street prostitution are relatively well known. They mainly occur in the larger cities, with Antwerp and Brussels accounting for about 80 per cent of window prostitution. Female sex workers dominate in window prostitution, most of them cisgender, with a smaller number of transgender women. In Antwerp the number of (cis and trans) women working in windows has declined significantly from about 1,500 in 2017 to less than 800 in 2021 (with a particular decline during the Covid period). Brussels, according to a 2008 study, would account for three to four hundred women working in windows. With stricter police repression in most cities, street prostitution has almost disappeared. No city counts more than a few dozen sex workers on the street, although over the course of a year, more people engage in it, off and on. About half of all street sex workers in Belgium identify as men; the rest are women and transwomen. Customers of window and street sex workers are almost exclusively men.

In both Antwerp and Brussels, the number of sex workers in more hidden workplaces (homes, hotels, pubs, brothels) is thought to be at least twice as high as in street and window prostitution. In the first decades of the twenty-first century, depending on the sources, estimates for Brussels ranged from 700 to 1,300 female, and 400 to 900 male sex workers operating annually out of sight of the general public. In Antwerp, in the same period, estimates also diverge widely, between 1,000 and 1,700 sex workers, more than a third of whom are men. An additional 2,000 sex workers were estimated to be active on an annual basis in the province of Antwerp.

The limited share of window and street prostitution is attributable to the rise of the Internet and mobile phones. Social media and websites help advertise services to attract new clients, avoiding immediate public visibility. Consequently, an increasing number of sex workers is moving from window or street prostitution towards private forms of commercial sex. Similarly, clients more than ever appreciate the privacy of Internet prostitution, now that red-light districts are more segregated from ordinary nightlife venues, rendering the purpose of one's presence in that area more noticeable. Customer-based review sites of sex workers have become a go-to source of information for clients. Sex workers, seeing the potential of these sites, encourage satisfied customers to post on them, or engage with them to correct or dispute negative reviews. The Internet, therefore, has provided ample opportunities to deepen interactions between sex workers and customers.

Following in the wake of the sex workers, regulatory organisations also went digital – albeit hesitantly. Given that male sex work in Belgium has always been more secretive and inaccessible to outsiders, social workers dealing with male sellers of sex and trained in approaches centred on flexible outreach were the first to open chat boxes and respond to sex ads online. Their example inspired organisations working with female sellers of sex to explore beyond the boundaries of the traditional red-light districts. Simultaneously, local police brigades introduced online monitoring systems. In 2014, the Antwerp police established a daily digital calendar recording the sex workers in each window. During police checks, officers could control online – with the aim to prevent subletting, exploitation, and human trafficking – whether a sex worker was registered, had a residence permit, or was working overtime. The Covid-19 pandemic triggered a further expansion of digital services from social workers. For instance, sex workers' advocacy group UTSOPI started a crowdfunding for sex workers who found themselves unemployed during the first lockdown. Public health organisations also use messaging apps and websites to disseminate information on sanitary regulations or vaccination options.

An Outlook

Over the past thirty years, window and street prostitution have been under increasingly close government monitoring and control, whether due to gentrification, health, or migration policies. A regime of unregulated tolerance has gradually given way to a flurry of local neo-regulatory practices. This new regime vacillates between repression and containment and is rendering window and street prostitution less accessible to precarious groups (for example, drug users and undocumented migrants) who engage in – occasional or permanent – sex work to make ends meet.

Clearly, the Internet will continue playing an ever more important role in the sex industry. That trend will increase the share of hidden forms of paid sex and will make it more difficult to protect sex workers. From Onlyfans to augmented reality sex, future online developments will further expand opportunities for and the variety of sex work. Moreover, the Internet facilitates globalisation and labour migration, which may have a lasting impact on sex work migration as well. Internet facilities decrease the need for a fixed base to work from, with sex workers already today regularly moving from place to place in the quest of new clients. If regulatory pressure on red-light districts increases, their disappearance, and replacement with more hidden or online activities, is far from unimaginable.

In Belgium, policy responses to the globalisation and digitisation of sex work were for a long time limited to the local level. As a result, sex-work policies differ greatly from city to city. Nonetheless, in their diversity, local initiatives all draw on a similar play book, focusing on the regulation of sex work through a mixture of policing, health care, and urban planning. The entrenchment of these local neo-regulationist initiatives has narrowed down the policy options at the national (federal) level, as they have strengthened the legal recognition of sex work in Belgium. This has rendered the option of a tightened abolitionist approach, as adopted in Sweden and France, unrealistic. It therefore came as no surprise when the Belgian federal government announced, in March 2022, a series of legal reforms to decriminalise and legalise various dimensions of sex work. The concrete cause triggering the reform were the Covid-19 lockdowns, which revealed the dire social consequences of sex workers' informal status. Sellers of sex were not allowed to work under Covid restrictions, but since they were not recognised as workers under Belgian labour law, they did not receive any Covid support nor replacement income. That explains the major legal reform of 2022, which distinguished paid service provisions to sex workers (such as renting rooms, banking and accountancy services, Internet advertising) from actual pimping and human trafficking. Removing the former activities from criminal law, while providing stronger punishments for the latter, grants self-employed sex workers better legal protection when engaging with third parties.

After the introduction of the decriminalisation law of 2022, further legal reforms were announced. The new labour law – approved in May 2024 – stipulates the conditions for formal employment of sex workers. This includes a permit system for recognised employers, conditions for employment contracts, e.g. the right of the employee to refuse work at all times, and the right to safe and healthy working conditions. The new regime aims at the strengthening of the legal status of sex workers, guaranteeing them access to the same social rights (such as social security, health insurance, and retirement benefits) as other workers, while also recognising the particularities and risks of commercial sex. It will be, in other words, a more flexible system than the one in existence in the Netherlands or Germany. Both New Zealand and Belgium are setting an example with their innovative legal framework. More importantly, the whole process for legal reform was undertaken in close collaboration with representatives of sex workers and victims of trafficking, who became increasingly organised and vocal in the past decades. Sonia Verstappen was one of them (see the next chapter).

The reforms also provide a firmer legal basis for local regulation and are likely to further encourage and possibly harmonise initiatives by local governments. In 2023, for instance, the Brussels regional government agreed – after a failed attempt fifteen years earlier – on a region-wide harm reduction policy and a consultation platform for intermunicipal policy coordination. The Brussels policy resolution refers explicitly to the decriminalisation of sex work by the federal government as a background to the initiative. The coming decades will tell what the effects of these and subsequent federal, regional, and local policy changes will be on the lives of women and men who sell sex in the cities and municipalities of Belgium.

7. 'I REALLY LOVED IT': A FORMER SEX WORKER'S TESTIMONY

Sonia Verstappen,
recorded by Pieter Vanhees

I was born in Brussels on 14 December 1951, to a rather bourgeois family. My childhood was not exceptional, but I had a difficult relationship with my parents, especially with my mother. My time at school cannot be called successful. In such a conservative milieu, sex work was never discussed.

When I was about eighteen years old, I started working as a barmaid in the Brussels nightlife. One day, I couldn't find my boyfriend, so I called his mother, who asked me to come see her. She had a bar in the Rue du Marché, which in the 1970s was an important red-light district near the North Train Station. Back then, sex was also sold in the Rue d'Aerschot, on the other side of the railway tracks, and in the *carrés* in Saint-Josse-ten-Noode, but young women usually started working in the Rue du Marché. Among the neighbourhoods with window prostitution, you found the best customers there. I got along well with this woman and started to work for her as a 'lady companion'. When the other girls worked at night, I was there for them in case they needed anything. The customers didn't see me. I did that for several months because I adored the atmosphere. The girls were beautiful, it was dark outside, there was a lot of champagne, there were lots of customers... I really loved it.

One day, one of the girls told me that she had a client who wanted a second girl. I accepted: it was my first customer. I liked it right away. At that time, we didn't have intercourse. Others maybe did, but I didn't. We stripteased, we drank champagne with the clients, we touched them and made them come. Only after a year or two did I start having sex with clients. We heard that some women were already doing that, and more and more clients were asking for it, too. In the beginning I only had sex with clients I liked. After a while, with others as well. It wasn't traumatic for me at all. Sometimes it's even easier, because you don't have to act at all. Throughout my career, I kissed only those clients I really liked. I always refused to kiss the others. But we drank lots of champagne.

Shortly after my first experience with a client, I asked the madam if I could start working there properly. My boyfriend didn't agree, but that didn't stop me: I wanted to do that work. I was really good looking at the time, so I had a huge number of clients. Sometimes I had one customer in the entrance hall, one waiting outside, and two more down the street. That was not only because I was beautiful, but also because I took my time with the customers. I talked to them, because I loved doing it; I didn't just have sex on autopilot. Clients also gave me so much: tenderness, love, and, of course, money. My childhood hadn't been easy. That's why I often say that each client helped me straighten my spine. All customers together made up the ideal man. Sex work satisfied all my needs at the time. Both on a physical and mental level, I loved having sex.

Moreover, I had much more money than my peers in other professions. In the 1970s, I received 2,000 Belgian francs for 'une passe'. There were days when, after giving half of my earnings to my madam, I still had 10,000 francs left. That was a lot of money. By comparison, at my first job in a print shop, when I was eighteen, I earned 750 francs a week. With that much money, life was a celebration: trips, restaurants, clothes. If the Inno department store still exists today, they have me to thank for it.

Of course, there were also risks: STDs, drug addictions. I was fortunate to be able to work for a long time without incurable diseases going around. Syphilis and gonorrhoea existed, but they were curable. I always took a condom for granted, for all sexual acts. In the 1970s, everything was done with a condom. I never practised my profession without it. Today, I think that is much more difficult. Of course, even then there were women with money problems or drug addictions who were willing to take more risks. However, when AIDS came up, we all started to panic a bit and became even more careful. But I didn't even consider leaving sex work.

Madams and Pimps

It was my madam who taught me the profession. She had been a sex worker herself. I was assigned one of her old clients, as a sort of test case. With him, in the presence of my madam I learned a lot: the do's and don'ts, how to make them come, how to find out about their fantasies by touching them in certain places. I learned from her that I could say no at any time. I learned how to do

Sonia Verstappen, recorded by Pieter Vanhees

my job well so that the client would come back, but also that I was master of the situation at any time. Just because a client pays, it doesn't mean he is allowed to do everything. Today that may not be true, but in my time, the old sex workers taught the trade to the young ones. I thought that was a good thing. The money provided a kind of contract, of course: a certain amount of money came with certain expectations, but when the contract was not respected, you could say no.

We were paid every day. I kept track of how much I had worked. Half of our earnings went to the madam. But, behind the curtains, we often got an extra note from a customer who wanted some more time or some other service. The madam knew, but we kept the extra money. By law, my madam was a pimp, but she was good to me and respected my work. She never forced me to accept a client I didn't want or made me do something I didn't want to do. If I didn't want to come to work, it wasn't a problem and she replaced me with someone else. There were probably also bosses who were not that kind, but they did not bother me. I always worked for women, never for men. I was very good so other madams wanted me to work for them, but I liked it where I was, and I didn't feel like leaving.

Except for women in very precarious situations, sex work was not and is not inevitable for those who have difficult lives. The vast majority of women who sold sex did it for the money. Although a lot of money circulated in the 1970s, nowhere else you could earn as much as in prostitution. Men in the 1970s sometimes stayed up all night drinking champagne. My mistress wanted me to keep them in until eight in the morning, so that she could bring in the cheques as soon as the bank opened, and the men could not protest over excessive fees. For women with no degree, it was really a way to make a lot of money, because there were few other well-paid alternatives. Through sex work, we gained freedom.

There were pimps, but they were different from today. They didn't have networks. You saw them going around with just two women, for instance. Back then, most women loved their pimp. Pimps took care of their 'merchandise'. By this I don't mean to say that all was sunshine and roses, but the French term *souteneur* was accurate: pimps supported their women. They kept things straight. When a woman charged too little or when she did things that were not done at the time, such as anal sex or facials, pimps intervened. They also intervened when someone harassed one of his girls. But since I didn't do unusual things, I had few problems. I respected the rules.

Unlike today, there were meaningful rules then, at least in the neighbourhood where I worked. Today's rules are enacted by petty pimps, all little scoundrels. Back then, we had a better mentality. People in the industry had honour; they could express themselves. That worked very well. When there was conflict, we didn't let it escalate. We negotiated to avoid worse. When a street-walker showed up in our neighbourhood, which was against the rules, we went and told her not to work there. If she didn't want to understand, a pimp was sent to tell her to stop.

In the 1980s, when I was thirty years old, I opened my own brothel. I rented a ground floor from which I worked. I was tired of giving up half of my earnings to a madam. I always worked alone. At one point, I did have someone working for me for a few months, but that was a catastrophe. Being a madam was not for me! But business was still good.

Behind the Curtains

I have always worked behind windows, and I loved it. You're in a protected environment where you can eat and drink, and on top of that, you can watch life on the street. You are not isolated. You are in contact with passers-by. People come in to have a chat. I worked at night, but it was always lively. The red-light district on Rue du Marché was more part of the urban fabric back then than it is today. Before its demolition as part of urban development plans it was a lively residential neighbourhood for people with limited resources. Plans to make way for office towers pushed the entire neighbourhood to a remote corner. Before that, the Rue du Marché was a safe place, even at night, and there was hardly any crime.

In the brothel there was first a small room through which the customer entered, with a small lounge and a bar, and behind it a curtain. When a client came, we would take them behind the curtain, where there was a sofa. There was no bed allowed, because by law it was a public place. We were also not supposed to close the door but of course we closed it when there was a customer. The police didn't bother us that much in the 1970s. They actually had fun with us, knocking hard on the door when they knew there was a client. They could catch us in the act, so we dressed quickly because we were not supposed to have sex there. The situation was really hypocritical; everyone knew what was going on. When we caught sight of the police, we would call from bar to bar to warn one another.

Streetwalking in 1970s Brussels took place mainly near the KVS theatre and on Avenue Louise. The women who worked on the streets were the lowest segment, which has always been the case and is still the case today. It's tough, cold in winter, always exposed to passers-by. I was also exposed but there was a window in between. I was in another universe. To many people, I was in a window showcase, but for me it was just the other way around: the world was behind a kind of screen.

Sonia Verstappen, recorded by Pieter Vanhees

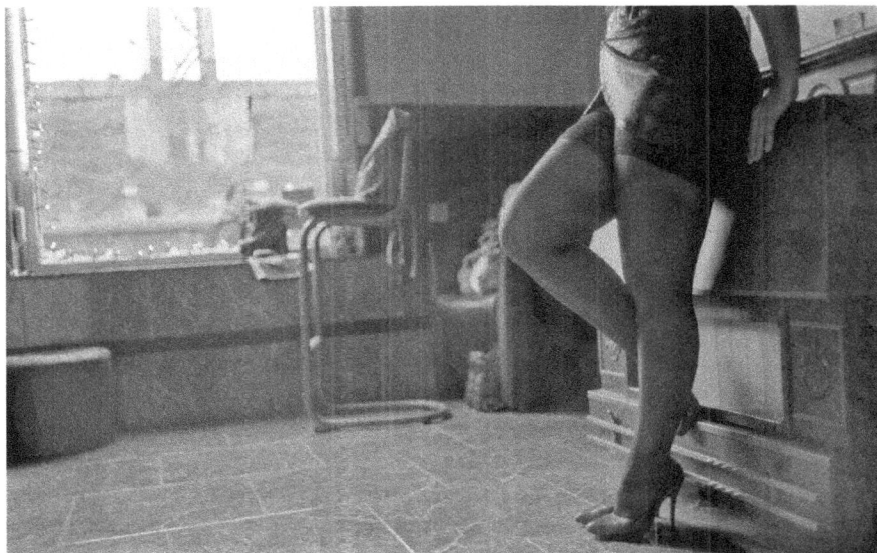

A sex worker waits for her next client in the Brussels North Quarter, the neighbourhood where Sonia Verstappen worked for more than thirty years. Raymond Dakoua, *Quartier Nord Bruxelles*, 2005.

On the Rue de Stassart, in the posh Ixelles municipality, women engaged in luxury prostitution from their cars. I don't know exactly how much they charged, but they were more expensive than us. They waited in their parked cars for clients with their lights on. Then they took their clients to fancy hotels, for a high price. Escorts were also at the top of the segment, but they had to spend entire nights with their clients. For me, that way of working was too lonely.

At some point in the late 1980s, my brothel was sold. Then I worked at a friend's place on the Rue du Marché for a while. But the rules had changed: handing over more than half of your earnings was no longer done. Instead, we had to pay a fixed daily amount. In this period, I took a break, because I had met a man who wanted me to quit. When we broke up, I didn't want him to see me behind a window again, so I went to work in Antwerp for a few months. I hated it! The customers were not friendly there. I'm a talker but that didn't work in Antwerp. Maybe the women there worked differently. Sometimes I would ask for a client's first name, and he would reply, 'That is none of your business.' I didn't like those customers. I felt like 'a whore' there.

At the beginning of the 1990s, I was about forty. Someone I used to work with in the Rue du Marché now owned a brothel in the Rue d'Aerschot, and I went to work with her for a while. In window prostitution you had three categories. The highest category worked in the Rue du Marché. When you got a little older, you went to the Rue d'Aerschot. When you got a little older still, you went to work in the *carrés*. It was sort of an age pyramid – and, of course, a price pyramid. I ended up working in the Rue d'Aerschot for about ten years.

After 2000, the red-light district around the North Station was in sharp decline. Meanwhile, window prostitution on the rue du Marché had disappeared altogether. A policy of decay and neglect led to an air of malaise that also had an impact on the clientele. The affluent clients of the 1980s and 1990s no longer dared to come to a 'bad neighbourhood' like the Rue d'Aerschot. Nowadays, you can no longer go there with a nice car. In the neighbourhood around the KVS theatre, too, customers are constantly harassed by the police, so they don't dare go there either. As a result, women are mainly confronted with the more difficult clients. Wealthier customers look for what they like on the Internet. Only some women who work in brothels along major roads still have customers like before.

Without Money, Problems Begin

My first madam put in a forty-five-rpm record when sex with a client began. It played a song about three minutes long. That gave an idea of how much time I spent with him. Sex with a client could go fast: it often lasted just a few minutes. You prepared them, of course. The guy had already been walking around the neighbourhood and was often excited before he entered the room. You obviously used the knowledge you had; after all, it was my profession. I could make a client come in thirty seconds. I chatted and caressed him a little and then it all went quickly.

It wasn't always that easy, of course. Some clients only stayed a few minutes, others much longer. Sometimes I had two customers in a day, sometimes ten. I was free to organise as I liked. Because I never had a pimp, I could always leave when I was tired. If I didn't feel like working one day, I could. Many people think that sex workers accept everyone and all requests. That's absolutely false.

The clients who made the strongest impression were the problematic ones. They were often masochists who wanted to be humiliated. It's not just about the pain, but really about humiliation. My profession taught me to love the person behind the man. Patriarchy exists, of course, but I became aware that not all

Sonia Verstappen, recorded by Pieter Vanhees

men are comfortable with the roles assigned to them. Those men came to me looking for a new balance. With some clients who started crying, it was really tough; it gets under your skin. Then I quit for the day. Seeing desperate people is really hard sometimes.

At the end of my career, things were not much different than when I was 20. But the arrival of the Internet did change a lot. Customers were not only looking for women on the Internet, but they also had new expectations. Pornographic films changed clients' desires. They wanted to do things they saw in porn movies. We had to start explaining to them that we didn't do many of those things. As a result, sex work became a little more difficult.

I had a number of regular clients. When I stopped working, I still had some clients from the very beginning. I knew everything about their lives, so they easily came to me. They knew I knew them well. They came to have sex, but also to talk. They were good acquaintances.

But I also had a private life, of course, and that was sometimes complicated. Since the beginning, all my partners were former clients. This had its advantages: I didn't need to explain my profession to them and, moreover, I knew them well even before they became my partners. At a certain point, I simply told them not to pay anymore and, from then on, we became lovers. And then the problems began… Everything became an emotional affair; jealousy popped up. Money acted as a shield. I can relate to something the psychoanalyst Jacques Lacan once wrote: money frees you from the yoke of recognition. As long as money is involved, people owe each other nothing.

I never lost my friends. I always had friends from middle- and upper-class backgrounds who were not part of the prostitution milieu. For them, my profession was not a problem. They knew that I didn't work for a pimp, that I didn't have a drug problem, that I was just Sonia. In the family context, I did wait to tell them about my profession. My family didn't play such a big role in my life, so I didn't think it was that important. It wasn't something that was tearing me apart or that I absolutely wanted to talk about. That wasn't a problem for me because it didn't reflect who I was. For some women, no doubt, it was different. They felt less comfortable with the trade. They felt shame. I had a friend in the neighbourhood whose husband didn't even know she was selling sex. Many people don't talk about it. Sometimes the reactions are also very negative. A colleague's son dropped her when he found out about her occupation. Fortunately, I had smart friends.

Especially in the beginning, I kept a little distance from the scene. I found the fights in the neighbourhood uninteresting. There were certain bars where women went before and after work, but that wasn't my thing. During my working hours, I was a sex worker. Afterwards, I was not engaged with my work. I read a lot behind my window, and I had friends who enriched me culturally. My profession was a part of my life, but certainly not all of it. The only thing I did in the beginning was to regularly put some money in a piggy bank with some colleagues in my brothel. When we had saved up some, we all went out to eat at a starred restaurant.

Coming Out

In the 1970s and 1980s, the majority of my colleagues were Belgian. There were some French, Spanish, and Italian women, but no girls from the Eastern Bloc yet. In the 1990s, however, Albanian sex workers and their pimps made their appearance in Brussels. That's when the problems started. Those pimps were really crazy. If women didn't hand over enough money, they were beaten. So, they dropped their prices and accepted unusual requests from clients. Moreover, Belgian and Albanian women didn't mix much. They were really terrorised by their pimps and were not allowed to have contact with us.

After a few years, the Albanians left and were succeeded by Romanian and Bulgarian women. Their pimps were a little less strict. I continued to work in the Rue d'Aerschot until 2001, but at a certain point I was simply fed up. I could no longer even tolerate the Romanians. In the brothel where I worked, I shared the room with another woman. I worked from noon until six in the evening. When I left at six, she arrived but when I returned the day after in the afternoon, she was still there. She worked eighteen hours a day! One day I had had enough, so I started arguing with her pimp. I had known the real pimps in the Rue du Marché, not the nasty ones from the Eastern Bloc who worked in the Rue d'Aerschot, but I knew how to deal with them. I had no fear. I said, 'Come, we need to talk,' and very calmly, I told him what the problem was. They only spoke with persons who respected them, and I knew how to do that. With pimps you shouldn't be hysterical. You have to speak firmly. The dust eventually settled, but I couldn't do it any longer. I wondered what I was still doing there.

Around that time, I became more militantly committed to the defence of sex workers' rights. One Sunday, I saw a television debate on prostitution. A woman and her daughter, both sex workers, had been invited. They worked in the Brussels North Quarter, not far from where I was active, and spoke without being made unrecognisable. Unfortunately, the broadcast had rather negative consequences. When the daughter brought her child to school the following day, the principal told her that he did not want a 'child of a whore' in his school.

Sonia Verstappen, recorded by Pieter Vanhees

Sonia Verstappen and Swiss sex work activist Grisélidis Réal at the shooting of *Sonia*, a documentary by Nathalie Delaunoy (2004). Photo by Elin Kirschfink.

I was angry. A little later, in about 1995, there were also riots in the neighbourhood. The trigger was an argument between a pimp and a local resident over a parking space. Then youngsters came and smashed all the windows. My anger and my sense of injustice really intensified.

My first deed as an activist, although still under the pseudonym Véronique, was to read a text on a Belgian public radio station. I addressed young people in the neighbourhood. The broadcast took place at eight in the morning and had a huge impact. That's how I got in touch with Espace P, an association for sex workers that existed since 1988. They provided medical tests, offered legal and psychosocial assistance, but also organised actions against stigmatisation. I began to participate more and more in these actions, but in the early days of the Belgian sex worker movement it was often a lonely struggle. I regularly spoke to journalists and went to colloquia to counter abolitionist voices. I began to lobby politicians. I spoke at universities and colleges to break the taboo surrounding my profession. I wanted to demystify prostitution, because sex workers are caught in the web of stigma surrounding their profession, which can destroy them. Through sensibilisation, I wanted to ensure that sex workers would no longer have to endure that.

My official 'coming out' as a sex worker took place on television in 2004, when Nathalie Delaunoy made a documentary about me. One day, a client told me that a friend of his wanted to make a film about a sex worker. Nathalie explained her project and I agreed. It was a fantastic experience: finally, a documentary that showed a different picture of prostitution than the usual story of sheer misery. A large part of the audience understood my message. I received nothing but encouragement and that strengthened me in my struggle. In time, however, it became tough to be virtually the only sex worker to testify. It weakened me because my word alone did not carry enough weight. I came across as the exception.

So, in 2015, with some colleagues, I founded an association for and by sex workers: UTSOPI. It became a success. Today, we are recognised by both the media and politicians as reliable and responsible partners. We are fighting to ensure that decisions that affect us are no longer made without us. We want our voice to be respected as much as that of any other citizen. The fight for basic justice remains necessary. In the absence of laws that protect us, many sex workers live in precarious situations. We are still not treated like other citizens.

I stopped working in 2011, at the age of sixty. I had health problems and the neighbourhood where I worked was deteriorating again. I really loved my profession and my clients. They made me who I am. I was not yet the oldest sex worker in my area, but it was time to quit. My struggle, however, will continue until no sex worker is ashamed of who he or she is.

Sonia Verstappen, recorded by Pieter Vanhees

BEYOND THE CLICHÉS

Magaly Rodríguez García

The more you know about the history of sex work, the easier it becomes to abandon simplistic ideas of the trade and its people. Alternative primary sources and input from contemporary social workers, sex workers, and colleagues of different disciplines allow historians to raise new questions and arrive at a more comprehensive understanding of the past. That is the dynamic nature of scholarly research.

The available material and the methodology employed by the authors of this book lead to several conclusions, debunking the clichés surrounding the sale of sex. Although the source material is fragmentary, a long-term analysis of discourses, policies, and practices of commercial sex offers an opportunity to unravel the complexity of sex work. We have paid special attention to sex workers' voices, for the simple reason that they are the best-placed to avoid the platitudes, half-truths, and myths that abound when it comes to prostitution – both for the past and present. All the topics discussed below relate to past and contemporary situations alike. The following paragraphs cite and unmask the most common clichés, prevalent in Belgium and many other countries.

'The Oldest Profession'

Prostitution is often called the oldest profession in the world. This view is linked to the discovery of a clay tablet with Sumerian cuneiform script from ca. 2400 BC, which contains a list of occupations and workplaces. The list included the Sumerian word *kar.kid*, which was long incorrectly translated as 'prostitute'. Signs for 'tavern' or 'brewery', too, were wrongly translated as 'brothel'. Experts on Ancient History now agree that priests, medicine men, cooks, writers, and even barbers are as old, if not older, as representatives of an occupation, than people who traded sex for material benefits.

Barter sex has been around for a long time, but it had a very different meaning than modern prostitution. Monetary economic systems – that is, payment with money instead of goods or services – emerged in about the seventh century BC, but for ordinary people transactions were of a different nature than in market economies. In ancient times, barter sex may also have taken place in the area now called Belgium. However, we chose the late Middle Ages as the starting period of our book because that is when markets increasingly gained in importance. Inns, taverns, and bathhouses flourished, as did the sale of sex. While the tighter controls of later centuries brought with them a certain professionalisation, the sex trade was never considered a conventional profession.

This book focused mostly on the usual suspects: policymakers, brothel owners, pimps, female sex workers, and male clients. Others appear less frequently in these pages because they are often difficult to track down in archives and publications. To date, it seems impossible to write a long-term and bottom-up history of male and queer sex work, let alone of female clients, which is why we primarily focus on women and men in the classic roles of seller, buyer, and intermediary. Yet the idea that women always stood on the supply-side and men on the demand-side of the prostitution market is also one we wish to refute here.

'Women Sell Sex, Men Buy Sex'

A constant in the image of prostitution across time and space, is the association of women with the provision of sexual services and of men with the purchase of sex. However, there is no question that male and queer commercial sex has existed as long as the female variant. Conversely, there were also women who paid for sex. In his guidebook *Bruxelles la nuit* (1868), the French writer Mario Aris (a pseudonym of Jean-Marie-Arice-Edmond Bizonnet de Rivau) described the following scene: 'At the Café de la Cour de Flandre, in the Rue du Marché, I saw a so-called professional lover for the first time. Without any hesitation, he let the necklaced woman pay. Once the shepherd's hour [that is, love hour] arrived, they both withdrew. The next day at eight o'clock, he, delighted, pocketed his earnings. The wage varies between 5 and 10 francs. Gifts are also accepted. In the better circles, these gentlemen are referred to as bed-boys.'

Aris's book belonged to a popular genre in Belgium and France that mixed journalism with fiction. It is therefore not clear whether the story of the lady who paid a young man for his sexual services was the product of Aris's imagination. The same is true of the references to female clients of prostitution that appear in medieval and early modern poems and folktales. But, as the American journalist Murray Kempton once wrote, 'the realm called fiction is ruled by what is real and the territory called fact has to make do with the dubieties of the fancied'.

Magaly Rodríguez García

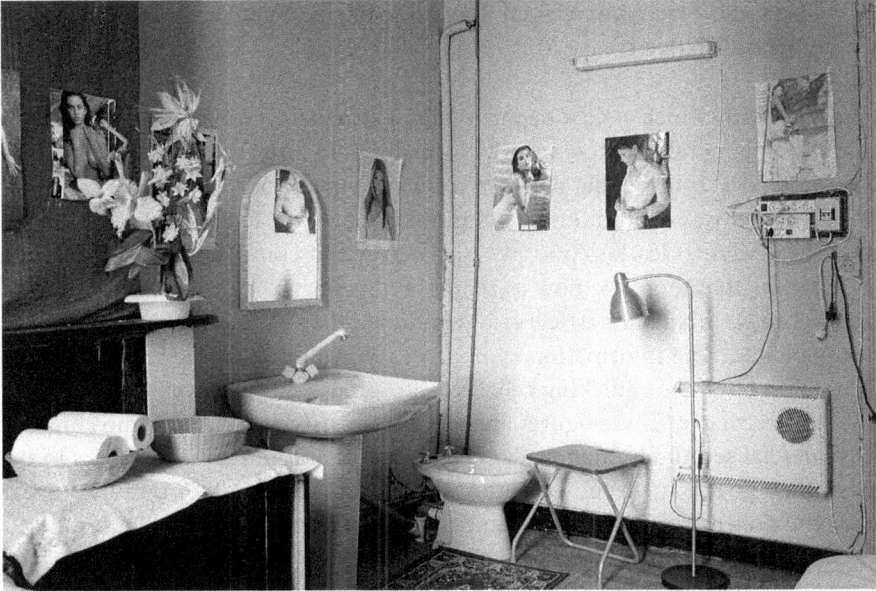

Karin Borghouts, *Abandoned Brothel*, 2001. In autumn 2001, Karin Borghouts photographed traces of sex work activities in an abandoned brothel in Antwerp's Sailors' Quarter.

Since the twentieth century, an increasing number of extant sources tell us about the profiles and experiences of women who paid for sex. Autobiographies and journalistic texts offer spicy details about women who sought pleasure and companionship from male, female, or queer sex workers. Prostitution and gay environments were often closely intertwined, and there is evidence that female sex workers occasionally served lesbian clients. Heterosexual women usually sought discretion. Although 'playboys' could be picked up on the street, female clients sought contact with young men through advertisements or in 'special bars'. The growth of the tourist industry and the advent of the Internet during the last decades of the twentieth century facilitated the promotion of male sex work and the search of paid sex by female customers. But we still do not know the extent to which (Belgian or resident) women seek solace from gigolos in Belgium, or from *sanky-panky's* somewhere in the Caribbean. The taboo on women who buy sex is perhaps stronger than the taboo that rests on prostitution itself. Hence it may take a long time before we are able to obtain precise numbers.

'Tens of Thousands of Involuntarily Women in Prostitution'

The ease with which police departments, journalists, and abolitionists bandy about numbers related to sex work is appalling. In 2015, the quality newspaper *De Standaard* reported that Belgium counted some 26,000 sex workers and that their number was continuously on the rise. In 2020, the federal police estimated that there were at least 30,000 persons engaged in commercial sex. If correct, that means that there are now as many sex workers as hairdressers (33,000 in 2017). The *De Standaard* article also mentioned that 'eight out of ten prostitutes are exploited'. The information came from Wim Bontinck, the federal police's head of the human trafficking cell. 'Prostitution is really everywhere', Bontinck told the journalist. These figures are also eagerly used by activists who consider commercial sex and human trafficking to be one and the same thing. As in the past, their goal is to alarm the authorities and society at large. Yet it is unclear how the police arrived at these numbers. This is also true for the figures in this book, as we do not always know what methods were used by the authors of our sources. What we do know for certain is that modern authorities and social reformers loved numbers.

The obsession with statistics began in the nineteenth century. A virtual 'war with numbers' took place between regulationists and abolitionists. Both groups claimed at the time that there was an 'invasion' of sellers and buyers of sex, pimps, and other demons. There is no doubt that the sex industry grew in the nineteenth century, but this was linked to population growth, increasing migration, the expansion of the entertainment industry, and of a state apparatus more eager to count things. The question, then, is whether there were *proportionately* more sex workers in the nineteenth and twentieth centuries than in the medieval or early modern periods. The clandestine nature of sex work does not allow us to draw firm conclusions on this.

Social support organisations for sex workers and victims of trafficking are more cautious when it comes to quantitative data. They are also transparent about their methodology. Violett, a non-profit organisation that offers (anonymous) medical, psychological, and legal support to sex workers in Flanders, wrote in its 2018 annual report that social workers reached 2,614 sellers of sex (women, men, trans, and queer). A joint count with organisations from Brussels and Wallonia yielded a result of some 6,500 sex workers for all of Belgium. Considering the large reach of those organisations, it is highly unlikely that the numbers propagated by the federal police and the press are realistic. PAG-ASA, a Brussels-based organisation that focuses on human trafficking, specifies that

Magaly Rodríguez García

'not every sex worker is a victim'. On its website, PAG-ASA states that since its inception in 1994, it has counselled some 1,750 victims of human trafficking. Out of those, 650 are victims of 'sexual exploitation', which includes not only prostitution but also pornography, work in champagne bars and massage parlours, as well as 'loverboy relationships' – relations in which young pimps use their seductive skills to exploit young women through commercial sex.

'Pimps and Traffickers are the Real Culprits'

Human trafficking is neither a fable nor a synonym for prostitution. The concept itself is fairly recent, as are related terms such as 'white slavery' and 'traffic in women and children'. Forced prostitution, on the other hand, is as old as commercial sex itself. As is the case for most occupations, economic necessity was nearly always present in the sex trade, but there were other pressures as well. Vicious pimps, exploitative brothel owners, and traffickers are not an invention of old-fashioned abolitionists or feminists. Yet scholarly analyses of labour relations in prostitution, in particular the relationship between sex workers and intermediaries, contradict the sensational stories about brutal pimps and naive girls who ended up selling sex against their will. Third parties were often persons who were themselves exploited and marginalised in the conventional labour market. Like sex workers, they sought a way out through the prostitution milieu, even though their strategy could involve the exploitation of (other) women. A comparative analysis is needed to find out whether the level of exploitation in the sex industry was higher than in other economic sectors.

In any case, recruitment did not go in one direction. The more closed and riskier the prostitution environment, the more efforts people made to find intermediaries who could help them with papers, contacts, and useful tips to circumvent police controls. Moreover, pimps were not always men and strangers. Sisters, nieces, and friends often acted as go-betweens. Parents who knew the sector well also introduced their daughters to the local prostitution milieu or induced them to sell sex in larger cities or abroad. The women in question were usually aware of the purpose of the trip. They perceived it as a family obligation and as a good opportunity to improve their standard of living and that of their loved ones.

If the economic benefits outweighed the disadvantages of prostitution, many sex workers were prepared to tolerate submission to intermediaries. Far away from home and without a social network, young women could find themselves in deplorable working conditions. But this was not the experience of all sex workers. As we demonstrate at length in this book, there is ample archival evidence of people in prostitution who do not appear as helpless victims at all. Prostitution often provoked anxiety, but women involved in the trade pointed more often to the stigma and the lack of protection from authorities, rather than to the sexual activity itself, as the major cause of distress.

'Prostitution Equals Violence and Trauma'

Starting in the nineteenth century, estimates were published not only on the size of the industry, but also on the 'terrible suffering' of women in prostitution. How moral reformers arrived at those conclusions is a matter of conjecture. This is also the case today. In one of its brochures, the Flemish Women's Council writes that '68 per cent of women in prostitution suffer from post-traumatic stress disorder, similar to victims of torture or veterans of war'. This is a remarkable conclusion, considering that the link between commercial sex and violence has not yet been studied in Belgium. Social workers from non-profit organisations and scientific experts know that violence occurs, but we cannot say much about its frequency or its nature. Is it mainly physical or psychological violence? Is violence a consequence of the work itself or rather the result of the vulnerable position of sex workers who often lead double lives? Do male, queer, and trans sex workers experience violence because of their involvement in prostitution or because of homophobia and transphobia? Does violence decrease or increase as street and window prostitution declines in favour of less visible forms of sex work?

Written sources and oral testimonies say much about the difficult situations streetwalkers and window sex workers faced. Dramas like the gruesome murder of Nigerian sex worker Eunice Osayande in Brussels in 2018, are thankfully rare. Other forms of aggression – like insults, spitting, and blackmail – are much more common. During an oral history project, one escort testified that she was blackmailed by a client at the beginning of her career in the early 2000s. He had fallen in love and wanted more. He would stand near the windows in Antwerp's red-light district, take pictures of her, and threaten to send them to her parents. The risk of blackmail already existed in the early modern period, as the religious condemnation of prostitution gained importance. The pressure to pay off debts to brothel owners or pimps must also have taken its toll on sex workers' mental health.

Physical violence was also present, although it did not always come from pimps, boyfriends, or clients. Neighbours, passers-by, and colleagues could make the lives of sex workers quite miserable. Some sellers of sex were themselves not afraid to engage in fights. Since most archival sources were produced

Magaly Rodríguez García

by public authorities, we have little evidence of police violence. The language of many reports, however, does suggest that women in prostitution – or any 'suspect' women – were often mistreated in police stations. The risk of burdensome interrogations and even arrest was always present. Furthermore, autobiographies and sex workers' oral testimonies reveal that police officers sometimes treated them more leniently in exchange for sexual services.

So, given all that misery, the question keeps surfacing: why did they do it? Archival research, oral histories, and contemporary analyses of prostitution centring on the voices of sex workers let us conclude that they did not consider the sale of sex as so very problematical. Sex workers tolerated the collateral damage because their experience in other sectors of the labour market was as bad, if not worse. Low wages, long hours, boredom, and aggressive bosses or colleagues led many people to the sex trade. Many combined traditional jobs – as maids, factory workers, or salesclerks – with occasional prostitution. All wished to boost their income and, if possible, to gain independence and participate on equal terms with men in the market economy.

Those motives never disappeared. In his journalistic book on sex work in Belgium, Hans Vandecandelaere reports on 'Belgian day labourers' who stood next to the Brussels KVS theatre waiting for their clients in the 1980s. He described them as 'mothers who earned extra money during school hours and caused little nuisance' to the neighbours. After an interview in 2019, I received an email from a Flemish school teacher who told me in all honesty that she occasionally engaged in the sale of sex. She had no bad experiences, but hoped to keep her side job a secret. In recent years, there is also more evidence of university students who engage in sex work on a temporary basis. Many do it out of curiosity and a desire for adventure, but also for the quick cash and flexible working hours. These are the same motivations that appear regularly in historical sources.

Whether all these people considered or consider their sale of sexual services to be prostitution remains to be seen. Nor do we know to what extent they viewed or view prostitution as a form of work. Ever since the late Middle Ages, many women did not see commercial sex as a job. For them it was an extra income, a temporary solution, an experiment. They identified themselves as lace workers or maids, even if they had not worked in those sectors for years. For other women, however, sex work was their main activity. They did not hesitate to call themselves 'girls of pleasure'. These diverse ways in which sex workers perceived and represented themselves live on to this day. Still, regardless of their self-perception and personal view of prostitution, the sale of sex was for many a good alternative, for some even a logical choice.

'Prostitution is a Job Like Any Other'

Some academics and many sex-work activists, in diametrical opposition to people who describe prostitution as sexual slavery, define commercial sex as a regular job. We consider it a high-risk profession. It involved many risks in the past, and still does today.

But what is striking about the history of prostitution ever since the Middle Ages is that sex workers were extremely creative when it came to dealing with the risks their activity entailed. The prostitution environment changed considerably over the centuries, but the strategies contemporary sellers of sex employ in the face of troublesome clients or pimps are strikingly similar to those of the past. They developed, for example, an impressive ability to assess clients. That sex workers did not dare refuse clients is therefore a myth. Only the most desperate, who used sex as a survival strategy, took any customer, sometimes for a piece of bread. Fortunately, there were also customers who took pity on the most marginalised women who often engaged in street prostitution. They gave them an extra penny or a pack of cigarettes. In emergencies, customers sometimes came to the rescue.

The solidarity in the industry is also striking. Sex workers exchanged information to avoid difficult situations. As early as the early modern era, they often solicited in groups of two or three. One of them stood guard while others served clients. If watchmen approached, the one on guard would sound the alarm. Sometimes it went even further. During a police interrogation in Antwerp in the 1920s, Angélique recounted that she had hit a drunken man for acting nasty with a 'gal'. Others called pimps, brothel owners, or neighbours for help to break free from the clutches of aggressive customers. 'Kicking ass' could also help. Agnes was arrested in Bruges at the beginning of the twentieth century for public nuisance. At the police station, she explained that she had made noise so that someone would come and help her. Joma, a Nigerian sex worker active near the Brussels North railway station, used the same tactic. 'If a client dares to do something, I take off my wig and run around like a crazy woman. It works. They run away', she told a team of researchers from Ghent University in 2019. But the stigma remains.

During the Middle Ages, sellers of sex sometimes risked banishment from the city and, from the early modern period onwards, incarceration in correction houses. With the introduction of modern migration laws and the Belgian passport in the early twentieth century, foreign sex workers risked expulsion from the country. So, to avoid repression and moral judgement from relatives, neighbours, and friends, many sex workers concealed their activities. When secrecy did not work, they often played the role of victim. For a long time, acute poverty was the main professed motivation; since the late nineteenth century, human trafficking became the magic word.

Commercial sex required more than just risk mitigation. Other skills were and are needed to cope with the profession. Patience, empathy, creativity, and self-discipline are a must in the industry. Sex workers who worked full-time had to be creative to kill time between one client and the next. Those with a strong character kept alcohol and other drugs at a safe distance during and after working hours. But many did not shy away from an old trick: making customers drink so much that they were unable to stand on their feet. Self-discipline also proved much-needed to deal with (a lot of) money, for 'easy money' can easily disappear as well. The temptation to spend it on new clothes, jewellery, and all kinds of entertainment – including lovers – could be great. Prostitution, moreover, is a cash economy. Sex workers were always at risk of being robbed or exploited by pimps, friends, relatives, or clients. But clients were not always dangerous predators or only looking for quick sex. Between the sheets, there was also just cuddling, laughing, and talking. For Sonia Verstappen, her room was 'un espace de parole', a place where her clients could simply go for a nice chat.

Prostitution is not an easy profession. It could even be humiliating. But many sex workers upheld an almost philosophical view of their work. When asked by writer Jack De Graef if she loved 'that life', Jenny, who worked in Antwerp in the 1960s, replied: 'What exactly is to love something? Who loves everything in life? It's *a* life. What more can a girl desire?' With that, she pointed to the enormous diversity of views and experiences that make up the history of sex work. It is a history that cannot be captured in mere platitudes.

SOURCES AND BIBLIOGRAPHY

Introduction: Anne-Marie's Tribulations

Several historiographical overviews of the history of sex work, some rather dated, are available for interested readers. Timothy's Gilfoyles 'Prostitutes in History: From Parables of Pornography to Metaphors of Modernity', *American Historical Review* 104 (1999) 117–141 remains worth reading. More recently, Judith Walkowitz, a pioneer of research into the history of prostitution in the 1980s, formulated some pertinent conclusions concerning the evolution of the field in 'The Politics of Prostitution and Sexual Labour', *History Workshop Journal* 82 (2016) 188–198. Both overviews focus heavily on English-language research. Françoise Blum, 'Prostitution(s). Construction et déconstruction d'un objet historiographique', *Actes de la recherche en sciences sociales* (2013) 105–108, is more focused on the French-speaking world. An indispensable overview of Belgian research on commercial sex in the nineteenth and twentieth centuries is Pieter Vanhees, 'Metafoor van de moderniteit: prostitutie in de Belgische geschiedschrijving', *Contemporanea* (2017) https://www.contemporanea.be/nl/article/2017-2-review-nl-vanhees.

Historical overviews in long-term and global perspective are thin on the ground. An accessible introduction is Kate Lister, *Harlots, Whores and Hackabouts: A History of Sex for Sale*, Thames & Hudson, 2021. A more academic work, but incredibly diverse, is Magaly Rodríguez García, Lex Heerma van Voss, and Elise van Nederveer Meerkerk (eds.), *Selling Sex in the City: A Global History of Prostitution, 1600s–2000s*, Brill, 2017, available in open access at https://brill.com/display/title/33391. Melissa Hope Ditmore (ed.), *Encyclopedia of Prostitution and Sex Work*, Greenwood, 2006 is written from a contemporary interest, but also includes historical accounts. Male sex workers remain out of the picture in many studies but are central to Peter Aggleton and Richard Parker (eds.), *Men Who Sell Sex: Global Perspectives*, Routledge, 2015. A brief global history of commercial sex is also presented in Magaly Rodríguez García, 'The Sale of Sex in History', in Mathew Kuefler and Merry Wiesner-Hanks (eds.), *The Cambridge World History of Sexualities*, Cambridge University Press, 2024, 335–338.

There are no long-term historical overviews for Belgium. Studies covering specific periods and cities are included in the literature reviews accompanying this book's chapters. The only work that covers a longer period and the whole of Belgium is an exhibition catalogue published in the 1990s: Lieve De Mecheleer (ed.), *Des étuves aux eros centers. Prostitution et traite des femmes du Moyen Âge à nos jours*, Archives de l'État en Belgique, 1995. Some chapters remain interesting, though the book does not provide an overarching narrative.

On the definition and terminology of sex work and prostitution, see more extensively Magaly Rodríguez García, 'Defining Commercial Sexualities, Past and Present', in Gavin Brown and Kath Browne, *The Routledge Research Companion to Geographies of Sex and Sexualities*, Routledge, 2016, 321–329.

The tribulations of Anne-Marie, which opened this chapter, derive from records found at the Antwerp City Archives (FelixArchief), inventory 731#420, no. 563-566.

1. Guilty Pleasure (1200–1550)

Archival sources on medieval sex work are difficult to track down: they turn up only sporadically in wider source sets. This chapter draws heavily on the bookkeeping and accounting documents made by the bailiff (also sometimes called *schout* or *maieur*) as the local representative of the duke or count. The bailiff recorded his expenses, for example to the executioner for the punishment of a criminal, as well as his income, including that from fines. Since he fined sex workers or clients who had misbehaved, we sometimes find more information about them in his accounts. Such accounts are kept in the Chamber of Accounts in the General State Archives in Brussels.

We also meet sex workers who came into contact with the law in urban judgement books (preserved in the city archives of Antwerp, Mechelen, Mons, Brussels, and Leuven). Texts that sellers of sex drew up themselves (such as lease contracts or the estate descriptions from which this chapter quoted) were preserved only sporadically, i.e. if they paid a notary or the aldermen's court to register a copy. Such copies have been preserved for Douai, Ghent, Antwerp, and Leuven, and can be consulted in the relevant city archives. However, finding sex workers in those archives is not easy. An index is often lacking, and if there is one, it is usually only by name, which does not make clear whether the contracts concern sex workers.

References to the life and work of Yde Veermans can be found in Jelle Haemers, 'Étuves, bordels et maisons de bains à Louvain au xve siècle: une édition des contrats de location des *stoven* trouvés dans les registres échevinaux de la ville', *Handelingen van de Koninklijke Commissie voor Geschiedenis* 185 (2019) 75–120; Jelle Haemers, 'Women and Stews: The Social and Material History of Prostitution in the Late Medieval Low Countries', *History Workshop Journal* 92 (2021) 29–50.

Much international research on sex work in medieval Europe has been conducted; see, e.g., Jacques Rossiaud, *Amours vénales. La prostitution en Occident, XIIe–XVIe siècle*, Flammarion, 2010; Ruth Karras, *Sexuality in Medieval Europe: Doing unto Others*, Routledge, 2005; Peter Schuster, *Das Frauenhaus. Städtische Bordelle in Deutschland, 1350 bis 1600*, Schöningh, 1992; Ruth Evans (ed.), *A Cultural History of Sexuality in the Middle Ages*, Bloomsbury, 2011. A new Bloomsbury volume on the cultural history of medieval sex work is in preparation (ed. Eleanor Janega, due 2025).

The key historical study for the Low Countries is Jelle Haemers and Chanelle Delameillieure, 'Vrijende vrouwen: instemming, seksualiteit en prostitutie', in Jelle Haemers, Andrea Bardyn, and Chanelle Delameillieure (eds.), *Wijvenwereld. Vrouwen in de middeleeuwse stad*, Vrijdag, 2019, 193–223 and Raymond Van Uytven, 'De ledige vrouwen van de middeleeuwen', in Lieve De Mecheleer (ed.), *Van badhuis tot eroscentrum: prostitutie en vrouwenhandel van de middeleeuwen tot heden*, Algemeen Rijksarchief, 1995, 11–21. For Bruges, see Guy Dupont, *Maagdenverleidsters, hoeren en speculanten. Prostitutie in Brugge tijdens de Bourgondische periode (1385–1515)*, Van de Wiele, 1996. Regulations of sex work have been studied by Raoul Van der Made, 'La prostitution dans l'ancien droit belge', *Revue du droit pénal et de criminologie* 29 (1948–1949) 763–773. On medieval literature concerning commercial sex, see Herman Pleij, *Oefeningen in genot. Liefde en lust in de late middeleeuwen*, Prometheus, 2020; and on medieval bathing culture: Fabiola Van Dam, *Het middeleeuwse openbare badhuis: fenomeen, metafoor, schouwtoneel*, Verloren, 2020.

Good studies on sex work in the localities mentioned in the chapter are Eric Bousmar, 'Marguerite d'York et les putains de Mons, entre charité dévôte et offensive moralisatrice (1481–1485). Autour d'une fondation de Repenties', in Jean-Marie Cauchies (ed.), *Marguerite d'York et son temps*, Centre européen d'études bourguignonnes, 2004, 81–102; Guy Dupont, 'Bad of bordeel? Middeleeuwse stoven aan Gentse wateren', in Geert Vermeiren, Marie-Anne Bru, and Anton Ervynck (eds.), *De Krook. Een leerrijk boek*, Snoeck, 2018, 134–157; Alain Marchandisse, 'La police du vice. Contrôle et répression de la prostitution dans la principauté de Liège à la fin du Moyen Age', *Bulletin de la commission royale pour la publication des anciens lois et ordonnances de Belgique* 43 (2002) 75–93; Mariann Naessens, 'Wat bordeelmadammen ons kunnen leren over het métier. Enkele opmerkingen over de bronnen voor de studie van de laatmiddeleeuwse Gentse prostitutie', *Handelingen der Maatschappij voor Geschiedenis en Oudheidkunde te Gent* 58 (2004) 147–162; Mariann Naessens, 'Seksuele delicten in Kortrijk in de late Middeleeuwen', *De Leiegouw* 44 (2002) 3–35; Laura Schoorens and Jelle Haemers, *Vogelvrije vrouwen? Prostitutie en bordelen in laatmiddeleeuws Brabant*, Stadsbestuur Leuven, 2018; Erik Spindler, 'Were Medieval Prostitutes Marginals? Evidence from Sluis, 1387–1440', *Belgisch Tijdschrift voor Filologie en Geschiedenis* 87 (2009) 239–272; Koen Van der Bracht, 'Prostitutie en zelfmoord in de Dendersteden Dendermonde, Aalst, Ninove en Geraardsbergen tijdens de Bourgondische periode (1385–1515)', *Het Land van Aalst* 61 (2009) 241–71.

Several more general studies on crime, urban governance, or social and economic history also provide clues to the history of prostitution. Among others, we used Bart Lambert, 'Double Disadvantage or Golden Age? Immigration, Gender and Economic Opportunity in Later Medieval England', *Gender & History* 31 (2019) 545–564; Isabelle Paquet, *Gouverner la ville au bas Moyen Âge. Les élites dirigeantes de la ville de Namur au XVe siècle*, Brepols, 2008; Fernand Vanhemelryck, *Marginalen in de geschiedenis: over beulen, joden, zigeuners en andere zondebokken*, Davidsfonds, 2004.

2. Wantons on the Scaffold (1550–1830)

Primary sources on prostitution in the early modern Southern Netherlands are scattered across numerous Belgian city and state archives, and consist mainly in documents created by the courts, ecclesiastical and municipal authorities. Some larger municipal archives, e.g. Brussels and Antwerp, include specific folders with records on prostitution. In many other cities and municipalities, the provisions, complaints, and correspondence relating to sex work are among other documents relating to criminal law or public order.

The bulk of our insight into the practice of prostitution comes from court files and police reports, in which witnesses and sex workers themselves sometimes paint a colourful picture of their existence. Case files contain a wealth of information but are not easy to interpret, for witnesses and defendants were always thinking of a possible conviction. Moreover, the relevant files are often difficult to track down because they are part of collections that are not always inventoried in detail. This chapter mainly drew on the eighteenth-century archives of the Antwerp Vierschaar (kept in the Antwerp city archives FelixArchief) and the series of historical trials kept in the Brussels city archives.

A specific register intended for 'public women' is also kept there (Historical Archives, Register 1143).

Literary and visual sources for prostitution are very scarce for the Southern Netherlands, especially after 1700. The text refers to Willem Ogier, *De seven hooft-sonden. Speels-ghewys, vermakelyck ende leersaem voor-gestelt*, Amsterdam, 1682 (original performance 1646).

The rise of regulation in the early nineteenth century engendered a virtual explosion of archival material. The archives of cities like Brussels and Antwerp harbour entire collections of applications to open or close brothels, complaints, draft regulations, and correspondence with other cities regarding prostitution. In the early nineteenth century, however, police reports and court records were often more concise than before, as full testimonies were rarely written down.

Existing historical research on prostitution in the sixteenth- and seventeenth-century Southern Netherlands is limited. Apart from chapters in general survey works, there is mainly Ann Du Pont's licentiate's thesis, *Prostitutie in de stad Antwerpen 16e–17e eeuw*, KU Leuven, 1985. Works on crime and jurisprudence can supplement the picture painted therein to a limited extent, notably Jozef De Brouwer, *De kerkelijke rechtspraak en haar evolutie in de bisdommen Antwerpen, Gent en Mechelen tussen 1570 en 1795*, Veys, 1971; Fernand Vanhemelryck, *De criminaliteit in de ammanie van Brussel van de late middeleeuwen tot het einde van het Ancien Régime (1404–1789)*, Koninklijke academie voor wetenschappen, letteren en schone Kunsten van België, 1981.

Most of the research on commercial sex in the early modern Southern Netherlands has, not coincidentally, focused on the eighteenth century, in which the authorities in many cities took a stricter stance against prostitution and also started drawing up more official documents. We can therefore paint a much richer picture of eighteenth-century paid sex. This chapter uses many findings from Maja Mechant's impressive PhD dissertation *Hoeren, pauwen ende ondeughende doghters. De levenslopen van vrouwen in de Brugse prostitutie (1750–1790)*, Ghent University, 2018. Mechant paints a nuanced and in-depth picture of prostitution in Bruges in the eighteenth century. She highlights specific aspects in several other publications; see, among others, Maja Mechant, "'Waerom sij met haeren man niet en woont ende waermede sij haer van haeren kant alleen geneirt": getrouwde alleenstaande prostituees in Brugge tijdens de achttiende eeuw', *Historica* 35:3 (2012) 7–13; Maja Mechant, 'Dishonest and Unruly Daughters. The Combined Efforts of Families and Courts in Handling Prostitution in Eighteenth Century Bruges', *Popolazione e Storia* 14:1 (2013) 129–150.

In addition to Mechant's research, recent research by Sarah Auspert and Elwin Hofman also provides a perspective on eighteenth-century prostitution in the Southern Netherlands: Sarah Auspert, 'La prostitution à Namur sous le régime français (1795–1813)', in Sarah Auspert, Philippe Bagard, and Vincent Bruch (red.), *Namur de la conquête française à Waterloo (1792–1815). Armées, société, ordre public et urbanisme*, Société royale Sambre et Meuse, 2015, 133–144; Elwin Hofman, 'Managing Stigma: Prostitutes and Their Communities in the Southern Netherlands, 1750–1800', *Histoire Sociale/Social History* 50:101 (2017) 3–18; Elwin Hofman, *Trials of the Self: Murder, Mayhem and the Remaking of the Mind, 1750–1830*, Manchester University Press, 2021.

Furthermore, the master's dissertations of Jean-François Eugene, *La prostitution à Bruxelles sous le Régime Autrichien (1715–1795)*, Université Catholique de Louvain, 1998, and Barbara Vos, *Meisjes van plezier. De prostituee te Gent in de zeventiende en de achttiende eeuw (casus 1775–1795)*, Ghent University, 2007, provide several interesting insights used in this chapter. For the impact of the French Revolution and paid sex in the early nineteenth century, Catharina Lis, 'Een politieel-medische orde: de reglementering van de prostitutie in West-Europa, in het bijzonder te Antwerpen tijdens de eerste helft van de 19de eeuw', in *Het openbaar initiatief van de gemeenten in België 1795–1940*, Gemeentekrediet, 1986, 559–579, is still very useful.

For an international perspective on early modern sex work, a number of excellent works exist. Lotte van de Pol, *The Burgher and the Whore: Prostitution in Early Modern Amsterdam*, Oxford University Press, 2011, remains invaluable for the history of commercial sex in the Dutch Republic. Faramerz Dabhoiwala's *The Origins of Sex: A History of the First Sexual Revolution*, Oxford University Press, 2012, provides a provocative look at commercial sex and sexuality more generally in the early modern age, especially in England. Joanne M. Ferraro, 'Making a Living: The Sex Trade in Early Modern Venice', *The American Historical Review* 123:1 (2018) 30–59; Tessa Storey, *Carnal Commerce in Counter-Reformation Rome*, Cambridge University Press, 2008; and Clyde Plumauzille, *Prostitution et Révolution, Les femmes publiques dans la cité républicaine (1789–1804)*, Champ Vallon, 2016 are also particularly valuable. These studies, like Mechant's and Hofman's publications, also contain extensive suggestions for further literature.

3. The Tyranny of Rules (1830–1918)

The nineteenth century and early twentieth are a rewarding period for historians of sex work. An entire administration was developed in cities and municipalities where prostitution regulations were in force. Police forces grew in size and produced an immense amount of archival material. Unfortunately, the preservation of these archives is very uneven. Among the major Belgian cities, the vice police archives of Antwerp are the best preserved. This is much less the case for Ghent, Brussels, Liège, and Charleroi. In the archives of some medium-sized cities, such as Kortrijk, Bruges, Leuven, and Mechelen, parts of the archives of the nineteenth-century vice police were well preserved. The great advantage of such archives is that just about everyone involved in the sex industry appears in them. Male prostitution was much less monitored by the vice police, resulting in far fewer records. A limited number of archives were preserved for this topic, mainly in the context of judicial prosecution in cases of public indecency or sexual relations with minors.

In addition, the nineteenth-century sex worker generated an enormous number of sources. She was at the crossroads of medical discussions (in medical journals, doctors' publications, and publications on venereal diseases), legal discussions (in archives of courts and legal journals), scientific research, the struggle against double moral standards and 'immorality' (by abolitionists and feminists), press articles (such as the white slavery scandal), and guides to nightlife. In all these sources, sex workers rarely spoke themselves: they were mainly talked, debated, and written about.

A final class of sources, which mainly tells us about the place the sex worker occupied in the imaginations of contemporaries, consists of art and literature. French naturalism and symbolism influenced Belgian writers such as Max Elskamp and Georges Eekhoud. Félicien Rops, in his graphic work, frequently linked prostitution to venereal disease and death. The German expressionist Otto Dix depicted commercial sex in Brussels during the First World War. A final, more atypical example is that of Neel Doff. This Dutch woman, who in later life belonged to bourgeois circles in Brussels and Antwerp, in her literary work described her own childhood in the world of prostitution.

In addition to some of these primary sources, we have also relied on the work of other historians of prostitution. Two studies on nineteenth-century prostitution outside of Belgium underpin the success of the topic in historical research. In *Les Filles de noce. Misère sexuelle et prostitution au xixe siècle*, Aubier, 1978 (trans. *Women for Hire: Prostitution and Sexuality in France after 1850*, Harvard University Press, 1990), the French historian Alain Corbin described the rise and disappearance of regulationism in France. American historian Judith Walkowitz studied the same period, but in Britain and through the eyes of abolitionism, in *Prostitution and Victorian Society: Women, Class and the State*, Cambridge University Press, 1980. More recent work also constitutes a source of inspiration for research on this period. This includes, e.g., Julia Laite, *Common Prostitutes and Ordinary Citizens: Commercial Sex in London,*

1885–1960, Palgrave, 2011 and Andrew Israel Ross, *Homosexuality, Prostitution and Urban Culture in Nineteenth-Century Paris*, Temple University Press, 2019.

Inspired by this research, many Belgian historians also took up the subject. Sophie de Schaepdrijver published on hyperregulationist Brussels, including 'Regulation Prostitution in Brussels, 1844–1877: A Policy and its Implementation', *Historical Social Research* 3 (1986) 89–108. Also on Brussels are Colette Huberty and Luc Keunings, 'La prostitution à Bruxelles au xixe siècle', *Les cahiers de la Fonderie* (1987) 3–22. For Antwerp, additional information can be found in Margo De Koster, 'Negotiating Controls, Perils, and Pleasures in the Urban Night: Working-Class Youth in Early-Twentieth-Century Antwerp', *Criminological Encounters* 3 (2020) 32–49; Eliane Van den Ende et al., *De Rossaert & zijn passanten*, Ludion, 2016.

For Belgian abolitionism, we mainly relied on Jean-Michel Chaumont and Christine Machiels (eds.), *Du sordide au mythe. L'affaire de la traite des blanches (Bruxelles, 1880)*, Presses Universitaires de Louvain, 2009 and Christine Machiels, *Les féminismes et la prostitution 1860–1960*, Rennes University Press, 2016. Prostitution during the First World War is covered by Piet Boncquet's popular publication, *Lief en leed: prostitutie in de Eerste Wereldoorlog*, Davidsfonds, 2015. Scientific analyses include Benoît Majerus, 'La prostitution à Bruxelles pendant la Grande Guerre: contrôle et pratique', *Crime, Histoire & Sociétés/ Crime, History & Societies* 7 (2003) 5–42; and Ellen Soetens's MA dissertation, *Prostitutie in de Eerste Wereldoorlog. Perceptie, visie en agency*, KU Leuven, 2017. Some publications by Liesbet Nys tell us more about the medicalisation of the 'prostitution problem' in the late nineteenth century: 'De grote school van de natie. Legerartsen over drankmisbruik en geslachtsziektes in het Belgisch leger (circa 1850–1950)', *Bijdragen en mededelingen betreffende de geschiedenis der Nederlanden* 115 (2000) 392–425; 'De ruiters van de Apocalyps: alcoholisme, tuberculose, syfilis en degeneratie in medisch België, 1870–1940', *Tijdschrift voor geschiedenis* 115 (2002) 26–46. Homosexual prostitution in nineteenth-century Brussels is discussed in Wannes Dupont, *Free-floating Evils: A Genealogy of Homosexuality in Belgium*, PhD dissertation, University of Antwerp, 2015.

4. Worlds Apart (Congo, 1885–1960)

Reconstructing the outlines of prostitution in Belgium's colonial territories is a challenge. The absence of an effective regulatory system and the weakness of police control deprive historians of the documentary basis they usually use – such as administrative censuses and police and medical reports – to produce a comprehensive analysis of the sex trade in overseas territories. Nevertheless, interesting, albeit fragmentary, archival documents can be found in the archives of the Belgian colonial administration (kept at the Belgian Ministry of Foreign Affairs and currently in the course of being transferred to the State Archives of Belgium). The archives of the Fonds du Gouvernement Général de Léopold-ville, which bring together files produced by the local colonial administration, are particularly useful not only for tracing the successive attempts and failures to control prostitution, but also for shedding light on the social realities behind these policies and the resistance they faced.

Another difficulty for reconstructing this history resides in the virtual absence of expert knowledge on prostitution practices in the Belgian colonial context: even the moral entrepreneurs – usually outspoken on the topic of prostitution – carried out few investigations on the subject, and the first ethnographic studies on 'free women' date from the period of decolonisation. The anthropological research of Suzanne Comhaire-Sylvain (*Femmes de Kinshasa hier et aujourd'hui*, Mouton, 1968) and Jean Lafontaine ('The Free Women of Kinshasa: Prostitution in a City in Zaire', in *Choice and Change: Essays in Honour of Lucy Mair*, Athlone, 1974, 89–113) provides invaluable information. The official periodical of the *évolués, La Voix du Congolais*, created in 1945, is a good indicator of the Congolese elite's investment in morality and women's affairs. Finally, less conventional sources such as popular songs and oral sources have also provided historians with key information on the place of free women in the towns of Central Africa under late colonialism.

Free women and prostitution in the Belgian colonies, therefore, have been the subject of limited historical research, perhaps because of the limitations of these documentary resources. In the early 1990s, however, research by Nancy R. Hunt, a pioneer in the history of women in colonial Africa, highlighted both the ambiguities of Belgian colonial control policies and the agency of free women in Congo and Burundi: Nancy R. Hunt, 'Noise over Camouflaged Polygamy, Colonial Morality Taxation, and a Woman-Naming Crisis in Belgian Africa', *The Journal of African History* 32 (1991) 471–494. This social phenomenon was also studied by the urban history specialist Charles Didier Gondola, in his book devoted to the history of the capitals of the two Congos, *Villes miroirs. Migrations et identités urbaines à Kinshasa et Brazzaville (1930–1970)*, L'Harmattan, 1997; and in a series of articles devoted to the key role played by women in the urban cultures of Central Africa: 'Popular Music, Urban Society, and Changing Gender Relations in Kinshasa, Zaire (1950–1990)', in Maria Grosz-Ngate and Omari Kokole (eds.), *Gendered Encounters. Challenging Cultural Boundaries and Social Hierarchies in Africa*, Routledge, 1996, 65–84 and 'Unies pour le meilleur et pour le pire. Femmes africaines et villes coloniales: une histoire du métissage', *Clio. Histoire, femmes et sociétés* 6 (1997) 87–104.

More recently, Amandine Lauro has been investigating the history of prostitution control policies in the Belgian Congo, the latest results of which will soon be published in *Sexe, race et politiques coloniales. Encadrer le mariage et la sexualité au Congo Belge 1908–1945*, Editions de l'ULB (forthcoming). The literature on the origins of HIV in the Congo Basin has made a strong case of colonial prostitution, but rarely on the basis of empirical studies; for an overview, see Charles Didier Gondola and Amandine Lauro, 'A Social Virus: The Emergence of HIV-1 in Colonial Kinshasa, 1920–1960', in William H. Schneider (ed.), *Histories of HIVs: The Origin of Multiple AIDS Epidemics*, Ohio University Press, 2021, 127–171.

5. Please Turn Off the Lights (1918–1970)

Until 1948, local governments ensured the production of vast amounts of sources on the sex trade. However, some archives did not survive destruction or neglect. The Brussels police archives, for example, are largely untraceable. In Ostend, the police archives were purposely destroyed in the 1970s and 1980s. Fortunately, there are other types of sources that offer precious details about the sex industry: newspaper articles, city guides, diaries, and visual material. The popularisation of photography and erotic images helped not only the sector but also later historians.

Based on those visual and literary sources, Eliane van den Ende's beautifully illustrated *De Rossaert & zijn passanten*, Ludion, 2016, reveals much about the 'girls of light morals and sailors' in Antwerp's Sailors' Quarter. Writer Jan Lampo, too, made clever use of journalistic texts and ego documents for his blog on the history of Antwerp, including one on the red-light district: https://janlampo.com/2011/11/26/kroniek-van-het-schipperskwartier/. Gonzague Pluvinage did something similar but in book form: *Sex in the City. Oorden van plezier in Brussel van de 19e eeuw tot de seksuele revolutie*, Museum of the City of Brussels, 2016, offers an accessible description of the normative framework around sexuality and the original ways in which individuals circumvented the rules in force from the nineteenth century to the 1960s. Both female and male prostitution are discussed here, as well as other sexual practices where the division between commercial and non-commercial sex was unclear. Author Jack De Graef, known for his publications on Antwerp dialect and folk life, in *Antwerpen bij nacht*, De Dageraad, 1970, also offers useful information on prostitution in the 1950s and 1960s. The information on 'Hoerenburg' comes from the work of Marita De Sterck, 'Moeder Sarov werd langzaam vermoord', *Brood & Rozen* (2014) 43–53.

The chapter is also based on the findings of scholars at Belgian universities and research institutions who used private archives, legal sources, police reports, letters, diaries, and newspapers: Margo De Koster, 'Girls' Journey to the Juvenile Court, Antwerp, 1912–1933', in Jéan Trépanier and Xavier Rousseaux (eds.), *Youth and Justice in Western States 1815–1850. From Punishment to Welfare*, Palgrave, 2018, 279–310; Aurore François, 'Juvenile Delinquence in Wartime and Peacetime: The Activity of the Belgian Juvenile Courts, 1912–1950', in Trépanier and Rousseaux, *Youth and Justice*, 311–332; Bart Eeckhout, Rob Herreman, and Alexander Dhoest, 'A Gay Neighborhood or Merely a Temporary Cluster of "Strange" Bars? Gay Bar Culture in Antwerp', in Alex Bitterman and Daniel Baldwin Hess (eds.), *The Life and Afterlife of Gay Neighborhoods: Renaissance and Resurgence*, Springer, 2021, 221–238; C.L. Kruithof, 'De bestrijding van de prostitutie', *Tijdschrift van de Vrije Universiteit van Brussel* 7:1 (1965) 116–151; Catherine Jacques and Christine Machiels, 'Féminisme et abolitionnisme aux xixe et xxe siècles en Belgique', in Jean-Michel Chaumont and Christine Machiels (eds.), *Du sordide au mythe: L'affaire de la traite des blanches (Bruxelles, 1880)*, Presses universitaires de Louvain, 2009, available online: https://books.openedition.org/pucl/755; Magaly Rodríguez García and Kristien Gillis, 'Morality Politics and Prostitution Policy in Brussels: A Diachronic Comparison', *Sexuality Research and Social Policy* 15:3 (2018) 259–270; Anne Van Haecht, *La prostituée. Statut et image*, Editions de l'Université de Bruxelles, 1973; Caroline Van Loon, 'De geschorene en de scheerster. De vrouw in de straatrepressie na de Tweede Wereldoorlog', *Bijdragen tot de eigentijdse geschiedenis* 19 (2008) 45–78. Paul Kinsie's reports were published in Jean-Michel Chaumont, Magaly Rodríguez García, and Paul Servais (eds.), *Trafficking in Women 1924–1926: The Paul Kinsie Reports for the League of Nations*, 2 vols., United Nations Publications Office, 2017. The second volume of that publication integrated explanatory chapters on the cities Kinsie visited, including Antwerp and Brussels, by Margo De Koster and Benoît Majerus.

Several MA dissertations also contributed enormously to the knowledge of prostitution policies, the main actors, and their living conditions during the interwar period. They are mostly based on local archives, which explains the focus on the history of a specific city: Vania Vande Voorde, *Prostitutie in Brugge tijdens de Eerste en de Tweede Wereldoorlog*, Ghent University, 2007; Lena Everaerts, *Prostitutie en agency: instap en werken in de Antwerpse prostitutie (1929–1940)*, KU Leuven, 2018; Jasper Smets, *Een nieuwe plaag? Opium en cocaïne in Antwerpen*, University of Antwerp, 2015. The work of Thierry Delplancq, city archivist of La Louvière, provides a wonderful microhistory of commercial sex during the Second World War: 'Félix et les femmes de mauvaise vie. Le contrôle de la prostitution à La Louvière durant la Seconde Guerre mondiale', *Quotidiana: tribute album Dr. Frank Daelemans*, Archives et bibliothèques de Belgique, 2011, 493–515.

Leading scholarly studies on sex work abroad from the late nineteenth century onwards include those of Elisa Camiscioli, *Selling French Sex. Prostitution, Trafficking, and Global Migrations*, Cambridge University Press, 2024; Paulo Drinot, *The Sexual Question: A History of Prostitution in Peru, 1850s–1950s*, Cambridge University Press, 2020; Julia Laite, *Common Prostitutes and Ordinary Citizens: Commercial Sex in London, 1885–1960*, Palgrave, 2011; Victoria Harris, *Selling Sex in the Reich: Prostitutes in German Society, 1914–1945*, Oxford University Press, 2010; Gail Hershatter, *Dangerous Pleasures: Prostitution and Modernity in Twentieth Century Shanghai*, University of California Press, 1999; Liat Kozma, *Global Women, Colonial Ports. Prostitution in Interwar Middle East*, SUNY Press, 2017; Jill Suzanne Smith, *Berlin Coquette: Prostitution and the New German Woman, 1890–1933*, Cornell University Press, 2013. For international debates on prostitution and human trafficking, see: Paul Knepper, *International Crime in the 20th Century: The League of Nations Era, 1919–1939*, Palgrave, 2011; Magaly Rodríguez García, 'Beware of Pity: The League of Nations' Treatment of Prostitution', *Monde(s)* 19 (2021) 97–117; Eileen Boris and Magaly Rodríguez García, '(In)Decent Work: Sex and the ILO', *Journal of Women's History* 33:4 (2021) 194–221.

6. Out of the Twilight Zone (1970–2024)

After the abolition of the regulation of prostitution in 1948, we can no longer rely on local archives or government-collected data to understand sex work. Official figures on and descriptions of sex work only become available again from the 1990s onwards. For window and street prostitution, registration and monitoring systems of police and social workers again provide reliable sources. As for hidden forms of sex work (i.e. escorts or in brothels, discotheques, saunas, massage parlours, hotels, private or strip clubs), however, evidence is only anecdotal. Moreover, information is only available on those who offered sexual services; to date, in Belgium no systematic large-scale research on customers exists. Policy texts and legislative proposals, supplemented by journalistic sources and interviews, constitute the main sources for research on the evolution of policy.

Journalistic texts and literary sources, e.g. Xaviera Hollander's *The Happy Hooker: My Own Story,* Sphere Books, 1971, offer insights into societal attitudes towards but also within sex work. On Antwerp, Jack de Graef's booklets (*Antwerpen bij nacht,* De Dageraad, 1970; *De erotiek in het Antwerpse nachtleven,* De Dageraad, 1978) are fascinating historical documents. Journalists such as Chris de Stoop (*Ze zijn zo lief meneer,* Kritak, 1992) and Hans Vandecandelaere (*En vraag niet waarom: sekswerk in België,* EPO, 2019) paint a broader picture of commercial sex in Belgium.

In the twenty-first century, academic research on sex work and prostitution policy in Belgium has greatly increased. Consultancy agencies such as Iris consulting and Seinpost, as well as academics like Marion van San, Koessan Gabiam, Maarten Loopmans, Gert Vermeulen, Stef Adriaenssens, and Jef Hendrickx, commissioned by various governments, have carried out research on the size, location, and turnover of sex work. These researchers, like Kristien Gillis, Dominique Boels, Anna Di Ronco, Marion David, and Ron Weitzer, also conducted more fundamental research on contemporary sex work and prostitution policy in Belgium. Marion David and Maarten Loopmans, 'Belgium', in Hendrik Wagenaar and Synneve Økland Jahnsen (eds.), *Assessing Prostitution Policies in Europe,* Routledge, 2019, 77–91 provide a general overview of recent prostitution policies in Belgium. In 2013, the Flemish criminological journal *Orde van de Dag* devoted a special issue to local policy changes in Belgium. Magaly Rodríguez García and Kristien Gillis, 'Morality Politics and Prostitution Policy in Brussels: A Diachronic Comparison', *Sexuality Research and Social Policy* 15:3 (2018) 259–270 provide a long-term analysis for Brussels, while Maarten Loopmans and Pieter Van Den Broeck, 'Global Pressures, Local Measures: The Re-Regulation of Sex Work in the Antwerp Schipperskwartier', *Tijdschrift voor economische en sociale geografie* 102:5 (2011) 548–561 analyse policy changes in Antwerp.

The impact of changing social perceptions on policies is discussed in Nina Persak and Gert Vermeulen (eds.), *Reframing Prostitution: From Discourse to Description, from Moralisation to Normalisation?* (Maklu, 2014) and Marion David, 'The Moral and Political Stakes of Health Issues in the Regulation of Prostitution (the Cases of Belgium and France)', *Sexuality Research and Social Policy* 16:2 (2019) 201–213. The effects of new local policies on red-light districts and sex workers are the focus, respectively, of Ronald Weitzer and Dominique Boels, 'Ghent's Red-Light District in Comparative Perspective', *Sexuality Research and Social Policy* 12:3 (2015) 248–260; and Anna Di Ronco, 'Law in Action: Local-Level Prostitution Policies and Practices and Their Effects on Sex Workers', *European Journal of Criminology* 19:5 (2022) 1078–1096.

Several authors, finally, zoom in on the practice of sex work. These include Stef Adriaenssens and Jef Hendrickx, who discuss the financial-economic side of sex work in 'Calculating Value Added of Prostitution with Multiple Data: A New Approach for Belgium', *Public Finance Review* 47:1 (2019) 58–86. Along with Anahita Azam, both authors also examine the effect of Covid on sex work in Belgium and the Netherlands: Anahita Azam, Stef Adriaenssens, and Jef Hendrickx, 'How Covid-19 Affects Prostitution Markets in the Netherlands and Belgium: Dynamics and Vulnerabilities under a Lockdown', *European Societies* 23:sup1 (2021) S478–S494. Male sex workers in Brussels are the focus of Koessan Gabiam and Cédric Piechowski, 'Les prostitutions masculines à Bruxelles', *Les Cahiers de la Fonderie* 44 (2011) 66–71, and Maarten Loopmans shows how customers perceived the turn-of-the-century changes in the Sailors' Quarter in 'De wensen van de wandelaar', *Rooilijn* 39:2 (2006) 70–75.

For the international context, Phil Hubbard, Roger Matthews, and Jane Scoular, 'Regulating Sex Work in the EU: Prostitute Women and the New Spaces of Exclusion', *Gender, Place & Culture* 15:2 (2008) 137–152 is a good starting point. Philippe Adair and Oksana Nezhyvenko, 'Love for Sale in All European Countries: Assessing the Figures of Prostitution', *Journal of Crime and Criminal Behavior* 3:1 (2023) 251–276 provide an estimation of the number of female sex workers in different EU countries. P.G. Macioti, Jennifer Power, and Adam Bourne, 'The Health and Well-being of Sex Workers in Decriminalised Contexts: A Scoping Review', *Sexuality Research and Social Policy* 20:3 (2023) 1013–1031 analyse the effects of decriminalisation on sex workers. Nicola Mai's documentary films on sex work also provide much food for thought: https://caer-film.org/.

7. 'I Really Loved It': A Former Sex Worker's Testimony

Sonia Verstappen was active in sex work for thirty-six years, mainly in Brussels, experiencing the recent history of the sex trade from a front-row vantage point. Her testimony was recorded in Wezembeek-Oppem, a municipality 10 kilometres east of the centre of Brussels, by Pieter Vanhees during an interview on 29 September 2021. Her personal account of the recent history of sex work in Belgium serves as a complement to the outside view in the other chapters.

Beyond the Clichés

The diverse quantitative evidence for prostitution and human trafficking can be found in the following sources: Pieter Huyberechts, 'Stijgend aantal prostituees in België', *De Standaard*, 15 May 2015; '18 mythes over prostitutie, Vrouwenraad, s.d., http://www.vrouwenraad.be/file?fle=36811&ssn= (Accessed 15 January 2022); 'Jaarlijks raport 2018', Violett, https://www.violett.be/storage/main/violett-2018.pdf; 'Human Trafficking. Who Are the Victims?', PAG-ASA, https://pag-asa.be/human-trafficking.

The quote on a female client was found in Mario Aris, *Bruxelles la nuit. Physiologie des établissements nocturnes de Bruxelles*, Aris, 1871, 130–131. Peter Sioen offers a fine account of boys in prostitution, and of his work with the Brussels relief organisation Adzon at the end of the twentieth century in *Het jongenskwartier: straatprostitutie in Brussel,* Dedalus, 1996. In an interview about the play *Paying for it*, which premiered in 2019, Sonia Verstappen spoke about her vision and experience in prostitution: www.youtube.com/watch?v=N43l1pjvJQ8. Jenny was interviewed by Jack De Graef for his book *Antwerpen bij nacht*, De Dageraad, 1970.

Several scholarly articles tackle definitions and statistics: Aurore François and Christine Machiels, 'Une guerre des chiffres. L'usage des statistiques par les discours abolitionniste et réglementariste sur la prostitution à Bruxelles (1844–1948)', *Histoire et mesure* 22:2 (2007) 103–134; Magaly Rodríguez García, 'Defining Commercial Sexualities, Past and Present', in Gavin Brown and Kath Browne, *The Routledge Research Companion to Geographies of Sex and Sexualities,* Routledge, 2016. 321–329. For a good analysis of the geography of commercial sex in nineteenth-century Brussels and the veracity of Mario Aris's publication, see: Fanny Paquet, Gaëlle Graindorge, and Camille Lhote, 'Géographie de la débauche', *Textyles* 47 (2015) 31–49.

Julia Laite provides a brilliant analysis of pimps and traffickers in the first half of the twentieth century in 'Traffickers and Pimps in the Era of White Slavery', *Past & Present* 237 (2017) 237–269. Research on Nigerian and Ghanaian women active in the Brussels North Station neighbourhood, by Sara Adeyinka, Sophie Samyn, Sami Zemni, and Ilse Derluyn, was published as *Nigerian and Ghanaian Women Working in the Brussels Red-Light District,* Routledge, 2021.

ABOUT THE AUTHORS

Jelle Haemers is Professor of Medieval History at KU Leuven. He studies urban political conflicts and gender history in late medieval Flanders and Brabant. He has previously co-edited *La femme dans la cité au Moyen Âge* (Racine, 2022).

Elwin Hofman is a cultural historian and writer. Assistant Professor in Cultural History at Utrecht University, he has (co)authored several books on cultural and social history, including a history of homosexuality in Belgium.

Amandine Lauro is a researcher and lecturer at the Université libre de Bruxelles specialising in African history, colonial history, and gender studies. She has co-edited *Colonial Congo: A History in Questions* (Brepols, 2024).

Ilias Loopmans is a historian and has contributed to the digitisation of nine-teenth-century police archives at the Antwerp City Archives.

Maarten Loopmans is Professor of Human Geography and Political Ecology at KU Leuven. He has a keen interest in the geographies of solidarity, diversity, and inequality. He has edited the section on paid sex for *The Routledge Research Companion to Geographies of Sex and Sexualities* (Routledge, 2016).

Magaly Rodríguez García is a specialist in the history of international labour organisations and subaltern history. She is a Professor at KU Leuven and collaborates with Belgian and foreign colleagues on projects regarding, among others, sex work and prostitution policy at the local, national, and supranational levels. In the context of oral history projects, she became closely involved with advocacy groups for vulnerable persons such as sex workers and homeless people.

Pieter Vanhees is a social historian and has researched the history of prostitution in the nineteenth and twentieth centuries at KU Leuven.

Sonia Verstappen is a sex work activist and former sex worker.